Cicero's Law

Rethinking Roman Law of the Late Republic

Edited by Paul J. du Plessis

EDINBURGH
University Press

Edinburgh University Press is one of the leading university presses in the UK. We publish academic books and journals in our selected subject areas across the humanities and social sciences, combining cutting-edge scholarship with high editorial and production values to produce academic works of lasting importance. For more information visit our website: edinburghuniversitypress.com

Edinburgh University Press Ltd
The Tun – Holyrood Road
12 (2f) Jackson's Entry
Edinburgh EH8 8PJ

First published in hardback by Edinburgh University Press 2016

Typeset in 10/12pt Goudy Old Style by
Servis Filmsetting Ltd, Stockport, Cheshire,
and printed and bound by CPI Group (UK) Ltd
Croydon, CR0 4YY

A CIP record for this book is available from the British Library

ISBN 978 1 4744 0882 0 (hardback)
ISBN 978 1 4744 3253 5 (paperback)
ISBN 978 1 4744 0883 7 (webready PDF)
ISBN 978 1 4744 0884 4 (epub)

Published with the support of the Edinburgh University Scholarly Publishing Initiatives Fund.

Contents

Contributors

Michael C. Alexander, Pittsburgh, PA: micalexa@uic.edu

Yasmina Benferhat, Nancy: yasmina.benferhat@univ-lorraine.fr

Benedikt Forschner, Erlangen: benedikt.forschner@fau.de

Jill Harries, St Andrews: Jdh2@st-andrews.ac.uk

Jennifer Hilder, London: jennyhilder88@gmail.com

Christine Lehne-Gstreinthaler, Rum: Christine.Lehne@uibk.ac.at

Saskia T. Roselaar, Delft: saskiaroselaar@gmail.com

Catherine Steel, Glasgow: catherine.steel@glasgow.ac.uk

Jan Willem Tellegen, Utrecht: bonifaci@xs4all.nl

Olga Tellegen-Couperus, Utrecht: O.E.Couperus@uvt.nl

Philip Thomas, Pretoria: philip.thomas231@gmail.com

Matthijs Wibier, Pavia: mh.wibier@unipv.it

Abbreviations

The abbreviations followed in this book are conventional and conform to those found in the *Oxford Classical Dictionary*, 4th edition. In addition, the following abbreviations may be found in the text:

aed.	*aedile*
cos.	*consul*
cos. suf.	*consul suffectus*
disp.	*disputatio*
fasc.	fascicle
fr.	fragment
leg.	*legatus*
Not. iur.	*De Notis Iuris* (by Marcus Valerius Probus)
OLD	Oxford Latin Dictionary
Plut. Cic.	Plutarch's *Lives*
pr.	*principium*
Ps. Ascon.	Pseudo-Asconius
Red. Quir.	'Post reditum ad Quirites' (Cicero)
tr. pl.	*tribunus plebis*

Chapter 1

Introduction

Paul J. du Plessis

The centre of gravity of legal development therefore from time immemorial has not lain in the activity of the state, but in society itself.

(Ehrlich 1962: 390)

In his 1995 book, *The Spirit of Roman Law* (Athens, GA 1995), Alan Watson included a chapter provocatively titled 'Cicero the outsider'. By locating this chapter towards the end of the book, Watson hinted that any discussion of Cicero in the context of the spirit of Roman law (a difficult concept in itself) could only really form part of an appendix (in this case Appendix A) to a book of this kind. The gist of this chapter, following the then dominant Romanist view, is that 'Cicero's outlook [was] remarkably different from that of the Roman jurists' (at 200).[1] As this statement implies, for Watson, Cicero stood outside the traditional narrative of the Roman jurists.[2]

This view of Cicero as 'an outsider' is based on two assumptions. The first is that a fundamental distinction between the 'jurist' and the 'advocate' (orator) existed in Roman law – a distinction that, according to its supporters, seems to have originated already in the mid to late Republic. Jurists were engaged in an intellectual endeavour, removed from the cut and thrust of legal practice, while orators were very much at its centre and utilised the art of persuasion (rhetoric) in courts of law, often with limited attention to (or indeed need for) the intellectual intricacies of Roman law. Such a system was made workable by the *formula* procedure operating in the Roman courts where the praetor and the jurists dealt with matters of law, while the lay *iudex* merely decided on the application of the law to the facts of the matter. The origins of this view about the perceived divide between the jurist and the orator are complex and may be traced at least to nineteenth-century German conceptions of law as a *Wissenschaft*, in which the 'scientific' study of law and those who were engaged in it were foregrounded at the expense of

---

[1] Cf. Dirksen 1858; Costa 1899; Greenidge 1901; Roby 1902a, 1902b; Costa 1927; Coşkun 2011 (reprint) as well as Thomas 11f. elsewhere in this volume.

[2] This also explains the title of this book, a play on the famous statement in *Top.* 51: 'Nihil hoc ad ius, ad Ciceronem.'

legal practice.[3] This view also finds support to some extent in Cicero's own statements about the endeavours of jurists, of whom he seems at times quite critical (although these should be treated with circumspection as they were produced within a specific context).[4]

The second assumption concerns the nature of Roman law in the late Republic itself. The narrative of the development of Roman law during this period (as found in many textbooks on Roman law) focuses on key figures (all great men belonging to the upper classes) such as Servius Sulpicius Rufus or the Scaevolae and their contribution to the creation of the 'science' of Roman law.[5] Although information about these individuals and their contributions to the law are very limited, they have nonetheless been elevated in most of these works to the status of the vanguards, steeped in Greek philosophical learning, of the 'classical period' of Roman law in the following three centuries. They have also been used to justify various key features of the narrative about the shape and function of juristic interpretation in 'classical' Roman law (intellectual isolation and scientification).[6] Owing to the belief that the 'science' of Roman law (whatever this means in the context of antiquity) was somewhat removed from the practice of law in the courts, the narrative concerning the development of Roman law in the late Republic has become largely insular (and rule-focused). Issues such as the impact of the political turmoil of the period (war, proscriptions, expropriation of land and the granting of greater rights to the Italian allies, and so on) on the development of Roman law and the operation of the courts are only occasionally investigated, and generally to a limited extent (for example largely with reference to criminal or public law).[7]

Since then, this view of Cicero as 'an outsider' has undergone revision. Cicero has become part of a larger debate concerning the divide between the jurist and the orator in the last century of the Roman Republic and concerning the nature of Roman law itself.[8] Not only has it been proposed that the dichotomy was not as watertight as previously assumed, but it has also been suggested that the legal world of the late Republic was far broader and more diverse than the picture presented by Cicero.[9] In light of these new insights, Cicero and the state of the law of the late Republic need to be re-examined.

This book is designed to engage with this debate. If, as has been suggested

---

[3] See comprehensively Tellegen-Couperus and Tellegen in du Plessis 2013. See also the same authors elsewhere in this volume. An important work in this regard is that of Tuori 2007.

[4] Cf. Gildenhard 2011. See the chapters by Benferhat 71f. and Hilder 166f. elsewhere in this volume.

[5] Cf. Harries 2006. See also Harries 123f. elsewhere in this volume.

[6] See, extensively, on law as a 'science' in antiquity, Giaro 2007.

[7] Notable exceptions are Riggsby 1999 and Alexander 2002 for criminal law and the many publications of Lintott on public law.

[8] Cf. Harries 2006; Saénz 2010.

[9] Cf. Lehne-Gstreinthaler 88f. elsewhere in this volume.

by recent scholarship, Cicero should no longer been seen as 'an outsider' in the narrative of Roman law of the late Republic, the question must be asked whether and to what extent this narrative will change if Cicero is treated differently. At this point, a word of caution is required. For a project of this kind to deliver meaningful results, it is important to treat Cicero's works with due sensitivity.[10] Cicero always had his prospective audience firmly in mind, whether in private correspondence or in published speeches. Furthermore, as an orator, he was not averse to bending the facts to match his version of events (Lintott 2008: 33; Steel 2004: 233–52). As Lintott (2008) has therefore rightly pointed out, Cicero's works can never be used as a factual account of historical events (at 3). Certain filters have to be applied in order to arrive at a more balanced picture. Nonetheless, if Cicero's own comments are approached with caution (using the tools of our sister disciplines such as philology, literary criticism and more specifically narratology) and interpreted in light of the existing narrative about Roman law in the late Republic, a more balanced picture can be achieved. This is one of the aims of this volume.

In this book, Cicero's contribution to modern understanding of the state of Roman law in the late Republic is treated under three headings: 'the nature of law', 'the nature of the legal profession' and 'the impact of legal practice'. These three subheadings have been specifically chosen to provide a broad-spectrum view of the 'legal world' to use Fantham's (2004) term, in which Cicero operated. This 'legal world' not only comprised legal theory as traditionally investigated by scholars of Roman law. It clearly also encompassed the practice of law in the courts. By sketching a panoramic view using these three broad headings, this volume aims to broaden the contemporary vision of the nature of late Republican Roman law by placing it in context (du Plessis 2013).

Already in his 1985 book on the rise of the Roman jurists, Frier argued that while the jurists played an important role during the late Republic, Roman law during this period was also influenced by larger societal factors.[11] Since 'society' is also the natural province of culture, it seems logical also to investigate the idea of Roman 'culture' in this context, especially in light of an emergent strand of scholarship based on Lawrence Friedman's concept of 'legal culture'.[12] First coined in the early to mid-1970s, the term has been

---

[10] Lintott 2008.

[11] Frier 1985: 273. Compare MacKendrick and Bennett 1995.

[12] Friedman 1969, 1969–70: 29–44. See also Smith and Reynolds 2014. Although contemporary socio-legal theory has moved beyond the idea of 'legal culture', it is my contention that 'legal culture' as a socio-legal concept remains particularly useful when dealing with the legal world of the late Republic, for two reasons. First, it draws many of its basic ideas from the first generation of socio-legal scholars such as Eugen Ehrlich (1862–1922) whose work grew directly out of their knowledge of Roman law. In second place, the concept of legal culture is particularly useful when analysing a period in Roman society when law and culture were

used with great effect in contemporary socio-legal scholarship.[13] Though useful as a concept, it is not without its critics, who have focused their criticisms primarily on two points, namely the inherent vagueness of the term and a general inability by its supporters to explain whether legal culture is the cause or the effect when it comes to legal change.

In light of these criticisms, it seems important to explain how the concept of legal culture will present itself in this work. While there is something to be said for maintaining an air of vagueness when using this term, 'legal culture' in this context will be used to denote a subset of Roman culture more generally.[14] Thus 'Roman legal culture' will be used to describe all those phenomena (including the economic) that can be related, whether directly or indirectly, to the workings of the law in the late Republic.[15] This casts the net rather wide, and deliberately so. It is important to state at this juncture, though, that Roman legal culture is not a static concept. It changes with time and all that can really be attempted here is a 'still picture', to use the phrase of Crook, that captures the events of the late Republic.[16] It is also important to remember that Roman legal culture is not modern legal culture and that conclusions about the behaviour of the legal profession in the modern period cannot necessarily be applied to the Roman situation. Thus, for example, Friedman, in his earlier works, distinguished between 'internal legal culture' (the culture of the legal profession) and 'external legal culture' (more general societal factors affecting the law).[17] While useful to describe certain aspects of modern law in the USA, this distinction should be approached with great care in relation to the late Republic. In fact, I would go as far as to suggest that it should be abandoned altogether when investigating the legal world of the late Republic. The reasons for this are, as more recent research by Tellegen-Couperus and Tellegen have shown, that the legal 'profession' of Republican Rome was more porous than first imagined.[18] Thus, Roman legal culture appears to have been far more embedded in Roman culture and society more generally.

One of the main criticisms of Friedman's concept of legal culture is that

---

closely linked, such as the late Republic. For a survey of the work of Eugen Ehrlich and a modern reassessment, see Hertogh and Oñati International Institute for the Sociology of Law 2009.

[13] See, for example, the criticisms of Cotterrell and Von Benda-Beckmann and Von Benda-Beckmann in their chapters in Nelken 2012.

[14] See the chapter by Friedman in Nelken 1997.

[15] Nelken 1994: 1–26. See Nelken for a survey of the range of meanings of the term. I have chosen the term 'relate to' rather than 'impact on' deliberately to enable the authors also to capture subtle influences.

[16] Crook 1967.

[17] Friedman and Schreiber 1996. The distinction between 'external legal culture' and 'culture' more generally has been one of the major sources of criticism of Friedman's theory.

[18] Compare the chapter by Tellegen-Couperus and Tellegen in du Plessis 2013. I use the term 'profession' here with some reservation as no 'legal profession' in the modern sense existed in the late Republic.

it fails to explain whether legal culture is the cause or the effect. It is not my intention to stake my claim regarding this matter here, since in my view much more work is required before an assessment can be made about the role of legal culture in the formation and change of law in Roman society.[19] It is perhaps best to state at this point both that culture can give rise to law, and that law can also change culture. Countless examples from history can attest to this. It is therefore perhaps wise not to draw the net too restrictively in this regard.

Having laid down these parameters, the astute observer may ask whether a focus on legal culture will add anything novel to the mix. Permit me to explain. Law is not insulated from society. It exists within and is surrounded by society. Law also responds to society in various ways. If this premise is used as a starting point, then the idea of legal culture becomes an important tool. The late Republic is a well-documented period in the history of Rome.[20] Not only was it a period of great socio-political change, accompanied by violence and instability, but there is also clear evidence of a legal system in turmoil – the suspension of the courts, accusations of corruption in the courts and in the administration of justice, and widespread political meddling.[21] Coupled with these are the profound changes to the legal system introduced under Sulla and a general sense, expressed by a number of influential figures during this period, that Roman law had become somewhat unmanageable and that it had to be written down. Among all of this, we find Cicero, legal practitioner and keen observer of the human condition. And it is in this respect that Cicero becomes indispensable. As someone who not only lived the period, but was also actively involved in legal practice, Cicero's 'legal consciousness' (that is, how he responded to the law and turned to the law when it was required) provides a fascinating insight into the period.

Meta-level studies such as those by Frier 1985 and Harries 2006, coupled with the comprehensive investigations by Watson into various branches of private law of the late Republic, as well as the insightful 2004 collection by Powell and Paterson on Cicero's practice as an advocate, provide a uniquely rich picture of Roman legal culture of the last century of the Republic. In addition, recent works on the Roman jurists and their dialogue with Cicero have done much to uncover the relationships between juristic pursuits and legal practice in this period.[22] The aim of this work is to call for a greater

---

[19] There is something to be said for reflecting back upon Ehrlich 1962 and his use of the term 'custom' as the source of all law. 'As late as the end of the Republic, the Romans considered their national customary law, the *ius civile*, at least as valuable as a source of law as the *leges*' (at 18).

[20] Treble and King 1930. See also the comprehensive recent works by May 2002 and Steel 2013 and the chapters collected therein. On Roman social history generally, see Alföldy 1975.

[21] It is noteworthy that many of the 'saviours' of the Roman Republic served a term as praetor.

[22] For example, Fantham 2004.

synthesis between all of these different strands of scholarship, using Cicero and the concept of legal culture as its central focus. While a history of Roman law in the late Republic is yet to be written, this book is an initial attempt to start the conversation.

BIBLIOGRAPHY

Alexander, M. (2002), *The Case for the Prosecution in the Ciceronian Era*. Ann Arbor.

Alföldy, G. (1975), *Römische Sozialgeschichte*. Wiesbaden.

Coşkun, A. (2011), *Cicero und das römische Bürgerrecht*. Göttingen (reprint).

Costa, E. (1899), *Le orazioni di diritto privato di M. Tullio Cicerone*. Bologna.

Costa, E. (1927), *Cicerone Giureconsulto*. Bologna (reprinted Rome 1964).

Crook, J. A. (1967), *Law and Life of Rome*. Ithaca, NY.

Dirksen, H. (1858), *Der Rechtsgelehrte Aulus Cascellius, ein Zeitgenosse Cicero's*. Berlin.

Du Plessis, P. J., ed. (2013), *New Frontiers: Law and society in the Roman world*. Edinburgh.

Ehrlich, E. 1962 (1913), *Fundamental Principles of the Sociology of Law*. New York.

Fantham, E. (2004), *The Roman World of Cicero's De Oratore*. Oxford.

Friedman, L. and Scheiber, H. (1996), *Legal Culture and the Legal Profession*. Boulder.

Friedman, L. (1969), *Legal Culture and Social Environment*. Indianapolis.

Friedman, L. (1969–70), 'Legal culture and social development', *Law and Society Review* 4: 29–44.

Frier, B. W. (1985), *The Rise of the Roman Jurists: Studies in Cicero's Pro Caecina*. Princeton.

Giaro, T. (2007), *Römische Rechtswahrheiten: ein Gedankenexperiment*. Frankfurt am Main.

Gildenhard, I. (2011), *Creative Eloquence: The construction of reality in Cicero's speeches*. Oxford.

Greenidge, A. (1901), *The Legal Procedure of Cicero's Time*. Oxford (reprinted New York 1971).

Harries, J. (2006), *Cicero and the Jurists: From citizens' law to the lawful state*. London.

Hertogh, M. L. M. and Oñati International Institute for the Sociology of Law (2009), *Living Law: Reconsidering Eugen Ehrlich*. Oxford.

Lintott, A. (2008), *Cicero as Evidence: A historian's companion*. Oxford.

MacKendrick, P. and Bennett, E. (1995), *The Speeches of Cicero: Context, law, rhetoric*. London.

May, J., ed. (2002), *Brill's Companion to Cicero: Oratory and rhetoric*. Leiden.

Nelken, D. (1994), 'Using the concept of legal culture', *Australian Journal of Legal Philosophy* 29: 1–26.

Nelken, D. (1997), *Comparing Legal Cultures*. Aldershot.

Nelken, D., ed. (2012), *Using Legal Culture*. London.

Powell, J. and Paterson, J., eds (2004), *Cicero the Advocate*. Oxford.

Riggsby, A. (1999), *Crime and Community in Ciceronian Rome*. Austin.

Roby, H. (1902a), *Essays on the Law in Cicero's Private Orations*. Cambridge.

Roby, H. (1902b), *Roman Private Law in the Time of Cicero and the Antonines*, 2 volumes. Cambridge.

Saénz, A. (2010), *Cicerón y la jurisprudencia romana: un estudio de historia juridica*. Valencia.

Smith, K. P. and Reynolds, A. (2014), 'Introduction: the archaeology of legal culture', *World Archaeology* 45: 687–98.

Steel, C. (2004), 'Being economical with the truth: what really happened at Lampsacus?' in J. Powell and J. Paterson, eds, *Cicero the Advocate*. Oxford. 233–52.

Steel, C. ed. (2013), *The Cambridge Companion to Cicero*. Cambridge.

Treble, H. and King, M. (1930), *Everyday Life in Rome in the Time of Cicero and Caesar*. Oxford.

Tuori, K. (2007), *Ancient Roman Lawyers and Modern Legal Ideals: Studies on the impact of contemporary concerns in the interpretation of ancient Roman legal history*. Frankfurt am Main.

Watson, A. (2008) *The Spirit of Roman Law*. Athens, GA.

Part I

On Law

Chapter 2

A Barzunesque View of Cicero:
From Giant to Dwarf and Back

Philip Thomas*

1. PROLOGUE

Cicero's cover letter to Trebatius introducing his *Topica* has been a frequent object of study in attempts to interpret the source of this work.[1] However, another letter to Trebatius is deserving of attention.[2] Cicero wrote to Trebatius since the latter had mocked him during drinks for saying that it was a moot point whether an heir can institute the *actio furti* for a theft committed from the *hereditas iacens*. Once back at home he looked it up and made a note, which he sent to Trebatius the following day, stating that this opinion, which according to Trebatius was held by no one, was in fact held by Sextus Aelius, Manius Manilius and Marcus Brutus, but that he, Cicero, agreed with Scaevola and Testa. This short, informal note to a friend persuades more that Cicero was indeed advocate and jurist, rather than the positivistic criticism that he was a mere rhetorician with superficial legal knowledge hiding his ignorance by over-reliance on equity.

* This work is based on research supported wholly by the National Research Foundation of South Africa (grant-specific unique reference number [UID] 85777); the Grant-holder acknowledges that opinions, findings and conclusions or recommendations expressed in any publication generated by the NRF-supported research are those of the author, and that the NRF accepts no liability whatsoever in this regard.

1. Cic. *Fam.* 7.19; Reinhardt 2003: 368f.
2. *Fam.* 7.22. 'Illuseras heri inter scyphos, quod dixeram controversiam esse, possetne heres, quod furtum antea factum esset, furti recte agere. Itaque, etsi domum bene potus seroque redieram, tamen id caput, ubi haec controversia est, notavi et descriptum tibi misi: ut scires id, quod tu neminem sensisse dicebas, Sext. Aelium, M. Manilium, M. Brutum sensisse. Ego tamen Scaevolae et Testae assentior.' ('You made game of me yesterday over our cups for saying that it was a moot point whether an heir can properly take action for theft in respect of a theft previously committed [fn. 837. i.e. in the interval between the testator's death and the heir's taking possession]. So when I got home, though late and well in tipple, I noted the relevant section and send you a transcript. You will find that the view which, according to you, has never been held by anybody was in fact held by Sext. Aelius, Manius Manilius, and M. Brutus. However, for my part I agree with Scaevola and Testa.' Translation by D. R. Shackleton Bailey.) It is difficult to understand how Harries 2006: 44 interprets this letter as 'a somewhat inebriated consultation of Q. Mucius'.

2. INTRODUCTION

The global modernisation of legal studies makes the perennial question whether the law is an art, a craft or a science topical. In his short story 'In the Park' Primo Levi[3] created a fantastic country inhabited by literary characters. There are five or six Cleopatras: Pushkin's, Shaw's, Gautier's, Shakespeare's version, and so on. Some years after his arrival Antonio notices that he is becoming diaphanous and understands that the memory of him is extinct. He takes leave of his new friends and waits for his flesh and spirit to dissolve into light and wind. The relevance of this fiction to this chapter is twofold: for centuries many versions of Cicero have competed, but in Capogrossi Colognesi's 'Un futuro senza storia?'[4] Cicero will become more transparent[5] eventually turning into the invisible man. Evelyn Waugh parodied this development in his novella 'Scott-King's Modern Europe': in 1946 Scott-King had been a classical master at Granchester for twenty-one years. When he arrived the school was almost equally divided into a classical and a modern side. Now out of 450 boys scarcely fifty read Greek. When the school reassembled in September the headmaster told him that the year started with fifteen fewer classical specialists as parents wanted to qualify their boys for jobs in the modern world and stated that there may be something of a crisis ahead.[6]

The above literary fragments are metaphors for Roman law and legal history. It is a tragic irony that as modern research in these disciplines subjects the tenets propounded in the great treatises of the nineteenth and twentieth centuries to critical analysis and develops new interpretative narratives, these contributions remain limited to a diminishing elite,[7] while the desired interdisciplinary collaboration proves an illusion even within the faculties. A regrettable by-product is that the supra-national codification of wisdom on the internet relies on the traditional version of dated or dating standard works. The purpose of this chapter is to link a number of new ideas, thus spinning a web that may hopefully provide a safety net for the casualties of unquestioning positivism. Gero Dolezalek explains his choice of expertise on the basis that the people and ideas at the beginning of a movement are interesting and important. In legal practice, however, the compilers at the

---

[3] Levi 2007: 57–71. Baldini 2006: 65–73 explains how in the first story the writer Antonio Casella encountered James Collins, a character he had created. Collins told him about the park in which all literary characters live as long as they are remembered. Casella writes his autobiography so he can live in this park as well.

[4] Capogrossi Colognesi 2011: 43–57.

[5] Chalkomatas 2004, in his review of Tobias Reinhardt's *Marcus Tullius Cicero, Topica*, rejoices in the number of modern commentaries on some of the major works of Cicero published in the recent past.

[6] Waugh 1967: 195–250.

[7] Elite simply means the best of a kind.

finish are indispensable tools and authorities. This has made Justinian's codification the focus of both study and practice of law during many centuries, while the pre-classical paradigm shift has been contained in an outdated continental European narrative.[8]

Diliberto has convincingly argued that the 'system' of the Twelve Tables is anachronistic,[9] but his work has also demonstrated that the source material makes the development of an alternative theory a gigantic if not fantastic enterprise. Reconstructing the sources of classical Roman law has met with more success, but as both humanists and interpellationists became a danger to legal certainty as well as legal theory, the codification bell has tolled for both paradigms. This chapter intends to follow the *communes opiniones* that classical Roman law represents the zenith of Roman law and Roman jurisprudence; that the latter was perfected by the great jurists of this period; that great changes in legal practice and jurisprudence had taken place during the last centuries of the Republic and that Greek culture pervaded Roman society during the same period. The proposition is that application of Barzun's theory of aspect[10] to the person of Cicero is overdue and that to view this thinker from a different perspective may lead to a reassessment of his place in the development of Roman jurisprudence. Arguments will be found in places as different as the so-called divides between common law and civil law and orators and jurists, Schulz's *Geschichte*,[11] legal argumentation and artificial intelligence, Tobias Reinhardt's *Marcus Tullius Cicero, Topica*, and the work of the Tellegens and Tuori.

3. THE COMMONALITIES BETWEEN ROMAN LAW AND ENGLISH LAW

The traditional view is to point out the divide between civil law and common law, which is then explained by the fact that civil law is based on Roman law. However, in the chapter 'Common law and civil law: neighbours yet strangers', Van Caenegem[12] draws attention to the fact that modern civil law is based on the academic teaching and study of the *Corpus Iuris Civilis*. However, Roman law of the classical period was much closer to the English common law than to modern civil law systems and their foundation, learned Roman law, as studied and taught at European universities. This observation

---

[8] Established during the second half of the nineteenth and most of the twentieth century by *communis opinio doctorum*. Mommsen (1856), Schulz (1961) and Wieacker (1965, 1967) are used in this chapter as examples of authoritative protagonists of this paradigm.

[9] Diliberto 2005: 217–39.

[10] Barzun 2000: 47–8, 174, 246–7, 250, 253, 430–1, 435–7, 568–74, 652–6, 759–63, 768–9.

[11] Schulz 1961: 44–117 describes his vision of 'Die Hellenistiche Periode der Römischen Rechtswissenschaft'. In spite of his scathing opinion of Cicero's legal knowledge, his footnotes show that he relies for his source material virtually exclusively on this 'non-jurist'.

[12] Van Caenegem 2002: 38ff.

had been made in 1935 by Pringsheim[13] and taken up and amplified by Stein.[14] Van Caenegem sets out the differences between the two legal traditions, but accentuates that the differentiating characteristics were shaped during the second period of Roman law, in other words between the twelfth and twentieth centuries.

It is obvious that Van Caenegem addresses the position of the judge and the adversarial/inquisitorial divide. Another aspect in this context, namely that the civil law adheres to the *curia ius novit* principle[15] while the common law relies on judicial unpreparedness,[16] is of relevance for the argument of this chapter. In the adversarial procedure of the common law the court is limited to the legal arguments raised by parties.[17] Viscount Kilmuir has remarked that the first and most striking feature of the common law is that it puts justice before truth,[18] and it can be argued that this characteristic shared between original Roman law and common law is often neglected. The predominance of the law of procedure as the engine of legal development and the oral courtroom tradition are other similarities of note,[19] which brings us to the distinction between jurists and orators.

4. THE DIVIDE BETWEEN ADVOCATES AND LAWYERS?

An interesting aspect of the *causa Curiana* is the legal representation of the respective parties, namely Quintus Mucius Scaevola and Marcus Licinius Crassus,[20] who had been consuls together previously. Volumes have been filled with the literature on this case from Cicero[21] onwards. It is impossible to address all interpretations and references to Stroux,[22] and Vaughn,[23] Wieacker[24] and Tellegen and Tellegen-Couperus,[25] must suffice to provide beacons of orientation. In particular the work of the last two authors has introduced persuasive arguments that the separation of the professions and the absolute beliefs in the law/rhetoric, jurist/orator divides are questionable, and the product of nineteenth-century *Dichtung* rather than *Wahrheit*.

---

[13] Pringsheim 1935: 347–65. *Contra* Watson 1990: 247–68.

[14] Stein 1991–2: 1591–603.

[15] Thomas 2012: 237–53; 2014c: 341–53.

[16] Mann 1977: 369; von Wobeser 2011: 201; Baxter 1979: *passim*.

[17] The *curia ius novit* principle is unknown in the common law tradition. Cowen 2004: 7; Mann 1977: 368; Zimmermann 1984: 306.

[18] Baxter 1979: 535. Viscount Kilmuir 1960: 42–3.

[19] Birks 1987: 446–50, in particular 447 fn.10; Laws 2002: 401–16.

[20] Wieacker 1967: 151–64.

[21] *Inv. rhet.* 2.122f; *Caecin.* 51ff, 67ff; *De or.* 1.180, 1.242ff, 2.24, 2.140f, 2.220ff; *Brut.* 39, 44f, 52, 149–53, 199; *Top.* 44.

[22] Stroux 1926: *passim*.

[23] Vaughn 1985: *passim*.

[24] Wieacker 1967: *passim*.

[25] Tellegen and Tellegen-Couperus 2000: *passim*.

It is ironic that the seed for the division of labour can be found in Cicero's own œuvre, in particular *Pro Murena*. However, the facts of this case should be remembered to place Cicero's argument that under the circumstances an experienced war hero should be at the helm of the Roman state rather than a jurist, however excellent. In his comparison between military and legal experience and their suitability to defend the state against her enemies, Cicero parodies legal practitioners as obsessed with bagatelles, but includes himself in their ranks.[26] Another text upon which the theory regarding the dichotomy between law and rhetoric has been built has been Cicero's *bon mot* on how Gallus[27] used to say that 'this is not a matter for the law, but for Cicero', when anyone came to him with a case revolving around facts.[28] The Tellegens have clearly and definitely dealt with this question.[29] However, it should be mentioned that the notion that factual questions are outside the domain of the jurist is questionable. In his inaugural lecture at the University of Cape Town, Gero Dolezalek stated the obvious, namely that most cases are decided on the facts and that in order to find some interesting points of law thousands of pages of mere fact-finding have to be read.[30] It is quite another matter that within the profession, division of labour and specialisation have established certain corners where the experts do not deal with factual questions. It is also a commonplace that within each profession a hierarchy develops and snide remarks abound. 'Nihil hoc ad ius; ad Ciceronem' may be one of these. Even today some advocates have very successful practices without setting foot in the courtroom, and Cicero has the last word in *Topica* 71:

> If to support citizens with advice and do it with help are to be held in the same esteem, then those who give advice on legal matters and those who defend people

---

[26] *Mur.* [21] 'Summa in utroque est honestas, summa dignitas; quam ego, si mihi per Servium liceat, pari atque eadem in laude ponam. Sed non licet; agitat rem militarem, insectatur totam hanc legationem, adsiduitatis et operarum harum cotidianarum putat esse consulatum. "Apud exercitum mihi fueris" inquit; "tot annos forum non attigeris; afueris tam diu et, cum longo intervallo veneris, cum his qui in foro habitarint de dignitate contendas?" Primum ista nostra adsiduitas, Servi, nescis quantum interdum adferat hominibus fastidi, quantum satietatis. Mihi quidem vehementer expediit positam in oculis esse gratiam; sed tamen ego mei satietatem magno meo labore superavi et tu item fortasse; verum tamen utrique nostrum desiderium nihil obfuisset.'

[27] The jurist Gaius Aquilius Gallus (c. 116–44 BC), a pupil of Quintus Mucius Scaevola. Gallus was a friend of Cicero and praetor during the same year as the latter (66 BC).

[28] *Top.* 51: 'Nihil hoc ad ius; ad Ciceronem, inquiebat Gallus noster, si quis ad eum tale quid retulerat, ut de facto quaereretur.'

[29] Tellegen-Couperus and Tellegen 2006: 381–408 and 382 fn.2 for their earlier publications on the topic.

[30] Dolezalek 1989: 18: 'All experienced lawyers know from practice that most cases do not pose any problem of law so that only the facts of the case need to be disputed. Evidence is brought to prove the contested facts and the judge merely has to decide whether the evidence was or was not satisfactory.'

in court must have equal share of glory; but the first holds; therefore what follows (holds).[31]

Wieacker professed his belief in this segregation in his monograph *Cicero als Advokat*, where he states categorically that as a rule in the courtroom none of the participants is a lawyer, as the jurists remain outside and above the case.[32] Nevertheless he also opined that Cicero was usually well-informed concerning the law,[33] but as an advocate had a cavalier attitude *vis-à-vis* the truth, as he used every trick in the book to persuade rather than convince.[34] However, his archetype jurist Scaevola had proven himself well versed in rhetoric and when so required would argue the opposite view.[35] Moreover, Wieacker's example of how a real Roman jurist would have condensed the case into two sentences and answered *respondi posse*, saving us the reasoning as trivial and a waste of words, provides no insight into the never-to-be-equalled art of decision making.[36] Finally, Wieacker's opinion that the *causa Curiana* had been wrongly decided[37] is illustrative of the continental professor[38] during the nineteenth and greater part of the twentieth century and outside the world of both common law and pre-classical Roman law.

Another literary character to provide context and support regarding the multiple divisions and hierarchies within the ranks of lawyers is Soames Forsyte, the main character in *The Forsyte Saga* and its sequel, *A Modern Comedy*.[39] A prosperous and well-respected solicitor, Forsyte respects Senior Counsel and the Bench, but feels insulted to be called an attorney.[40] This not only proves that it is extremely difficult to understand the different echelons of lawyers in another society, but indicates how difficult and dangerous it is to make judgements about the position of lawyers during the late Roman Republic on the basis of little inside jokes by Cicero, for example.[41] However, the belief in the dichotomy between jurist and orator has taken root so much that it appears impossible to eradicate it. Thus, Jill Harries in

---

[31] Reinhardt's translation of: 'Si consilio iuvare cives et auxilio aequa in laude ponendum est, pari gloria debent esse ii qui consuluntur et ii qui defendunt; at quod primum est; quod sequitur igitur', Reinhardt 2003: 339.

[32] Wieacker 1965: 7.

[33] Idem: 14 and 25.

[34] Idem: 13ff.

[35] D. 34.2.33 Idem (= Pomponius) 'libro quarto ad quintum Mucium.'

[36] Wieacker 1965: 26: 'eine Entscheidungskunst, die sich allein durch das spezifische juristische Sachproblem leiten liess.'

[37] Wieacker 1967: 161.

[38] Van Caenegem 2002: 45f.

[39] The author John Galsworthy was the son of a solicitor and studied law at New College, Oxford. He was called to the bar at Lincoln's Inn in 1890.

[40] Galsworthy 1926: 54: '"He called me an attorney," said Soames with a grim smile, "and she called me a liar. I don't know which is worse."'

[41] De Brauw 2006: *passim*.

her important contribution to the history of Roman law categorically states that the realities of Roman 'interdisciplinary' thinking are not accurately reflected by adherence to anachronistic 'disciplinary' boundaries,[42] and describes Cicero as a student of both Scaevolae who had a lifelong conversation with the law. She discusses his versatile legal authorship,[43] but repeats the mantra that Cicero was never a jurist.[44] Nevertheless, this chapter will express the belief that Cicero was a jurist and that he played an important role in the development of Roman law.

5. THE FOUNDING OF LEGAL SCIENCE

Tuori has made an impressive contribution to the debate on the birth of legal science.[45] He clearly points out that beliefs about what constitutes science have always been far from uniform; in short science is all things to all men. Another interesting feature of his work is an obsession with system and science. The conclusion may be drawn that in the absence of a *communis opinio*, personal beliefs sway the scales, and even authoritative authors waver. In his introduction to the *causa Curiana* Wieacker states that every Romanist knows that the decisive achievements of Roman law had already been concluded during the late Republic,[46] but admits limited knowledge and division of opinion on the influence of Greek civilisation during this period. In *Cicero als Advokat*, the same author calls the Roman achievements an art and places the origin of legal science in the High Middle Ages.[47]

In consequence, it may be advisable to abstain from seeking the origins of legal science and rather investigate the methodology of Roman law, as methodology is a less loaded term since it refers to the methods, principles and rules of a discipline, whether in the arts or the sciences. It is common knowledge that during the later Republic a paradigm shift took place, which laid the foundation for classical Roman law. It is also uncontested that the cause of this development was the influence of Greek science. However,

---

[42] Harries 2006: 232. See also 34, where Schulz's definition of 'legal science' and 'jurist' are cited with approval, but without drawing the conclusion that Cicero was a jurist (neither did Schulz himself).

[43] Idem: 52–5, 93 where it is stated that *De Inventione* reads at times like a law textbook; 134f, 146–8 where Cicero's work regarding civil rights and citizenship are discussed; 210ff where Cicero's preoccupation with Roman constitutional law in the *Philippics* are dealt with. See Hilder 166f. elsewhere in this volume.

[44] Even the title *Cicero and the Jurists* gives an indication. Express statements of this belief are numerous, for example at 27, 37, 56, 68, 101, 104, 230. See also 50, where a definition of lawyer is not offered. Also Watson 1991: 101.

[45] Tuori 2007: 21–69.

[46] Wieacker 1967: 151.

[47] Wieacker 1965: 27: 'Als die Europäer im Hochmittelalter durch die Digesten mit dieser grossen Kunst der römischen Juristen bekannt wurden, entwickelte sich daraus für alle Zeiten eine sachlich und technisch bestimmte Rechtswissenschaft.'

agreement is limited to eliminating Euclid as a force in this regard, as no unanimity appears possible as to whether philosophy or rhetoric, and which school and/or which scholar, was influential.

6. MARCUS TULLIUS CICERO, *TOPICA*

Corpus Christi professor Tobias Reinhardt provides impetus to the renaissance of Cicero with his *editio maior* of the neglected *Topica*.[48] Reinhardt has established a modern, authoritative text with critical apparatus, translation and commentary, preceded by an extensive introduction, that makes invaluable contributions to the various disciplines of which he is a *maestro*,[49] as well as to Roman law, legal history and legal argumentation. However, the unavoidable hazard of interdisciplinary work is that it is impossible to gauge whether the authorities of other disciplines reflect submerging or emerging paradigms. As to be expected, Reinhardt's focus is more directed to Cicero's sources in the Greek and Hellenistic literature than to any potential original contribution to legal methodology by Cicero himself. Thus the introduction to *Topica* and the cover letter to Trebatius are taken at face value and not as false modesty.[50]

6.1 Thetical rhetoric

Reinhardt draws attention to the fact that Cicero had a predilection for abstraction and in consequence made a distinction between thetical and hypothetical rhetoric.[51] A perfect example is found in *Pro Caecina*, where Cicero moves from the hypothesis of Caecina to the thesis of the rule of law.[52] Cicero credits Aristotle for this methodology and refers to the latter's teaching of topics as indications of where to find arguments to speak *generatim*, that is on a general level.[53] In the *Orator* Cicero refers to the importance

---

[48] Reinhardt 2003: *passim*.

[49] Ancient rhetoric and poetics, Latin literature and ancient philosophy.

[50] Cic. *Fam.* 7.19. Reinhardt 2003: 177–81, 369f. The same excuse for writing as well as the 'no books available' story was still in use more than sixteen centuries later. De Groot wrote a book, *Inleidinge tot de Hollandsche Rechtsgeleerdheid*, ostensibly for the instruction of his nephews as he claimed in the preface, but in reality the book had other aims. It was the first systematic treatment of Dutch law as a national legal system. He wrote this book while imprisoned in the Loevestein Castle. Since he was the foremost intellectual of his time, he was allowed books and these were brought to him daily in a large book chest. He escaped by hiding in the chest and fled abroad where he spent the rest of his life. The only other reference to the nephews is found in Boswell's *The Life of Samuel Johnson*, where a nephew of Hugo Grotius asked for charity as he was poor and infirm, see Butler 1826: 208.

[51] For the origins of thetical rhetoric, Philo of Larissa and Cicero's championship of thetical rhetoric see Reinhardt 2003: 7–17.

[52] *Caecin.* 70–7; also *Sest.* 91–2; Cf. Harries 2006: 160 where she values Cicero's excellence as an advocate as based on the fact that he argued not on fact but on principle in *De Domo Sua*.

[53] *De or.* 44–6; Reinhardt 2003: 3ff.

of the invention of arguments and calls this a matter of intelligence, which should, if possible, be moved to a general level. His reference to the *status* theory as defined by Hermagoras of Temnos[54] indicates Cicero's combination of an abstract application of this method to determine the legal question with topical argumentation in his *Topica*.[55] After a short introduction to *topoi*, Cicero elaborates on the diverse sources of argument. Thereafter he sets out his ideas on *thesis*[56] and links topics with the *status* theory.[57] In paragraphs 91ff he indicates how to find correct topics for certain *theses*. This is not the place to enter the *topoi* debate, and the chapters entitled 'The short history of the *topos*' and 'The anonymous Seguerianus' by Reinhardt provide an excellent and clear exposition of the topic.[58]

6.2 Cicero's *Topica* and Roman legal methodology

Reinhardt devotes a special section of his introduction to the legal aspects of the *Topica*. He follows the orthodox narrative established during the nineteenth century and the ruling paradigm for most of the following century, namely that jurist and advocates belonged to totally different professions;[59] that Cicero had limited legal knowledge[60] and that Quintus Mucius Scaevola was the founder of Roman legal science.[61] As set out above these assumptions are no longer generally accepted. Not only has the role of private law been over-emphasised,[62] but the absolute ignoring or ignorance of the common law distinction between barristers and solicitors has been made common knowledge by increasing awareness of comparative law, globalisation and legal harmonisation. However, more than anything else the unquestioning acceptance that for centuries 'legal science' operated without any theoretical underpinning, but on intuition and authority has become difficult to acknowledge.[63] Reinhardt admits Cicero's interest in law,[64] and

---

[54] See Reinhardt 2003: 346–54.

[55] Idem: 5–7.

[56] *Top.* 79–83.

[57] *Top.* 83–91.

[58] Reinhardt 2003: 18–35 and 36–52.

[59] Idem: 54, 56, 59, *passim*.

[60] Stein 1978: 184: '(C)icero, whose knowledge of law was superficial rather than profound'; Reinhardt 2003: 54, fn.4: 'Cicero himself was not considered a *iurisconsultus* by his contemporaries.'

[61] Reinhardt 2003: 53–72.

[62] Idem: 54–7, 68. It should be kept in mind that in everyday life criminal law plays a bigger role for people and lawyers.

[63] Idem: 54. Rationality always relies on method, which is one of the subtexts of Kahnemann 2011.

[64] Idem: 59: 'Cicero has a keen interest in legal matters, which is not as obvious for a Roman advocate as it might seem.'

views Cicero's prolepsis in *De Oratore*[65] as announcing the future publication of the (fictional) *De iure civili in artem redigendo*. Reihardt never considers the *Topica* to have been the promised book. It is submitted that the so-called lost work (*De iure civili in artem redigendo*) qualifies as a suitable subtitle to the *Topica*.[66] However, a close reading of Reinhardt's analysis of passages in Cicero's other work, the *causa Curiana*, and the contemporary intellectual context justify the hypothesis that Cicero's combination of *thesis* with *topos* in his *Topica* was meant to be the definitive textbook of legal methodology. It is submitted that Reinhardt himself veers in this direction: he refers to Cicero's ideas about juristic methodology,[67] and he suggest as much in his discussion of Cicero's proposals for a reform of the *ius civile*[68] and rhetorical versus legal invention,[69] where he concludes that a number of Cicero's *loci* still feature as types of legal arguments; that Cicero was the first to develop a theory of causality in law and how the *Topica* set out the methodology of legal argumentation.[70] However, Reinhardt's objectives were different and he relied on the continental legal tradition and a legal historical narrative constructed by authorities ranging from Schulz and Wieacker to Frier,[71] Stein and Watson to provide his context.[72]

Indications of the internal contradictions are for example Reinhardt's comment on Crassus' remark in *De Oratore* that orators have made fools of themselves by not knowing the law properly and Reinhardt's explanation that this refers to cases before the praetor in the *formula* procedure.[73] The *causa Curiana* clearly shows that Scaevola, an educated patrician and most prominent jurist, was well versed in rhetoric and a skilled advocate at the bar,[74] which explains the character of his writings.[75]

---

[65] In *De or.* 1.188 Cicero proposes by way of Crassus that after defining the objective of law the methods of division, partition and definition should be used to develop a system.

[66] At 60–6.

[67] At 59.

[68] At 59–66.

[69] At 66–8. At 66 the classical point of view that a jurist will look at a case in an impartial way is proposed. An interesting example of the *locus ex contrario* is one of the foundational texts of international law, *De jure praedae*, written by Grotius, commissioned by the monopolistic Dutch East India Company to defend freedom of the seas and freedom of trade. See www.brittannica.com/EBchecked/topic/153610/De-Jure-Praedae (consulted on 6 March 2015); also Thomas 2003: 361–82.

[70] At 67f.

[71] Frier 1985: *passim*; Birks 1987: *passim*; Cohen 1988: *passim*.

[72] For the exalted role of the Roman jurist in this tradition see Thomas 2014a: 41–59.

[73] At 60: 'I have remarked above how the replacement of the system of the *legis actiones* by the formulary procedure had made the law more flexible and more adaptable to the particular case. However, this flexibility came with an increased complexity of the legal material an orator had to be familiar with (at least if compared with the relatively concise framework provided by the Twelve Tables and the *legis actiones*).'

[74] Thomas 2014b: 727–41.

[75] Reinhardt 2003: 57ff.

The belief that during the second and first century BC Roman legal science came into being without theoretical underpinning, and that the accession of *equites* to the ranks of jurists was the main reason requiring argumentation for legal opinions[76] should be met with scepticism. It is suggested that even before the Twelve Tables some form of theory underpinned Roman jurisprudence, of which unfortunately little information exists.[77] It is also highly plausible that during the last two centuries BC societal changes necessitated transparency and rationalisation in jurisprudence and that Scaevola formed part of this movement. This is not the place to go into detail about the *topoi*, and the question as to which were Cicero's sources. It is submitted that if the late Republican legal development is re-assessed without the myth of antagonism between jurists and orators, but rather in the context of increased specialisation within the legal profession, the *Topica* would receive not only a different reception, but another evaluation as well.

7. ARTIFICIAL INTELLIGENCE AND LEGAL ARGUMENTATION

The champions of 'legal science' believe in codification and/or in natural law, the system and the correct legal solution, that is to say they accept a number of premises as axiomata and syllogistic logic suffices. Legal historians are subversives as they point out that many of these axiomata have actually undergone change or disappeared in the course of legal history, for example the *paterfamilias* and his *ius vitae necisque*; the legal position of women; the concept of ownership[78] and freedom of contract and testation. Another interesting critique is found in the world of artificial intelligence. Bench-Capon, Prakken and Sartor[79] commence their essay by pointing out that a popular belief is that artificial intelligence can do no more than deduce the consequences of a precisely stated set of facts and legal rules. They surprisingly continue that this makes many lawyers sceptical as such a mechanical approach leaves out the most important part of legal reasoning. After setting out the development of the AI systems for legal argumentation they conclude:

> Legal reasoning has many distinctive features, which include: any proposed set of rules inevitably contain gaps and conflicts; many of its concepts are imprecisely defined meaning that interpretation is required; precedent cases play an

---

[76] Idem: 56.

[77] Watson 1991: 9: '(l)aw in the legal period . . . (t)he provisions taken together form a harmonious system.'

[78] *La Déclaration des Droits de l'homme et du citoyen.* Décret des 20,21,23 et 26 Août 1789. Article XVII. 'La propriété étant un droit inviolable et sacré, nul ne peut en être privé, si ce n'est lorsque la nécessité publique, légalement constatée, l'exige évidemment, et sous la condition d'une juste et préalable indemnité.'

[79] Bench-Capon et al. 2015: 1–20.

important role; procedural issues can influence the status of arguments; much legal argumentation is adversarial and dialectic in nature; the facts of a case need to be selected and characterised; many decisions express a preference for particular values and purposes; and all its conclusions are defeasible, subject often to formal appeal. All of these features mean that deduction cannot provide an adequate model of legal reasoning and instead argumentation must take centre stage to allow for these contextual, procedural and interpretative elements.[80]

A similar conclusion is voiced by Reinhardt who states: 'Legal decision-making refers to values and value-hierarchies, and corresponding considerations may affect or determine the scope of a legally relevant term; it is partly for this reason that legal argument resists to some extent a "logical" treatment'.[81]

8. CONCLUSION

The crux of this chapter is the paradox that the main source of late Republican law has been written off as an orator, a non-jurist, by continental legal historians. In 1965 Wieacker begins his *Cicero als Advokat* with the statement that this facet of Cicero, that is his being an advocate, is usually not part of the general knowledge of a cultured person. He described Cicero's place in the curriculum of the gymnasiast and how his work on rhetoric, philosophy, ethics and politics has formed Roman and European culture well into the nineteenth century. However, the sheer mass of the body of Cicero's work, his varied talents and interests, the date and mode of his death, the discovery of his private correspondence and the concomitant insight into the variance between the public mask and the private person, as well as the less savory aspects of his character, all combined to denigrate this proto-renaissance man as a failed politician, a translator and simplifier of Greek rhetoric and philosophy, a mere orator.

Tuori has dissected the foundation myth and found that in spite of widely diverging narratives general agreement appears to exist that for the foundation of legal science two elements were required, namely Roman law and Greek science. The methodological foundation of Roman jurisprudence has remained obscure as the Romanists who researched the influence of Greek science on Roman law focused on Greek philosophy and followed Plato's denigration of rhetoric. The discussion stagnated around the question as to which Greek philosophical school exercised influence, which may well have been one of the questions of the sphinx. It is more than interesting that on the basis of a few words, for example *generatim*, whole theories have been lanced, but the notion that Cicero, the principal source of information on

---

[80] At 17.
[81] Reinhardt 2003: 219.

both of these elements, might have been more than a mere reporter has never even provided the seed, let alone the thesis, that this multi-talented, Greek-educated, versatile intellectual could have stood at the cradle of Roman legal methodology. Reinhardt's commentary on Cicero's *Topica* provides a clear indication that the methodology of argumentation derived from a variety of Greek authors and paradigms, which were absorbed by Cicero and reworked by him for application in Roman law. Although constricted by his own areas of interest and the extrinsic *locus* of Romanist authorities, Reinhardt's comments clearly state that Cicero had a thorough knowledge of Greek philosophy in the widest sense and was prone to theoretical reflection; he also expected his readers to be acquainted with the basics of logic that made him take the underlying principles for granted. Finally, the division between philosophy and rhetoric varied through antiquity and of the two aspects of the latter the theatrical has overshadowed the theoretical, which facilitated the painting of Cicero's portrait by Mommsen and continues to minimise his originality and contribution to legal methodology.

BIBLIOGRAPHY

Baldini, A. (2006), 'Primo Levi's imaginary encounters: *Lavoro Creativo* and *Nel Parco*', *Arcadia-International Journal for Literary Studies* 41: 65–73.

Barzun, J. (2000), *From Dawn to Decadence: 500 years of Western cultural life*. London.

Baxter, L. G. (1979), 'Civil litigation and *jura novit curia*', *South African Law Journal* 96: 531–40.

Bench-Capon, T., Prakken, H. and Sartor, G. (2015), *Argumentation in Legal Reasoning*, Chapter 1, 1–20. Available at www.cs.uu./groups/IS/archive/henry/argbooksps.pdf, accessed 6 May 2015.

Birks, P. (1987), 'Review: The rise of the Roman jurists', *Oxford Journal of Legal Studies* 7: 444–53.

Butler, C. (1826), *The Life of Hugo Grotius: With brief minutes of the civil, ecclesiastical, and literary history of the Netherlands*. London.

Capogrossi Colognesi, L. (2011), 'Un futuro senza storia?' *Index* 39: 43–57.

Chalkomatas, D. (2004), 'Review: Tobias Reinhardt's *Marcus Tullius Cicero, Topica*', *Bryn Mawr Classical Review* 12.32, available at http://bmcr.brynmawr.edu/2004/2004-12-32.html, accessed 1 February 2016.

Cohen, D. (1988), 'Review: The rise of the Roman jurists', *Classical Philology* 83: 163–5.

Cowen, D. V. (2004), 'Early years of aspiration', in D. V. Cowen and D. P. Visser, eds, *The University of Cape Town Law Faculty: A history 1859–2004*. Cape Town. 1–23.

De Brauw, M. (2006), 'Cicero, Servius, and the Lawyer Jokes at *Pro Murena* 19–30', available at https://camws.org/meeting/2006/abstracts/debrauw.html, consulted 3 May 2015.

Diliberto, O. (2005), 'Una palingenesi "aperta"', in M. Humbert, ed., *Le Dodici Tavole: Dai Decemviri agli Umanisti*. Pavia. 217–38.

Dolezalek, G. (1989), 'Stare decisis': Persuasive Force of Precedent and Old Authority (12th–20th century). Cape Town.

Frier, B. W. (1985), The Rise of the Roman Jurists: Studies in Cicero's Pro Caecina. Princeton.

Galsworthy, J. (1926), 'The Silver Spoon', in J. Galsworthy, A Modern Comedy. London (published in Penguin Books 1967).

Harries, J. (2006), Cicero and the Jurists: From citizens' law to the lawful state. London.

Kahneman, D. (2011), Thinking, Fast and Slow. London/New York.

Laws, J. (2004), 'Epilogue: Cicero and the modern advocate', in J. Powell and J. Paterson, eds, Cicero the Advocate. Oxford. 401–16.

Levi, P. (2007), 'In the park', in P. Levi, A tranquil star: unpublished stories (translated by A. Goldstein and A. Bastagli). New York/London. 57–71.

Mann, F. A. (1977), 'Fusion of the legal professions?' Law Quarterly Review 93: 367–77.

Mommsen, Th. (1856), Römische Geschichte. Bd. 3. Von Sullas Tode bis zur Schlacht von Thapsus. Leipzig, available at http://www.deutschesarchiv.de/mommsen_roemische03_1856/0581–0586, accessed 1 February 2016.

Pringsheim, F. (1935), 'The inner relationship between English and Roman law', Cambridge Law Journal 5: 347–65.

Reinhardt, T. (2003), Marcus Tullius Cicero Topica. Oxford.

Schulz, F. (1961), Geschichte der römischen Rechtswissenschaft. Weimar.

Shackleton Bailey, D. R. (1978), Cicero's Letters to his Friends. 2 vols. Harmondsworth/New York/Victoria/Ontario/Auckland.

Stein, P. (1978), 'The place of Servius Sulpicius Rufus in the development of Roman legal science', in O. Behrends, M. Disselhorst, H. Lange, D. Liebs, J. G. Wolff, and C. Wollschläger, eds, Festschrift für Franz Wieacker zum 70. Geburtstag. Göttingen. 175–84.

Stein, P. (1991–2), 'Roman law, common law, and civil law', Tulane Law Review 66: 1591–603.

Stroux, J. (1926), 'Summum ius summa iniuria. Ein Kapitel aus der Geschichte der interpretatio iuris, in Festschrift Paul Speiser-Sarasin. Basel. 115–58. Reprinted in J. Stroux (1949), Römische Rechtswissenschaft und Rhetorik. Potsdam.

Tellegen, J. W. and Tellegen-Couperus, O. E. (2000), 'Law and rhetoric in the causa Curiana', Orbis Juris Romani 6: 171–202.

Tellegen-Couperus, O. E. and Tellegen, J. W. (2006), 'Nihil hoc ad ius, ad Ciceronem', Revue Internationale des droits de l'Antiquité 53: 381–408.

Thomas, P. J. (2003), 'Piracy, privateering and the United States of the Netherlands', Revue Internationale des droits de l'Antiquité 50: 361–82.

Thomas, P. J. (2012), 'Die resepsie van Romeinse reg in die Suid-Afrikaanse regstelsel: stare decisis en curia ius novit', LitNet Akademies (Regte) 9: 237–53, available at http://www.litnet.co.za, accessed 1 February 2016.

Thomas, P. J. (2014a), 'Ars aequi et boni, legal argumentation and the correct legal solution', Zeitschrift der Savigny-Stiftung für Rechtsgeschichte, romanistische Abteilung 131: 41–59.

Thomas, P. J. (2014b), 'The intention of the testator from the causa Curiana to modern South African law', in J. Hallebeek, M. Schermaier, R. Fiori, E. Metzger and J.-P. Coriat, eds, Inter cives necnon peregrinos: *essays in honour of Boudewijn Sirks*. Göttingen. 727–41.

Thomas, P. J. (2014c), 'Some reflections on the role of the judge from the perspective of a mixed legal system', in S. Corrêa Fattori, R. Corrêa Lofrano and J. L. N. Magalhães Serretti, eds, *Estudos em homenagem a Luiz Fabiano Corrêa*. São Paulo. 341–53.

Tuori, K. (2007), *Ancient Roman Lawyers and Modern Legal Ideals: Studies on the impact of contemporary concerns in the interpretation of ancient Roman legal history*. Frankfurt am Main.

Van Caenegem, R. C. (2002), *European Law in the Past and the Future: Unity and diversity over two millennia*. Cambridge.

Vaughn, J. W. (1985), 'Law and rhetoric in the *causa Curiana*', *Classical Antiquity* 4: 208–22.

Viscount Kilmuir (1960), 'The migration of the Common Law: 1. Introduction', *Law Quarterly Review* 76: 41–5.

Von Wobeser, C. (2011), 'The effective use of legal sources: how much is too much and what is the role for *iura novit curia*', in A. J. van den Berg, ed., *Arbitration Advocacy in Changing Times*. Deventer. 201–18.

Watson, A. (1990), 'Roman law and English law: two patterns of legal development', *Loyola Law Review* 36: 247–68.

Watson, A. (1991), *Roman Law and Comparative Law*. Athens, GA.

Waugh, E. (1967), 'Scott-King's modern Europe', in *Work Suspended and Other Stories*. Harmondsworth/Baltimore/Victoria. 195–250.

Wieacker, F. (1965), *Cicero als Advokat: Vortrag gehalten vor der Berliner Juristischen Gesellschaft am 29. April 1964*. Berlin.

Wieacker, F. (1967), 'The *causa Curiana* and contemporary Roman jurisprudence', *Irish Jurist* 2: 151–64.

Zimmermann, R. (1984), 'Die Rechtsprechung des Supreme Court of the Cape of Good Hope am Ende der sechziger Jahre des 19. Jahrhunderts', in J. V. van der Westhuizen, P. J. Thomas, S. Scott, D. van der Merwe, J. Th. de Smit, and R. Feenstra, eds, *Huldigingsbundel Paul van Warmelo*. Pretoria. 286–307.

Chapter 3

Reading a Dead Man's Mind: Hellenistic Philosophy, Rhetoric and Roman Law

Olga Tellegen-Couperus and Jan Willem Tellegen

1. INTRODUCTION

A recurring topic of discussion, both in Roman antiquity and in modern times, is the connection between philosophy, rhetoric and law. Of the many philosophers and their schools that existed in Roman antiquity there are two that may have been particularly relevant to the development of Roman law: the Hellenistic schools of Stoicism (Middle Stoa) and the New Academy. In the second century BC, the Roman military conquest of Greece led to the Greek cultural conquest of Rome, introducing Greek philosophy and, in its wake, rhetoric. In that very same century, the praetor was put in charge of jurisdiction, legal procedure was innovated with the formulary procedure, and many new legal institutions were introduced. It is now generally assumed that there was a connection between the rise of Roman law and the arrival of Greek philosophy and rhetoric in Rome. However, the question which of the two philosophical schools was most relevant to the development of Roman law has not yet been answered satisfactorily.[1]

In attempting to answer this question, we will use the concept of *voluntas testatoris* as a case study. We will first briefly consider to what extent the sources – mainly Justinian's Digest and the rhetorical and philosophical works of Cicero – can be of use (section 3.2). Next, we will summarily explain the modern views on the *voluntas testatoris* and the knowledge theories of the Stoa and the New Academy in antiquity (section 3.3). We will then describe the modern interpretation(s) of the *causa Curiana* (the first case in which the *voluntas testatoris* is mentioned), relate it to Stoic epistemology, and compare it with the rhetorical sources (section 4). Finally, having analysed four *responsa* from the Digest that are generally assumed to deal with the *voluntas testatoris* (section 5), we will conclude (section 6) that even though the Roman jurists did not develop a blanket theory of *voluntas testatoris*, if they did follow a particular philosophical school when solving legal problems like those caused by an unclear will, it would more likely have been the New Academy rather than the Stoa.

---

[1] For a clear and differentiated overview, see Wieacker 1990: 618–21.

2. THE SOURCES AND THE DEBATE

In trying to determine which of the two schools had the greater impact on the development of Roman law, we submit as an initial observation that the guidance or direction offered by the sources is relatively sparse. True, the early Roman works on philosophy and rhetoric, of which those written by Cicero in the first century BC are the most important ones, do contain references to law. In his *De Legibus*, Cicero describes law as 'the highest reason, implanted in Nature, which commands what ought to be done and forbids the opposite', using ideas and concepts that are typical of the Stoa.[2] Yet in his *Academica*, Cicero argues against the knowledge theory (epistemology) of the Stoa. Then again, in this context he does not refer to law. In *De Oratore*, Cicero describes the ideal orator as being well versed in philosophy and law, and in the context of *inventio* – the first duty of the orator – he shows that the New Academy is much more useful for inventing legal arguments than the Stoa (2.157–9). His other works on rhetoric too, such as the *Partitiones Oratoriae* and the *Topica*, are clearly linked to the Academy.[3] The upshot is that Romanists tend to view Cicero as an eclectic and, more to the purpose of our argument, believe that his works on philosophy and rhetoric cannot reliably help ascertain which philosophical school held sway in the evolution of Roman law.

How about specifically legal sources? Whether the Roman jurists referred to philosophy in their opinions on legal problems we simply cannot know, because the original opinions have not come down to us. We know them mainly through the sixth-century collection of Justinian's Digest, in which they were probably included in a much shortened form. These excerpts contain hardly any references to philosophy at all, the well-known exception being Marcian's reference to the once famous Stoa leader Chrysippus (D. 1.3.2). In sum, the legal sources do not appear to offer tangible, usable clues about the prevailing philosophical influence on Roman law either.

The middle of the nineteenth century saw the beginning of the debate on the indebtedness of Roman law to philosophy. It was argued and assumed that Stoicism had been very influential on, for instance, the concepts of *ius naturale*, *ius gentium*, and *ratio naturalis*, and that Cicero and the Roman jurists alike would have known something that is comparable to the modern concept of human rights. To this day this view has its adherents,[4] but it has also been disputed; while opponents admit that the

---

[2] Cic. *Leg.* 1.18: 'lex est ratio summa insita in natura, quae iubet ea quae facienda sunt, prohibetque contraria.' For the Stoic concepts of nature and reason, see Sandbach 1989: 31–4.

[3] So Gaines 2002: 475. In his early treatise *De Inventione*, Cicero was still struggling how to find a place for philosophy in rhetorical theory; thus Corbeill 2002: 40.

[4] For an overview of the discussion, see Crifó 2005: 240–69. See also Mantovani and Schiavone 2007 and Giltaij 2011.

Roman jurists would have been well acquainted with the various philosophical schools, they are adamant that the Roman jurists, when giving
opinions about legal problems, would have done so without heeding
philosophy.[5]

In the course of the twentieth century, the debate on the influence of
philosophy on Roman law extended to other topics, such as the method
the Roman jurists used. A particular bone of contention was (and is)
whether they applied Stoic logic; this was much debated. A large number of
prominent Romanists have assumed that they did.[6] In his recent book *The
Invention of Law in the West*, Schiavone argues that jurists like Q. Mucius
Scaevola integrated Stoic logic into Roman law, thereby creating 'a new
way of conceiving law, which would transmute its protocols into those
of a science without equal in antiquity, no less compact and conceptually
dense than the great classical philosophy'. There was no room for rhetoric.[7]
Nonetheless, the Roman jurists themselves do not explicitly call themselves
adherents of Stoicism, and so the question remains whether Stoic theory and
lifestyle really did help shape Roman jurisprudence.[8]

It is remarkable that in this debate it is Stoicism that has virtually
monopolised attention. Whether the New Academy has had any influence
on the development of Roman law has hardly been investigated.[9] This lop-
sidedness may have something to do with the Romanists' view of Roman
law as a science, that is, as an organic system based on logic.[10] The scientific
character of Roman law is usually explained by connecting it with the dialectical method that was introduced by Plato and that was also practised by
the Aristotelian and Stoic schools. To Plato, this method meant the study
of forms (*genera* and *species*) and was to lead to the discovery of principles
governing the forms and explaining individual cases.[11]

What is usually not explained is that as a form of logic the dialectical
method is based on two principles: the *principium contradictionis* – two contradictory statements cannot both be true in the same sense at the same time
– and the *principium tertii exclusii* – of two contradictory propositions one
must be true, the other false: there is no third alternative. Stoicism used these
two principles within the framework of its knowledge theory. Not only were
these principles not generally accepted, they were in fact fiercely opposed by
the adherents of the New Academy. Stripped down to its essence, the debate
between the two schools turned on the question of whether it is possible

---

[5] Thus, for instance, Van der Waerdt 1990.
[6] See Wieacker 1990: 630–9.
[7] Schiavone 2012: 186. Elsewhere, 198, he adds that there was no room for rhetoric.
[8] Thus Bund 1980: 145.
[9] Formigoni 1996 is an exception.
[10] On this topic, see Tellegen and Tellegen-Couperus 2013.
[11] Thus Schulz 1953: 62–3. There are, however, no sources to prove that the Roman jurists
     used the dialectic method to construct a legal system.

to know anything for certain: according to the Stoa it was, according to the New Academy it was not.[12]

The question whether any knowledge can be certain may also be relevant in a legal context. An almost archetypal case in point is when someone has made a will that is unclear or that may not hold in the light of changed circumstances. In Romanist literature, it is assumed that Roman jurists, when interpreting such a will in accordance with the testator's intention, wanted to ascertain the testator's real, or at the very least presumed, intention. Consequently, and inevitably so, it is also assumed that in the jurists' view it was possible to know that intention. Since infallible knowledge was at the heart of the debate between the Stoa and the New Academy, attempting to find out whether the jurists really held that view is a worthwhile pursuit. In this way, we may learn more about the relationship between Roman law, rhetoric and the Hellenistic schools of philosophy.

3. INTERPRETATION OF THE *VOLUNTAS TESTATORIS* AND EPISTEMOLOGY

In this section we will briefly outline modern views on the interpretation of the *voluntas testatoris* and the knowledge theories of the Stoa and the New Academy.

The concept of *voluntas testatoris* is related to the law of succession. When someone has made a will that is unclear or that may not hold in the light of changed circumstances, the question arises how the will should be interpreted. In Roman antiquity, textbooks on rhetoric like Cicero's *De Inventione* provided various answers to that question. Similarly, the *responsa* of the Roman jurists contain many examples of the interpretation of unclear or ambiguous wills. In modern Romanist literature, both types of sources have been used to study the concept of *voluntas testatoris*.

Over the past century or so, the interpretation of wills in Roman law has generated a variety of views.[13] Around 1900, it was generally assumed that the classical jurists interpreted unclear wills in accordance with the wording of the will, that Justinian favoured an interpretation based on the testator's intention, and that the compilers adapted the classical texts accordingly. However, in 1926, Johannes Stroux argued that as early as the late Republic the Roman jurists had begun to interpret unclear wills on the basis of the testator's intention and that they had done so by using the *status* theory of rhetoric and particularly the *status verba-voluntas* as introduced by the Greek rhetorician Hermagoras (second century BC). Stroux' view triggered a lively discussion, which resulted in a wide variety of opinions, but on one issue most scholars agreed: there was no connection between law and rhetoric.

[12] See Hankinson 1995: 105–8, with sources.
[13] Wieling 1972: 56–65.

Today, the view most commonly held is that the Roman jurists originally interpreted wills literally, that in the late Republic they also used other criteria, such as definition, the *voluntas testatoris* and the *favor heredis*, but that in Justinian law the *voluntas* prevailed.

The only Romanist to provide an elaborate explanation of the *voluntas testatoris* and its interpretation is Voci. In Chapter 4 of his handbook on the Roman law of succession, Voci discusses the *voluntas* in the dispositions *mortis causa* and particularly the relationship between declaration and intention. In this context, he argues that they are of equal importance, the declaration being instrumental to the intention. If the declaration does not correspond with the intention, the clause is invalid. If the declaration and intention differ only partially, the declaration must be interpreted on the basis of language or logic.[14] In Chapter 5, Voci discusses the interpretation of dispositions *mortis causa*: when interpreting a will, one should try to discover the testator's intention. Difficult though it may be to probe the testator's mind, it can be done, because the testator is assumed to have been a reasonable human being who can be assumed to have made a reasonable will.[15]

According to Voci, the interpreter must first try to discover the testator's real intention on the basis of historical, thus provable facts (the *volontà effettiva*). If that proves impossible, the interpreter can use the criterion of reasonableness to attribute a presumed intention (the *volontà induttiva*) to the testator. Voci distinguishes two forms of presumed intention: the *volontà verosimile* (it is likely that the testator will choose the most reasonable and opportune of two possible results) and the *volontà implicita* (it is assumed that the testator implicitly means to include a certain disposition in his will). The only time the criterion of reasonableness cannot be applied is when the testator's intention appears to be *contraria*.[16]

Moving on to the second topic of this section – the knowledge theories of the Stoa and the New Academy – what we know of them mainly stems from two sources, Cicero's *Academica* dating from 45 BC and the second-century works of Sextus Empiricus. Both sources deal with Stoic epistemology in the light of the criticism that Arcesilaos (New Academy, third century BC) levelled against the views of Zeno, the founder of the Stoa, and of the objections Carneades (second century BC) raised against the views of Chrysippus. The debate between the Stoa and the New Academy on the question of the certainty of knowledge belongs to the history of Greek philosophy. Since

---

[14] Voci 1963: 823–5.

[15] Idem: 885–989.

[16] In this context, Voci 1963: 887 and 894 refers to Cic. *Inv. rhet.* 2.123 twice, namely when introducing the real intention and when introducing the implicit intention. In this section, Cicero states that an advocate who pleads *contra scriptum* will sometimes show that the writer always had the same end in view and sometimes that the writer's purpose has to be modified to fit the occasion as a result of some act or event. He does not refer to the writer's real or implicit intention.

our interest is in the history of Roman law, we will only address this debate insofar as it is relevant to our argument.

For our purpose, two issues or questions in this debate are relevant: 'what can we know?' and 'how do we know the world?'.[17] Both issues belong to the sphere of philosophy that was called Physics, the study of the physical world. Regarding the first question, the Stoa held that the *kosmos* is not the result of chance; it is a living organism. All things in the *kosmos* consist of an active, divine principle (*pneuma*, breath) and a passive principle (*hule*, matter), and the tension between these two principles (*tonos*) varies. The soul, for instance, has a very refined form of *pneuma*, being at the same time rational and corporal. Only these things exist, that is, they can act and be acted upon. Other things are incorporeal, such as time, place and emptiness.

The second question ('how do we know the world?') was the central issue in the debate between the Stoa and the New Academy. In the Stoic theory of knowledge, the main concept is impression (*phantasia*).[18] According to the Stoics, our senses receive constant impressions that pass from objects through the senses to the mind. The mind can judge whether an impression gives a true representation of reality or a false one. Some impressions contain such a strong guarantee of reality that they force our mind to 'assent'; they then become a kataleptic, that is, recognisable, presentation of reality. The crux of the controversy between the two schools was this concept of *katalepsis*, recognition.

The question was whether perception by means of *katalepsis* was true. In his *Academica*, Cicero summarises the discussion as follows. According to the Stoics, he says, *dialectica* was invented to serve as a 'distinguisher' or judge between truth and falsehood (2.91). Cicero, however, echoing Carneades' criticism, brings two arguments to refute this statement. First, he states that *dialectica* as such is unable to provide certainty. As an example, he describes the so-called *sorites*: when from a heap of corn the grains are taken away one at a time – at what point does the heap cease to be a heap? (2.92). The second argument against the use of *dialectica* for judging what is true or false is the weakness of the principle that every proposition is either true or false. Cicero demonstrates this with the famous liar paradox: if you say that you are lying and you say it truly, are you lying? If such a disjunctive proposition (consisting of two contrary statements) can be false, neither is true (2.95–7).

According to Cicero, Stoic *dialectica* will not help settle the question of the certainty of knowledge. It is better to hold, with Carneades, that some presentations can be qualified as probable and others as not probable. Probability comes in degrees. In order to qualify a particular presentation as probable it is essential that it be unhindered by anything. Thus the wise man

---

[17] See Sandbach 1989: 85–94.
[18] See Rist 1969: 133–51.

will make use of whatever probable presentation he encounters, if nothing presents itself that is contrary to that probability (2.99).

When comparing Voci's theory of the *voluntas testatoris* with the theories of knowledge developed in Hellenistic philosophy, we cannot help but notice a certain similarity between Voci's ideas and Stoic epistemology: where the Stoics regarded all things that exist as consisting of breath and matter, Voci considered the will as consisting of the document and the intention. Whatever one may think of this equation, it does inspire the question whether the way in which Romanists interpret the *voluntas testatoris* has a parallel in Stoic epistemology. Asking the question is easy: answering it, alas, may not be as straightforward, but in the following two sections, on the *causa Curiana* and four *responsa* from Justinian's Digest respectively, we will attempt to do just that.

4. THE *CAUSA CURIANA*

In Roman oratory as well as in Romanist literature, the textbook example of the interpretation of unclear wills is the *causa Curiana*. Details of this lawsuit, which was tried in about 92 BC, have come down to us in the works of Cicero. Certain passages in Cicero's *De Oratore* and *Brutus* give the following specifics.[19] A man called M. Coponius drew up a will in which he instituted any son(s) that might be born to him as his heir(s). Coponius added a *substitutio pupillaris* stipulating that a certain M. Curius was to inherit the estate if his, that is, Coponius', son(s) should die before reaching adulthood. Coponius died without issue and when his will had been opened and read, the inheritance passed to Curius, because it was assumed that the condition relating to the substitution had been fulfilled. However, the heir by intestacy, who was also called Coponius, denied it had and claimed the inheritance. In the trial that followed, Quintus Mucius Scaevola, speaking for this Coponius, argued in favour of a literal interpretation of the will, whereas Marcus Licinius Crassus, speaking for Curius, defended an interpretation that relied on the testator's intention. Crassus won.

In antiquity, the *causa Curiana* was a *cause célèbre* for reasons of rhetoric. It is also famous today, but for a different reason: it is regarded as having introduced an important innovation into the Roman law of succession, that is, the idea of the testator's 'presumed intention'. It is for that reason that

---

[19] *De or.* 1.180, 238, 242–5; 2.24,140 and 220–2; *Brut.* 143–5, 194–8, and 256. Also references in *Top.* 44 and *Caecin.* 53, 67 and 69. In *Inv. rhet.* 2.122, Cicero describes a similar case but does not add any names. These sources do not give a completely uniform description of the case, for instance, only in *De Inventione* is the testator said to have had a spouse, in *Topica* is the son said to be born within ten months, and in *Caecin.* 53 is the son called a *postumus*. Since these additions are irrelevant to the legal problem, we prefer to omit them in our description of the case.

Romanists tend to direct their gaze towards the *voluntas testatoris* and, by extension, Crassus' plea. A good example of this orientation is Voci's analysis of this case.

Voci regards the discussion in the *causa Curiana* as an important moment 'per la ricerca induttiva della volontà'.[20] He summarises Scaevola's argument on behalf of the heir by intestacy as follows: the will is invalid because of the inefficacy of the pupillary substitution and the non-existence of the vulgar substitution. The latter is the institution of a second or further heir in case the institution of the heir is or becomes invalid.[21] Rebutting Scaevola's argument, Crassus is said to have stated that the testator must be understood to have implied the vulgar substitution, because he who presupposes to appoint any son of his own as his heir and appoints a substitute for him, does all the more want a substitute for himself. In his plea, Crassus contrasts strictness with *aequitas*, written words with *voluntas*, *verba* with *res*. Voci explains the word *res* as the objective situation that by itself imposes the solution on the reasonable man: the testator can be supposed to be a reasonable man. In this connection, *res* is one and the same thing as *voluntas*. According to Voci, the practical value of Crassus' defence was that it led to the recognition of the implicit intention and more in general of the presumed intention; theoretically, it sired the twin ideas of the presumed intention as the testator's intention and of the testator as a prudent person.

Many scholars have adopted Voci's interpretation, although they do not always mention the implicit vulgar substitution.[22] The most recent example is the explanation of the *causa Curiana* offered by Schilling.[23] He suggests that – according to Crassus – the 'testator had erroneously assumed that he would have a descendant. He had not anticipated that he could die without issue. Had he considered this possibility, he would probably have appointed Curius as heir'.

How do these theories relate to Stoic epistemology? Although neither Voci nor Schilling (nor any other scholar for that matter) refers to any philosophical school, their way of reasoning strongly recalls Stoic epistemology. Let us first examine Voci's comment on Crassus' plea and particularly the implicit vulgar substitution. Voci tries to reconstruct the presumed intention of testator Coponius by means of logical reasoning. The major premise is that Coponius was a reasonable man who wanted his will to be valid. The minor premise is that Coponius could prevent his will from failing by adding a vulgar substitution to the pupillary one. Voci's conclusion is that Coponius must have intended to include a vulgar substitution

---

[20] Voci 1963: 912–14.

[21] For an example, see Gai. *Inst.* 2.174.

[22] For an overview, see Tellegen and Tellegen-Couperus 2000: 174–81. Now also Liebs 2012: 46–9.

[23] Schilling 2014: 316.

even though he did not literally do so. What is clear from Voci's argumentation is that he used Stoic philosophy in two ways: one, by assuming that
the intention of the testator was a *res* that exists and that can be known for
certain by means of *katalepsis*, and two, by constructing a line of reasoning
based on logic.

Schilling's reasoning also comes close to Stoic epistemology. He distinguishes two possible situations:

1. The testator had considered the possibility that he could die without
   issue.
2. The testator had not considered the possibility that he could die without
   issue.

It is impossible for both possibilities to be true at the same time, Schilling
argues, so either (1) or (2) is true. According to Schilling, possibility (1)
can be ruled out because, if the testator had considered this possibility, he
would probably have appointed Curius as his heir. So possibility (2) must
be true. Schilling then constructs Coponius' intention as follows: he wanted
the substitute Curius to be his heir. His reasoning brings to mind one of
the principles of Stoic *dialectica* referred to, that of the excluded third (any
proposition is either true or false).

This summary of the modern views on the *voluntas testatoris* in the *causa
Curiana* and their comparison to Stoic epistemology prompt the question
whether these views are borne out by the sources. We think they are not,
for two reasons. First, Voci's assumption that a vulgar substitution formed
part of the discussion in the *causa Curiana* is not supported by any of the
sources describing this case. Nor did Scaevola qualify Coponius' will as
invalid because of the non-existence of a vulgar substitution, and nor did
Crassus argue that Coponius had implicitly included such a substitution.
Second, Voci's premise that a *substitutio vulgaris* would have saved the will
is not true. Both types of substitution presuppose the existence of a primary
heir. Coponius, however, had added a condition to the *institutio heredis* ('if a
son is born, he must be heir'). Scaevola's argument ('in order to die, one first
has to be born') would therefore also hold against a *substitutio vulgaris*. Even
if a *substitutio vulgaris* had been added, the testator's intention would have
been equally unclear.

Schilling's interpretation is not based on the sources either. He reasons
that there were two situations Coponius could have taken into account,
that is, that he would have children and that he would not have children.
However, the wording of the will leaves open various possibilities. The
conditional wording of the *heredis institutio* as quoted by Cicero (*si mihi filius
genitur unus pluresve, is mihi heres esto*) indicates that he did not know whether
he would have one or more children or none at all. The fact that he did not
explicitly provide for the situation that he would have no children does not

mean that he did not consider this possibility. Maybe he assumed that the *substitutio pupillaris* would apply in that case as well, because as Crassus' reference to common practice suggests that had happened before.[24] In short, the wording of the will is such that the possibilities (1) and (2) mentioned by Schilling can in fact both be true and that it is unfeasible to reliably reconstruct the *voluntas testatoris* by means of dialectical logic.

In fact, if Crassus had used any reasoning suggested by modern Romanists, not he but Scaevola may well have won the trial. Our point is that logic of any kind would not have been helpful in this case. Carneades' criticism would still hold: there is no criterion for establishing the truth and dialectics do not help. It is virtually impossible to ascertain either the testator's real or his presumed intention.

What is more, the dispute between Scaevola and Crassus was not about the *voluntas testatoris* but about the interpretation of the words in Coponius' will.[25] The pleas of both advocates make this clear. Scaevola referred to the words of the will, and particularly to the wording of the *substitutio pupillaris*: in combination with the conditional institution of the heir, it was invalid. Crassus did not deny that the wording of the pupillary substitution was inadequate, but he referred to common practice showing that for want of a better one this wording had been long accepted. He then added that this was what the testator wanted.

Crassus' plea is a perfect example of the strategy used by the speaker who is attacking the letter of the will, as described by Cicero in his *De Inventione*, 2.138: he will first of all argue the equity of his case. After that, he will use other arguments, such as stating that the author having risen from the dead would approve of this act or interpretation. Crassus did not found his plea on the testator's intention in the sense of his 'real' or 'presumed' intention; he only used the *voluntas* in the sense of probable, presumable intention and he did so to support his main argument of equity. In other words, if any Hellenistic school of philosophy were relevant here, it would be that of the New Academy.

5. VOLUNTAS TESTATORIS IN JUSTINIAN'S DIGEST

In Justinian's Digest, hundreds of texts concern the law of succession but only sixty mention the *voluntas testatoris*.[26] Most of them date from the second century. In modern literature it is assumed that in the early Empire some jurists began to use the concept of the testator's presumed intention that had first been recognised in the *causa Curiana*. According to Schilling,

[24] According to Cicero, *Brut.* 197 *in fine*, Crassus argued that 'most people wrote their wills in this way and that it was valid procedure and always had been'.

[25] In the same vein, Wieacker 1967: 178.

[26] According to the *Vocabularium Iurisprudentiae Romanae* V (1939), s.v. testator.

these jurists were not interested in subdividing the testator's real and presumed intention in the abstract so as to develop proper technical terms. Only Papinian used the term *coniectura voluntatis* – and he did so twice – to describe the construction based on the testator's presumed intention.[27] In addition to the cases in which the *voluntas testatoris* is actually mentioned, a large number of other *responsa* in the Digest are today explained in terms of the testator's intention, even if they do not mention it.

Do the latter *responsa* support the commonly held view that when interpreting an unclear will the Roman jurists aimed at ascertaining the testator's real or presumed intention? And did Papinian really develop a theory of the testator's presumed intention? Of course, a discussion of all of these *responsa* falls well beyond the scope of this chapter. We selected four to begin answering these questions. The first two are *responsa* that Romanists link to *voluntas* even though the word is not used in them. The other two texts are the *responsa* in which Papinian used the words *coniectura voluntatis*.

5.1 D. 32.62

The first *responsum* we will discuss is D. 32.62. It stems from the second-century jurist Salvius Iulianus (Julian).

> Iulianus, liber singularis de ambiguitatibus. Qui duos mulos habebat ita legavit: 'mulos duos, qui mei erunt cum moriar, heres dato': idem nullos mulos, sed duas mulas reliquerat. Respondit Servius deberi legatum, quia mulorum appellatione etiam mulae continentur, quemadmodum appellatione servorum etiam servae plerumque continentur. Id autem eo veniet, quod semper sexus masculinus etiam femininum sexum continet.

> Julian, *Ambiguities*, sole book: A man who had two mules left a legacy as follows: 'Let my heir give two *muli* which shall be mine when I die.' He left no *muli* but two *mulae*. Servius replied that the legacy was due, for *mulae* are included under the term *muli*, just as *servae* are generally included under the term *servi*. This may be caused by the fact that the male sex always also includes the female.[28]

In this *responsum*, Julian quotes Servius Sulpicius Rufus (Servius), a contemporary and friend of Cicero's, and the most prominent jurist of his day. It is important to note that this *responsum* was selected by the compilers from Julian's *liber singularis de ambiguitatibus*; it is included in book D. 32 entitled *De legatis et fideicommissis*. D. 32.62 deals with a *legatum per damnationem* in which the testator bequeathed two mules with the additional remark *qui mei*

---

[27] Schilling 2014: 317–20 lists opinions of Labeo (D. 33.2.41), Celsus *pater* (D. 31.29 pr.), Celsus *filius* (possibly as advisor of Emperor Hadrian, in Paul. D. 5.2.28), Africanus (D. 32.64), and Q. Cerv. Scaevola (D. 31.89.1). However, in none of these texts can the testator's intention be regarded as a presumed intention.

[28] The translations of this and the following Digest texts are based on those in Watson 1985.

erunt cum moriar, 'which shall be mine when I die'. When he wrote his will, he owned two he-mules. When he died, he owned two she-mules. The question arose whether the bequest of the mules was owed. Servius said it was, because she-mules are regarded as having been included under he-mules. He underpins his opinion by comparing this case with female slaves, who are usually understood to be included in the word slaves. Julian agrees with Servius and rephrases his *responsum* in a general sense: 'This may be caused by the fact that the male sex always also includes the female.'

The last sentence of this *responsum* has evoked a considerable amount of comment in modern Romanist literature.[29] We will look at the observations of two scholars who interpreted it referring to the testator's intention: Wieling and Harke. In his book on the interpretation of wills in Roman law, Wieling analyses this *responsum* in the context of interpretation by means of definitions and grammar.[30] He states that definitions were often used by Roman jurists to ascertain the meaning of concepts. In all these cases, the point in question is whether a particular word is defined in a strict sense or whether the intention of the testator may have influenced the meaning of the concept. A number of such definitions suggest that they have an absolute meaning, as in the last sentence of D. 32.62, where Julian states that the male sex always includes the female. Wieling, however, argues that there cannot have been such a general view: it is easy to think of examples in which this view would lead to preposterous outcomes and in which Julian would certainly decide otherwise. Even so, Wieling thinks it is clear that Julian did not allow the testator's intention to influence the meaning of the word *muli* and that Julian conceivably abided by this decision as long as it did not clearly lead to results that are 'unsachgemäss' (wrong).

Harke, on the other hand, thinks that Julian did allow the testator's intention to influence the interpretation of the word *muli*.[31] In his view, Julian assumed that the testator's experience in life would determine what could be expected to be the testator's intention regarding the mules. This view forms part of Harke's theory that *verba* and *voluntas* were supplementary, not competitive, criteria.

We disagree with Wieling's comment on D. 32.62, because, in our view, the legal problem in this case does not turn on definition. Cicero describes definition as a phrase that explains what the thing defined is (*quid sit*).[32] In this case, however, neither Servius nor Julian explains what a mule is; they merely explain that the word *mulus* is used in various ways. The legal problem, then, is caused by the vague, imprecise use of this word in the will in question. In

---

[29] See Fiuris (*Archivio elettronico per l'interpretazione delle fonti giuridiche romane*: CD-ROM by Pierangelo Catalano and Francesco Sitzia) *ad loc.*

[30] Wieling 1972: 120–1.

[31] Harke 2012: 64.

[32] Cicero, *Top.* 26.

other words, the legal problem turns on ambiguity, which may well be precisely why Julian included this case in his book *De ambiguitatibus*. He solved
the problem by referring to the general usage of the word.[33] Julian did not in
any way consider the testator's intention, presumed or otherwise.

Harke's comment does not seem very convincing either; Julian does not
refer to the testator's experience in life, let alone to his intention, and we
therefore cannot accept that this *responsum* supports Harke's theory about
the use of *verba* and *voluntas* in Roman law.

We think Julian's opinion can best be explained by means of Cicero's
description of the rhetorical *status ambiguitas* in his *De Inventione*. In 2.116,
he begins to describe the controversies that turn upon written documents,
that is, when some doubt arises from the nature of the writing. Such doubt
comes from ambiguity, from the letter and intent, from conflict of laws,
from reasoning by analogy and from definition. A controversy arises from
ambiguity when there is doubt as to what the writer meant because the
written statement has two or more meanings. After giving an example of
such a controversy, Cicero offers various arguments that can be useful:

> Primum, si fieri poterit, demonstrandum est non esse ambigue scriptum, prop-
> terea quod omnes in consuetudine sermonis sic uti solent eo verbo uno pluri-
> busve in eam sententiam in quam is qui dicet accipiendum esse demonstrabit.

> In the first place it should be shown, if possible, that there is no ambiguity in the
> statement, because in ordinary conversation everyone is accustomed to use this
> single word or phrase in the sense in which the speaker will prove that it should
> be taken.[34]

When we compare Julian's approach of the *mulae* problem with this instruction, it is clear that Julian did exactly what rhetorical theory as described
by Cicero suggested. No reference is made to the testator's intention; the
problem turns on the ambiguous wording of the will and is solved with a
reference to customary language.

5.2 D. 34.5.28

The second text that lacks the word *voluntas* but that Romanists regard as
referring to the testator's presumed intention stems from Javolenus: D.
34.5.28:

> Iavolenus libro tertio ex posterioribus Labeonis. Qui habebat Flaccum fullonem
> et Philonicum pistorem, uxori Flaccum pistorem legaverat: qui eorum et num
> uterque deberetur? Placuit primo eum legatum esse, quem testator legare sensis-

---

[33] In the same vein, Voci 1963: 832 fn. 30 and Torrent 1971: 666–7. Winkler 2013: 216 states
that the Stoics would have called this case an example of simple homonymy.

[34] Translation of this and the two following sections by Hubbell 1976.

set. quod si non appareret, primum inspiciendum esse, an nomina servorum dominus nota habuisset: quod si habuisset, eum deberi, qui nominatus esset, tametsi in artificio erratum esset. Sin autem ignota nomina servorum essent, pistorem legatum videri perinde ac si nomen ei adiectum non esset.

Javolenus, *From the Posthumous Works of Labeo*, Book 3: A man who owned a fuller called Flaccus and a baker called Philonicus legated: 'Flaccus the baker' to his wife. Is only one of them to be delivered and, if so, which one? Or are both to be delivered? It was decided that in the first instance that slave was legated whom the testator thought he was legating, but that if this was not clear, the first thing to consider was whether the owner knew the names of his slaves. If he did, then it is the slave who is named that should be delivered, the error being supposed to lie in the description of his trade. But if he did not, then it is the baker who should be deemed to have been legated just as if no name had been given to him.

Javolenus' third book on Labeo's posthumous work deals with legacies.[35] The *responsum* has come down to us in D. 34.5 *De rebus dubiis*. The case is fairly straightforward, but is complicated by what looks like an unfortunate mix-up. Someone had two slaves: Flaccus who was a fuller and Philonicus who was a baker. In his will, the testator left *the baker Flaccus* to his wife. Almost inevitably, the question arose which of the two slaves was owed, or perhaps whether both were.

To date, this text has been explained in terms of the testator's intention.[36] By way of example, we will look at Voci's comment. He deals with D. 34.5.28 in the context of *falsa demonstratio*, the problem that arises when the testator has added a wrong description to a person or thing mentioned in his will, for instance in a legacy.[37] Does such a *falsa demonstratio* invalidate the legacy? According to Voci, it does when the description is essential, and it does not when the description is only accessory; it is the testator's intention that determines whether the description is essential or accessory. Voci refers to D. 34.5.28 to make his point. Does it support his conclusion?

According to Voci, the question to be decided in this case is which of the two slaves has been validly bequeathed. He begins his analysis by stating that the *responsum* contains a distinction that links up with a general rule of interpretation: first, one has to ascertain the testator's real intention, and if that is not possible one can try to assess what the testator can most likely have wanted. Voci recognises this distinction in D. 34.5.28. As to the first part of the *responsum* ('eum legatum esse, quem testator legare sensisset'), he discusses several situations in which it is clear what the testator meant. Here, the testator's real intention determines whether the *falsa demonstratio*

[35] Lenel 1889: I 307 (no. 192).
[36] See for instance, Gandolfi 1966: 92–3 with older literature; Wieling 1972: 53; Backhaus 1981: 122–5.
[37] Voci 1963: 850–3.

is essential or accessory. In the second part of the text, dealing with the situation in which it is not clear which slave was meant, Javolenus offers a double criterion based on the common practice that an owner did not always know his own slaves: whatever he knew – the name or the profession – should be essential. Here, the testator's presumed intention determines whether the *falsa demonstratio* is essential or accessory.

In our view, Javolenus referred neither to the testator's real nor to his presumed intention. Not a single word in the *responsum* supports this conclusion. It is even questionable whether the rule 'falsa demonstratio non nocet' is applicable here: the question to be decided in this case is whether only one slave is owed, and if so which one, or both. The validity of the legacy itself was not at stake. This being so, Javolenus' *responsum* cannot be relied on to support Voci's conclusion.

The problem in this case is not what the testator thought, but what he wrote down. In other words, this *responsum* does not turn on the *voluntas testatoris* but on the ambiguous wording of the legacy. That Javolenus and/ or Labeo very likely thought so too becomes clear if we again compare this *responsum* with Cicero's discussion of *ambiguitas* in his *De Inventione*. After the introduction (2.116), which was mentioned in connection with the *mulae* text, Cicero continues as follows (2.117):

> Deinde, qua in sententia scriptor fuerit ex ceteris eius scriptis et ex factis, dictis, animo atque vita eius sumi oportebit, et eam ipsam scripturam, in qua inerit illud ambiguum de quo quaeretur totam omnibus ex partibus pertemptare, si quid aut ad id appositum sit quod nos interpretemur, aut ei quod adversarius intellegat, adversetur. Nam facile, quid veri simile sit eum voluisse qui scripsit ex omni scriptura et ex persona scriptoris atque eis rebus quae personis attributae sunt considerabitur.

> In the next place, one ought to estimate what the writer meant from his other writings, acts, words, disposition and in fact his whole life, and to examine the whole document which contains the ambiguity in question in all its parts, to see if anything is apposite to our interpretation or opposed to the sense in which our opponent understands it. For it is easy to estimate what it is likely that the writer intended from the complete context and from the character of the writer, and from the qualities which are associated with certain characters.

In this entry, the writer's intention is mentioned twice. When we apply Cicero's discussion to linguistic ambiguity in legal cases, do his comments imply that the testator's real intention should be discovered? We think they do not; the words *sententia* and *voluisse* only refer to the crux of the problem. As Cicero says in 2.116, a controversy arises from ambiguity when there is doubt as to what the writer meant because the written statement has two or more meanings. When that happens, the advocate can try to solve the problem by examining the writer's other writings, acts, and so on. In line with these instructions, Javolenus/Labeo examines the testator's habits with regard to his slaves. He does not pretend to discover the testator's real or presumed intention, but to assess what the testator *probably* meant and so solve the problem of the ambiguous wording of the legacy. The compilers most likely also thought he did, for they included this *responsum* in title 34.5 *De rebus dubiis*, on ambiguous cases.

5.3 D. 31.78.1

The other two texts we will discuss are the *responsa* in which Papinian used the words *coniectura voluntatis*. The first one is D. 31.78.1:

> Papinianus libro nono responsorum. Cum post mortem emptoris venditionem rei publicae praediorum Optimus Maximusque Princeps noster Severus Augustus rescindi heredibus pretio restituto iussisset, de pecunia legatario, cui praedium emptor ex ea possessione legaverat, coniectura voluntatis pro modo aestimationis partem solvendam esse respondi.

> Papinian, *Responsa*, Book 9. When after the death of the buyer our best and greatest Emperor Severus Augustus ordered that a sale of public property should be rescinded and the price restored to his heirs, I replied in the matter of this money that following the conjectured intention of the testator the appropriate part of the value should be paid to the legatee to whom the buyer had made a legacy of part of the public land possessed in this way.

Book 9 of Papinian's *Responsa* addresses *fideicommissa*.[38] The compilers included the *responsum* in D. 31 *de legatis et fideicommissis*. The case is rather complicated. Around the year 170, someone bought public land. Later, he drew up a will in which he left part of this land to a legatee. When in due course he died, his heirs accepted the inheritance and the legatee became owner of the land. Sometime later, the Emperor Septimius Severus decided to rescind the sale of the land and to pay back the purchase price. The land became public property again and the heirs as successors to the buyer received the purchase price. The legatee who had lost his legacy claimed part of the price from the heirs. Papinian was asked for advice and his reply was that the testator would probably want the heirs to pay the legatee an equivalent of the value of the land that had been bequeathed to him.

This *responsum* has attracted very little attention from modern Romanists.[39] Recently, Schilling referred to it in his paper on *coniectura voluntatis*. He states that:

---

[38] Lenel 1889: I 923 (no. 614).
[39] *Fiuris* reports six references, all in footnotes only.

the testator could not have foreseen what had happened at the time of the succession and so Papinian asked what he would have wanted. He explicitly construed the will according to the presumed intention of the testator (*coniectura voluntatis*) and contrary to the clear wording of the will.[40]

In his comment, Schilling does not address the legal problem involved and that is why we wonder if this *responsum* can really demonstrate that Papinian 'established a theoretical understanding and technical formulation of our subject-matter'.[41] What was the legal position of the legatee and how did Papinian safeguard his interests? Only when we know the answers to these questions can we assess the meaning of the words *coniectura voluntatis*.

Since the legacy concerned the ownership of land, we suppose that it was formulated as a *legatum per vindicationem*. The legatee had acquired ownership upon the heirs' acceptance of their inheritance, only to lose it when the emperor nullified the sale.[42] Apparently (as seems likely), the legatee heard of the purchase price having been returned to the heirs and he wanted to claim part of it to make up for his loss. But how could he set about that? He could not use the *legatum per vindicationem*, because, unlike the *legatum per damnationem*, this type of legacy could be used only to claim one's own property and the land now belonged to the state. Two ways for Papinian to solve the problem spring to mind: to convert the legacy into a *legatum per damnationem* or to convert it into a *fideicommissum*.

At the initiative of the Emperor Nero, a senatorial decree had been issued that made it possible for an invalid *legatum per vindicationem* to be converted into a valid *legatum per damnationem*.[43] The paying over of such a legacy could be claimed from the heirs with an *actio ex testamento*. If the bequeathed object was a *certum*, as in the case in question, then the *formula* would contain the clause 'quanti ea res est': if the judge were to decide that the claim was justified, he would condemn the heirs to pay the value of the *res* to the legatee. In the case of the rescinded sale, however, a conversion like this would not help. It was meant for cases in which the legatee had been unable to acquire his legacy from the outset. Here, the legatee had acquired the land but had lost it later, so the heirs could successfully deny his claim. For this reason it is unlikely that Papinian would have used this strategy.

But the invalid *legatum per vindicationem* could also be converted into a valid *fideicommissum*. This was a request made by a testator to one or more persons who would benefit from his inheritance to do something for or give something to a third party.[44] It was originally used in cases where the *ius civile* would not

---

[40] Schilling 2014: 320.
[41] Idem: 319.
[42] The land will have been delivered by means of *traditio*, cf. Kaser 1971: 415. When the *causa* of the *traditio* lapsed, the delivery became invalid.
[43] Gai. *Inst.* 2.197; see also Voci 1963: 225–8.
[44] Gai. *Inst.* 2.246–89; see also Voci 1963: 231–4.

allow a legacy, for example, to benefit someone who was not a Roman citizen. There were no formal requirements for a *fideicommissum*; it could be made in any way, even by means of a nod. The *fideicommissum* had been in use since Republican times, but at that time the beneficiary would not have had recourse to legal remedies to enforce performance. The emperor Augustus introduced a special *praetor fideicommissarius* who was authorised to judge claims based on *fideicommissa*, and in the second century, legacies that for some formal reason were null and void could be qualified as a valid *fideicommissum*.

Although the *responsum* as we know it does not say so, there are two reasons to assume that Papinian opted for converting the invalid *legatum per vindicationem* into a valid *fideicommissum*. The first is quite uncomplicated: Papinian included this *responsum* in a book on *fideicommissa*. The second is more elaborate: Papinian used the words *coniectura voluntatis* to support his view that the heirs should indemnify the legatee. For a *fideicommissum* to be valid it sufficed that the testator's intention had been clearly expressed. In this case, the testator had clearly expressed his intention to leave part of the public land he had bought and possessed to the legatee. Unfortunately, the legacy had become invalid. Following the testator's conjectured intention, Papinian regarded this invalid legacy as a valid *fideicommissum*. While the *fideicommissum* is not mentioned, the *coniectura voluntatis* is.

Papinian did not construe the will in accordance with the testator's presumed intention (*coniectura voluntatis*) and contrary to the clear wording of the will, as Schilling suggested. Rather, Papinian used the clear wording of the will, particularly that of the *legatum per vindicationem*, to convert the invalid legacy into a valid *fideicommissum*. In other words, there is no reason to conclude from this *responsum* that Papinian 'established a theoretical understanding and technical formulation' of *coniectura voluntatis*. All he did, and all he had to do, was avail himself of the options Roman law placed at his disposal.

5.4 D. 31.77.8

The second *responsum* in which Papinian used the words *coniectura voluntatis* is D. 31.77.8. The text runs as follows:

> Papinianus libro octavo responsorum. Evictis praediis, quae pater, qui se dominum esse crediderit, verbis fideicommissi filio reliquit, nulla cum fratribus et coheredibus actio erit: si tamen inter filios divisionem fecit, arbiter coniectura voluntatis non patietur eum partes coheredibus praelegatas restituere, nisi parati fuerint et ipsi patris iudicium fratri conservari.

> Papinian, *Responsa*, Book 8. When a son is evicted from lands which his father, believing himself to be the owner, had left to him by the terms of a *fideicommissum*, there will be no action against the brothers and co-heirs. If, however, he made a division among the sons, the arbitrator will – upon conjecture of the father's

intention – not allow this son to re-establish the parts that have been bequeathed to the co-heirs to be taken in advance, unless they too are prepared to hold up their father's decision in favor of their brother.[45]

Like Book 9, the eighth book of Papinian's *Responsa* deals with *fideicommissa* and like the former *responsum*, this one was included by the compilers in Book 31, *De legatis et fideicommissis*.[46] The words *coniectura voluntatis* belong to the second part of the *responsum*. What do they mean in this context? We again quote Schilling's comment:

> In the second case, a testator had left particular pieces of land, of which he thought he was the owner, to one of his sons and gave the rest of his lands to his other sons. It transpired that the particular pieces of land did not belong to the testator, such that the disposition was void and the son would receive nothing. This was an outcome the father obviously would not have wanted. Papinian held that according to the testator's presumed intention (*coniectura voluntatis*), the other sons should purchase the particular pieces of land for their brother or alternatively they should pay him an equivalent.[47]

Schilling's description seems to be based on Wieling's.[48]

In our view, Schilling (and, for that matter, Wieling) explains the words *coniectura voluntatis* in a way that is not backed by the text. These words do not refer to what the testator would want his heirs to do for their evicted brother, but to what he would want the arbiter to do for his heirs. The case may be more complicated than Wieling and Schilling suppose. For a proper understanding of the text and particularly of the words *coniectura voluntatis* it is necessary to reconstruct the case, to assess the legal problem, and to analyse Papinian's reaction.

The case: a father had left some pieces of land to one of his sons by means of a *fideicommissum*. He also divided his estate among his sons by means of *praelegata*, that is, legacies left to heirs in addition to their portion. Since legacies and prelegacies had to be included in a will, the father must have drawn up a will and he must have instituted his sons as heirs. The father died and the son who had received the *fideicommissum* took possession of the lands. However, he was evicted, because somebody else turned out to be the real owner. The evicted brother wanted his brothers to compensate him for his loss but he could not make them do so. Probably, it was then that an arbitrator was asked to divide the inheritance. The evicted son made a request to the arbitrator but, unfortunately, it is not clear what he asked.

His question is hidden in Papinian's opinion on what the arbiter should

---

[45] This translation is based on that in Watson 1985, but the latter part differs considerably.

[46] Lenel 1889: I 917 (no. 599).

[47] Schilling 2014: 320. On the *divisio inter liberos*, see Voci 1963: 476–8.

[48] Wieling 1972: 181–2. However, Schilling does not refer to Wieling.

do. The relevant sentence is 'arbiter . . . non patietur eum partes coheredi-
bus praelegatas restituere'. It has been translated in various ways, none of
which is satisfactory.[49] The main problem is the verb *restituere*, which usually
means 'to restore', or 'to return'. However, it cannot have that meaning here
because the subject of *restituere* is *eum*, that is, the son, and he cannot return
what had been bequeathed to his co-heirs. Moreover, it is not clear to whom
he should return it. *Restituere* can also be translated as 'to re-establish', that
is, the parts that had been assigned as prelegacies to his co-heirs.[50] In our
view, this is the only translation that makes sense. The evicted son asked
the arbitrator for permission to bring the *fideicommissum* into the undivided
inheritance in order to secure the value of the land he had lost.

The legal problem in D. 31.77.8 is caused by the fact that the land from
which one of the sons had been evicted had been left to him by means of a
fideicommissum. If it had been left by means of *a legatum per damnationem*,
things might have been different. When a testator had made a *legatum per
damnationem* of someone else's property, the heirs charged with paying over
the legacy were obliged to buy the land or, if that was not possible, to pay
the value of the land to the legatee. About *fideicommissa* of someone else's
property, however, jurists held different opinions: according to Gaius, some
held that such a *fideicommissum* should be dealt with as if it were a *legatum
per damnationem*; others thought that if the owner did not want to sell, the
fideicommissum became invalid.[51]

In this case, the son had had possession of the land on the basis of the
fideicommissum, but he had been evicted. His situation was comparable
with that of someone to whom something had been bequeathed by means
of a *fideicommissum* which had from the outset belonged to someone else.
Therefore, the main question in this case was whether the heirs should
regard the *fideicommissum* as a *legatum per damnationem* and pay to their
brother the value of the land (it is not likely that the successful evictor would
want to sell the land), or whether they could regard it as invalid. A second,
related question was whether the evicted son could make the arbiter include
the *fideicommissum* in the division made by the father.

Papinian divided his *responsum* into two parts. First, he dealt with the
validity of the *fideicommissum*: he did not agree with those who wanted to
regard a *fideicommissum* of someone else's property in the same way as a
legatum per damnationem, but instead regarded it as invalid. Second, Papinian

---

49 Watson 1985: 'the arbitrator . . . will not allow him to restore to the co-heir (but: *coheredi-
bus*) the part (but: *partes*) bequeathed to be taken in advance'; Otto et al. 1831: 'so wird der
Schiedsrichter . . . nicht zugeben dass jener Sohn die den Miterben zum Voraus vermachten
Antheile sollte herausgeben müssen'; Spruit 1997: 'zal de scheidsman . . . niet toelaten dat
die zoon aan de mede-erfgenamen de hun bij prelegaat vermaakte porties afgeeft.'

50 Oxford Classical Dictionary 1980: fasc. VII, ad loc. sub 4.

51 Gai. *Inst.* 2.262. According to Voci 1963: 254 fn.17, only D. 32.30.6 and D. 32.14.2 respectively by Labeo and Gaius testify to the view first mentioned by Gaius.

dealt with the division that the father had made in his will. There is no reason to assume – like Wieling and Schilling do – that the evicted son had been excluded from this division. The *fideicommissum* may have been an extra bonus. Because Papinian regarded it as invalid, he gave as his opinion that the arbiter should not consider it when dividing the inheritance. By dealing separately with the validity of the *fideicommissum*, Papinian prevented a situation in which the testator's intention in the *fideicommissum* could be used against his intention in the division.

Let us now return to the main question: what do the words *coniectura voluntatis* mean in this *responsum*? Papinian used them as an argument for the arbiter not to consider the *fideicommissum* when dividing the inheritance; the father had made a division by means of *praelegata* indicating how he wanted his property to be divided among his sons. For one son, he had also included a *fideicommissum*. He probably would not want his division to be upset by the fact that this *fideicommissum* turned out to be invalid. The words *coniectura voluntatis* were not meant to compensate the evicted son, but to protect the portions assigned to the other sons. It seems rather far-fetched to qualify this view as a 'theoretical understanding and a technical formulation' of the testator's presumed intention.

5.5 Hellenistic epistemology revisited

How do these *responsa* and their modern-day interpretations compare to Hellenistic epistemology? Romanists interpret these *responsa* in terms of the testator's real or presumed intention, whether or not it is mentioned by the jurist in question, and from this interpretation they deduce the solution to the legal question they believe to be correct. The assumption that it is possible to know the testator's intention meshes remarkably well with the ideas of Stoic epistemology. Yet, while the Roman jurists, following suggestions in rhetorical handbooks, do sometimes refer to the testator's intention, they only appear to do so in the sense of *probable* intention and as an argument to support a desirable resolution of the legal issue. There is not even a hint of a suggestion that it is the testator's real or presumed intention they are after. If the influence of any epistemology can be traced in the jurists' argumentation, it is that of the New Academy.

6. CONCLUSION

We have attempted to show that there is a discrepancy between the Romanists' interpretation of *voluntas testatoris* and the way the Roman jurists used these words. The former interpret them so that they fit their theory on the testator's intention: by regarding him as a reasonable person who is supposed to have made a reasonable will, they can reconstruct his real or presumed intention. In the *causa Curiana*, this reconstruction generated the hypothesis that the testator would have included a vulgar substitution in his will, and in the four *responsa* it led to rather complicated exegeses of two simple cases (D. 32.62 and D. 34.5.28) and to rather simplified exegeses of two complicated cases (D.31.78.7 and D. 31.77.8).

We on the other hand believe that, like Cicero, the Roman jurists used the words *voluntas testatoris* in the sense of probable intention, sometimes in the context of the *status verba-voluntas*, sometimes in another context, but always as an argument to support an opinion. In the fourth *responsum* (D. 31.77.8) both parties would have used the testator's intention to support their claim: the son by referring to the *fideicommissum* and his brothers by referring to the division made by their father. Clearly, in such a case, it is impossible to know the testator's real or presumed intention. There is no single correct solution based on logical reasoning. The same holds for the other three *responsa* and for the *causa Curiana*.

In the introduction we raised the question of which philosophical school was most relevant to the development of Roman law, the Middle Stoa or the New Academy. We think they can both claim predominance, but in two different periods. The New Academy was most relevant to *le droit romain romain*, while the Stoa is most relevant to *das heutige römische Recht*. The Roman jurists referred to the *voluntas testatoris* in the sense of the testator's *probable* intention, assuming that it is impossible to know something for certain. The Romanists, however, tend to interpret *responsa* about unclear wills on the basis of the testator's real or presumed intention, assuming that it is possible to read a dead man's mind. As Schilling has pointed out, this theory is closely related to modern German law and it is therefore tempting to qualify this theory not only as Pandectism, but – since Romanists try to design a modern theory on the interpretation of wills in the Roman sources – as 'retro-Pandectism'. Of course, the philosophical basis of modern legal science belongs to our time, but it seems to share some fundamental elements with the Middle Stoa. In Roman antiquity, on the other hand, jurists facing the challenge of interpreting texts may more readily and successfully have turned for support to the New Academy. Cicero showed the way.

BIBLIOGRAPHY

Backhaus, R. (1981), Casus perplexus: *die Lösung in sich widersprüchlicher Rechtsfälle durch die klassische römische Jurisprudenz*. Munich.

Bund, E. (1980), 'Rahmenerwägungen zu einem Nachweis stoischer Gedanken in der römischen Jurisprudenz', in M. Harder and G. Thielmann, eds, De iustitia et iure, *Festgabe für U. von Lübtow*. Berlin. 127–45.

Corbeill, A. (2002), 'Rhetorical education in Cicero's youth', in J. M. May, ed., *Brill's Companion to Cicero: Oratory and rhetoric*. Leiden. 23–48.

Crifó, G. (2005), 'Per una prospettiva romanistica dei diritti dell'uomo', in K. M.

Girardet and U. Nortmann, eds, *Menschenrechte und europäische Identität: Die antiken Grundlagen*. Stuttgart. 240–69.

Formigoni, W. (1996), Pithanōn a Paulo epitomatorum libri VIII: *sulla funzione critica del commento del giurista Iulius Paulus*. Milan.

Gaines, R. N. (2002), 'Cicero's Partitiones *Oratoriae* and *Topica*: rhetorical philosophy and philosophical rhetoric', in J. M. May, ed., *Brill's Companion to Cicero: Oratory and rhetoric*. Leiden. 445–80.

Gandolfi, G. (1966), *Studi sull'interpretazione degli atti negoziali in diritto romano*. Milan.

Giltaij, J. (2011), *Mensenrechten in het Romeinse recht?* Nijmegen.

Hankinson, R. J. (1995), *The Sceptics*. London.

Harke, J. D. (2012), '*Verba* und *voluntas* – was bedeutet Testamentsauslegung für die Hochklassiker?' in J. D. Harke, ed., *Facetten des römischen Erbrechts: Studien zur Geschichte und Dogmatik des Privatrechts*. Berlin/Heidelberg. 55–77.

Hubbell, H. M. (1976), *Cicero, De Inventione, De optimo genere oratorum, Topica*. London.

Kaser, M. 1971[2]. *Das römische Privatrecht I*. Munich.

Lenel, O. (1889), *Palingenesia iuris civilis*, 2 volumes. Berlin.

Liebs, D. (2012), *Summoned to the Roman Courts: Famous trials from antiquity*. Berkeley.

Mantovani, D. and Schiavone, A., eds (2007), *Testi e problemi del giusnaturalismo romano*. Pavia.

Otto, K. E., Schilling, B. and Sintenis, C. F. F. (1830–3), *Das Corpus iuris civilis (romani)*. Leipzig.

Rist, J. M. (1969), *Stoic Philosophy*. Cambridge.

Sandbach, F. H. (1989[2]), *The Stoics*. London.

Schiavone, A. (2012), *The Invention of Law in the West*. Cambridge, MA.

Schilling, J. D. (2014), '*Coniectura Voluntatis, Ergänzende Testamentsauslegung* and construction by necessary implication: a historical comparison of Roman, German and English law', *Zeitschrift für Europäisches Privatrecht* 22: 313–56.

Schulz, F. (1953[2]), *History of Roman Legal Science*. Oxford.

Spruit, J. E., Feenstra, R. and Bongenaar, K. E. M., eds (1993–2011), *Corpus iuris civilis: Tekst en vertaling*. Zutphen.

Stroux, J. (1926), '*Summum ius summa iniuria*. Ein Kapitel aus der Geschichte der *interpretatio iuris*', in *Festschrift Paul Speiser-Sarasin*. Basel. 115–58. Reprinted in J. Stroux (1949), *Römische Rechtswissenschaft und Rhetorik*. Potsdam.

Tellegen, J. W. and Tellegen-Couperus, O. E. (2000), 'Law and rhetoric in the *causa Curiana*', *Orbis Iuris Romani* 6: 171–202.

Tellegen, J. W. and Tellegen-Couperus, O. E. (2013), '*Artes urbanae*, Roman law and rhetoric', in P. J. du Plessis, ed., *New Frontiers: Law and Society in the Roman World*. Edinburgh. 31–50.

Torrent, A. (1971), *Salvius Iulianus: Liber singularis de ambiguitatibus*. Salamanca.

Vocabularium Iurisprudentiae Romanae (1903–1985), Berlin.

Voci, P. (1963[2]), *Diritto ereditario romano II*. Milan.

Waerdt, P. A. van der (1990), 'Philosophical influence on Roman jurisprudence? The case of Stoicism and natural law', *Aufstieg und Niedergang der Römischen Welt II*. 36.7: 4851–900.

Watson, A., ed. (1985), *The Digest of Justinian*. Philadelphia.

Wieacker, F. (1967), 'The *causa Curiana* and contemporary Roman jurisprudence', *Irish Jurist* 2: 151–64.

Wieacker, F. (1990), *Römische Rechtsgeschichte I*. Munich.

Wieling, H. J. (1972), *Testamentsauslegung im römischen Recht*. Munich.

Winkler, M. (2013), 'Zur Logik und Struktur in Julians *liber singularis de ambiguitatibus*', *Zeitschrift der Savigny-Stiftung für Rechtsgeschichte, romanistische Abteilung* 130: 203–33.

Chapter 4

Law's Nature: Philosophy as a Legal Argument in Cicero's Writings

Benedikt Forschner

1. INTRODUCTION

Cicero's reputation as a legal philosopher seems to be somehow discredited by his role as a politician and advocate. Despite admiration of his intellectual capacity, there is a prejudice that politics as well as legal practice require a day-to-day pragmatism incompatible with the aim of searching for a reliable, timeless truth. The move towards reading Cicero's writings *in context* did not change the particular reluctance to believe in *what* Cicero says or – more importantly – to believe that Cicero *himself* believed in what he said. Given his different faces, one is prone to read his writings against the background of a multi-layered set of rhetorical, political or tactical functions forming his words and making them understandable in the eyes of a modern reader. As far as substance follows function in this sense, there is no place for a pure, abstract *theory* of law.

However, during the years of his political retreat after the Luca Conference, Cicero did develop a comprehensive and coherent theory of law and its nature. This theory, mainly found in his *Laws* and the *Republic*, is not – as often assumed – a theory contrasting man-made laws and natural law. It is a theory of law in the widest sense of the word, dealing with *natura iuris*, that is, the nature of law in general. This theory finds its origins in Stoic writings, especially in the *oikeiosis* doctrine; but Cicero amalgamates *nomos* and *physis* towards a new holistic understanding of law, which is not grounded in any dichotomy of *leges* and a higher-ranking ideal of natural law. For Cicero, law is nature – and what is not nature, is not law. Given this background, Cicero's understanding of law goes beyond the idea of law as a specific tool among others to *regulate* society. Law has no function in this sense; it rather *is* the very essence of practical wisdom in a society of rational human beings. This practical wisdom is described as the highest form of human insight; it results from the very moment when gods and men join up to constitute a *societas communis*.

There is no evidence that Cicero's legal philosophy strongly influenced legal practice in the long term; but I will try to show that (1) Cicero made use of truly *philosophical* arguments in legal practice and (2) the structure of legal practice was open enough to implement these reflections as specifically *legal* arguments. The understanding of law as a closed doctrinal normativity fails to grasp the infinite and situational character of legal decision-making in the late Republic. There are a number of arguments, in particular in Cicero's forensic speeches, which can clearly be understood against the background of his specific theory of the nature of law. Many of these arguments can be – and often have been – read simply as invectives or rhetorical tools. But a pure functional reading underrates their substantial plausibility, which grounds on their philosophical substance rather than on mere tactical aims.[1]

2. CICERO ON THE NATURE OF LAW

It is commonly assumed that Cicero's idea of 'right' and 'wrong' law is based on a juxtaposition of a divine category of natural law and a man-made category of positive law.[2] This reading strongly reflects a modern distinction that dates back – *inter alia* – to the natural law doctrines of the early Enlightenment,[3] but one can also find traces of this 'dichotomist' approach in philosophical thought before and within Cicero's time. The antithesis of *nomos* and *physis* had broadly been discussed by the Sophists, in particular by Antiphon in his treatise *peri aletheia*;[4] and also the Stoics, even though they tried to reunite *nomos* and *physis* in an all-embracing cosmic principle,[5] did not aim at closing the theoretical rift between man-made laws and the principle of nature.[6] However, there is no evidence about similar discourses on the relation of positive law and any higher-ranking laws in Roman law. An early example of a dichotomist understanding of natural and positive law can be seen in Cato's speech for the Rhodians;[7] but as with the distinction between *ius naturale*, *ius civile* and *ius gentium*, Roman law did not read any consequences into a conflict between these different kinds of law. Thus, a dichotomist reading of Cicero's legal philosophy is not anachronistic with respect to its distinction between natural law and positive law; but it contradicts Roman law as far as it tries to establish a hierarchy among these laws.

---

[1] In what follows, I will present aspects I have partly published earlier; cf. B. Forschner 2014: 21f. and B. Forschner 2015: esp. 52f., 60f., 71f.

[2] Kenter 1972: 170; Nörr 1974: 25; Colish 1990: 98; Lintott 2002: 225f. Powell 2001: 17f., admits that Cicero 'had in mind no systematic dichotomy between natural law and positive law', but he still adheres to a dichotomic reading; cf. Powell, ibem, 37: 'true law (. . .) is (. . .) law (. . .) consonant with natural justice'; 38: 'definition of law (. . .) from which a set of general laws is supposed to be derived.'

[3] See Hochstrasser 2004.

[4] Heinimann 1965. See also Ostwald 2009: 158f.; Scholten 2003: 206; Kerferd 1981: 111; Gagarin 2002: 65; Honsell 1993: 179f.

[5] Cf. recently M. Forschner 2014: 73–84.

[6] Chrysipp, SVF 3.308; Diog. Laert. 7.128.

[7] Cf. Gell. NA 6.3.45f.: 'Ac primum ea non incallide conquisivit, quae non iure naturae aut iure gentium fieri prohibentur, sed iure legum rei alicuius medendae aut temporis causa iussarum[.]'

However, as will be demonstrated, Cicero's position was even more unique than a superficial reading might suggest. At the very beginning of his *Laws*, Cicero lays out the purpose behind his treatise. Here it becomes clear that he is not searching for a definition of different sorts of law – for example natural law or positive law – or a hierarchic structure putting these laws in any relation to each other. Rather, Cicero is trying to develop an understanding of the nature of law – *natura enim iuris explicanda nobis est.*[8] Thus the *Laws* should not be regarded as an attempt to challenge or renew the Roman perception of natural law. As we will see, the Roman sources dating from Cicero's time do not provide any consistent natural law theory at all, and the term *ius naturale* does not appear in the *Laws* even once.[9] Cicero's approach turns out to be radical in the true sense of the word.[10] He aims to investigate the source from which all law originates (*tota causa universi iuris ac legum*); a source that is not to be found in the praetorian edict or the Twelve Tables, but is to be derived from the *intima philosophia.*[11]

Philosophy, as understood by Cicero, deals with the conditions and traits of a community as it exists among humans by nature. In this context, 'law' is described as the ideal – that is, natural – way of organising a human community.[12] Therefore, understanding the true nature of law requires an understanding of the nature of men: *Natura enim nobis explicanda est, eaque ab hominis repetenda natura.*[13] Albeit Cicero's approach seems to be collective at first glance, his starting point is not the community, but the human being as part of this community. However, law – as Cicero sees it – is not a means to organise a community of men against their nature. It is not an external command forcing the man to set aside his natural desires, and its primary goal is not to discipline unregulated human interests by way of coercive power. Law rather emerges within the man as the very essence of his reason.[14]

Cicero's idea of human rationality is broadly based on Stoicism, in particular on specific aspects of the doctrine of *oikeiosis*. I will briefly shed some light on this philosophical background, even though the impact of Stoicism on Cicero's concept of virtue is not surprising and is – by and large – common sense. What is more important is to consider how Cicero slightly changes the Stoic legacy and draws conclusions from his concept that a purely Stoic tradition would never have accepted.

For Cicero, human beings are the only living creatures among all others that are capable of sharing reason. However, reason is not primarily a human

---

[8] Cic. *Leg.* 1.17. For a different approach, see recently Atkins 2013: 169f.

[9] Girardet 1983: 35f., 54f.

[10] From *radix* = root.

[11] Cic. *Leg.* 1.17.

[12] Idem: 1.17.

[13] Idem: 1.17.

[14] Idem: 1.18: 'Eadem ratio, cum est in hominis mente confirmata et perfecta, lex est.'

trait. Nature in its entirety is ruled by the immortal gods;[15] and the gods let men participate in reason as the highest among divine capacities.[16] Reason serves as a hinge connecting human and divine thinking; it is the feature separating men from other living creatures by way of establishing a specific kinship and thus a cosmic community between men and gods.[17]

It is important to see that Cicero, while claiming that all men are equal due to their reason, does not have in mind equality comparable to a Christian or a modern liberal understanding.[18] For Cicero, the equality of all men is not grounded in their status as 'persons', who own an untouchable value simply *qua* being humans; and he does not even believe that all men succeed in gaining reason. He merely states that all men are equal with respect to their *capacity* to gain reason.[19] Through this capacity, however, all men are distinguished from animals merely in a formal – that is, a potential – sense.[20] It is men's duty to make use of this capacity by developing reason and bringing it to perfection. As nobody owns the skills to teach himself to cultivate and use reason, for the open-minded man divine nature serves as tutor: by seriously taking into account what he sees above him in the sky and around him on the hills and meadows, and by being responsive to natural – that is, divine – occurrences, man starts to communicate with the immortal gods.[21] This communication will sharpen his understanding of 'right' and 'wrong', and will lead him to act in accordance with nature. On the highest level of *ratio*, human nature gains perfection; here, human and divine reasoning converge.[22] According to Cicero, this sort of *ratio* – which he calls *recta ratio* – is the law.[23]

Thus, human *ratio* is of an evolving nature. There exists a broad range between those who gain *ratio perfecta* (who are rather few) and those who gain a lower form of *ratio*; and a few do not even possess any traces of rational insight– as we will see later, those are ranked on the level of animals or below. This idea of an evolving human rationality is rooted in the Stoic doctrine of *oikeiosis*.[24] Men and animals alike share a common instinct to preserve their own natural constitution and their community,[25] and as a very first impetus, this instinct is inherent in all newborn creatures.[26] But in the

---

[15] Idem: 1.21.
[16] Idem: 1.22.
[17] Idem: 1.23–5.
[18] Spaemann 1987: 295.
[19] *Ex neg.* Cic. *Leg.* 1.18, 1.22, 2.11.
[20] On this aspect, see B. Forschner 2014: 36.
[21] Cic. *Leg.* 1.26: 'Artes vero innumerabiles repertae sunt, docente natura, quam imitata ratio res ad vitam necessarias sollerter consecuta est.'
[22] Idem: 1.23.
[23] Cic. *Rep.* 3.33; *Leg.* 1.18.
[24] Cicero's affiliation with Stoic philosophy is strongly disputed in detail. For diverse approaches see Görler 2004: 240f.; Hirzel 1883: 488; Glucker 1988: 34f.
[25] On the social aspect of these instincts see Cic. *Fin.* 3.65; *Stob. ecl.* 2.7.109.10 = SVF III, 686.
[26] Diog. Laert. 7.85.

case of human beings, a *logos* emerges in the course of their lives and over-
lies these instincts. Even though a newborn child is free of experience and
behaves merely by instinct, it already has an unspecific capacity that enables
it to develop human rationality later on.[27] This capacity is understood by
the Stoics as a prior grasp (*prolepsis*) of specific concepts, such as 'useful',
'good' and 'bad'. The Stoic *prolepsis* can be compared to a very first sketch[28]
or a blank writing tablet.[29] It does not provide the child with the capacity
to understand a specific issue in detail and to reflect on it; but it enables it
to collect impressions in a still undifferentiated way. Through experience,
methodological study and habit the grown man will be able to structure his
perceptions and to develop concepts to reflect his environment. On this
developed level, man turns out to be a moral character. He leaves his animal
starting-point of pure self-reference and opens his mind towards the world.[30]

In Stoic writings, one finds different strands of arguments explaining how
the capacity to gain reason became part of the human mind.[31] Insofar as the
Stoics take up a theological position, they consider the whole cosmos as a
common home of gods and men imbued with divine reason. Based on their
shared reason, gods and men constitute a well-ordered and just society.[32]
Here, the gods are seen as the source of human rationality. The Stoics also
developed a more empirical approach, which is primarily grounded on the
visible developments of newborn children and animals; and this approach
seems not to be shaped by any divine metaphysics.[33] But in the *Laws* (and,
for instance, in contrast to *De Finibus*), Cicero associates himself with the
theological strand of the Stoic heritage. This might also be for pragmatic
reasons.[34] Writing the *Laws*, Cicero pursued practical political aims. He
did not intend to contribute to a purely academic debate, but he tried to
save exactly this sort of *res publica, quam optumam esse docuit in illis sex libris
Scipio*.[35] Cicero's ambitions as a politician were still (and again) high at this
time, but in the aftermath of the Luca Conference he was forced by Pompey
to adhere to the rules and end his fight against the reunited triumvirs.
However, whereas the 'official' Cicero of this time is often regarded as a
politically flexible or even slick academic thinker, he remained a strong and

---

[27] Cf. Pohlenz 1959: 56.
[28] Pohlenz 1959: 56.
[29] M. Forschner 1995: 155.
[30] M. Forschner 2008: 169–91, 174. For a purely sociobiological understanding of the *oikeiosis*
       doctrine, which denies that the Stoics made a categorical difference between men and animal,
       see Bees 2004: 200f. For a critical discussion of Bees' position see B. Forschner 2015: 61f.
[31] Schofield 1995: 191f. See already B. Forschner 2014: 30f.
[32] Cf. Schofield 1991; Vogt 2008. For a balanced account of Stoic theology see Algra 2003:
       153–78.
[33] Schofield 1995: 191f.
[34] On this aspect see B. Forschner 2014: 31.
[35] Cic. *Leg.* 1.20.

dedicated republican. Believing that the Republic was suffering mainly from moral decay,[36] he tried – for the first time in Roman history – to set out the intellectual preconditions on which a republican society depends. Cicero's theological approach was perfectly compatible with religious belief in the late Republic, and it surely helped him to get noticed by his contemporaries.

As demonstrated, Cicero's concept of the nature of law is based on Stoic references. According to Cicero as well as to (some) Stoics, gods and men constitute a community grounded on their commonly shared reason; both Cicero and the Stoics understand law as the highest reason (*recta ratio*/ὀρθὸς λόγος), which emerges when human reasoning meets with divine reasoning; and both believe that men own the *capacity* to gain reason, but still have to develop reason over time. But despite these apparent similarities, Cicero's understanding of law differs from the Stoic doctrine in a significant way. The Stoics, even though they believe in an all-embracing cosmic principle, never question the dichotomy of man-made laws (*theseis*) and the principle of nature (*physis*).[37] Cicero, however, does not define *lex* in relation to – and thus as a potential counterpart of – *ius*, but as source of all *ius*: In *Leg.* 1.19, *lex* appears as *exordium iuris* and, more specifically, as a yardstick to distinguish *ius* and *iniuria*.[38]

Unlike the dichotomist Stoic approach, Cicero's concept, as it appears in the *Laws*, turns out to be holistic. Man-made laws are not measured against a higher-ranking natural law; they exist as law only if they are concordant with nature. Otherwise, they are not just seen as invalid law, but they do not count as law at all. This is a problem of the status of law, but it is also of terminological importance: identifying invalid law as law causes an *error sermonis*, which easily makes one forget the true character of law.[39] Cicero's theory, as developed in the *Laws*, does not only amalgamate *lex*, *ius* and *natura*; it also neutralises the terminological dichotomy of *theseis* and *physis*. Legal statutes inconsistent with nature must not be called law; they have to be removed from the legal discourse.

3. THE TYRANT: A MONSTER IN HUMAN DISGUISE

Cicero's concept of the nature of law is closely connected to his theory of human nature. Being the substance of *summa ratio*, law is a product of the rational human mind. However, as not all men succeed equally in developing

---

[36] Cic. *Rep.* 1.69.

[37] On this dichotomy in Stoic writings see Long 1996: 218. But see Lehoux 2012: 57f.

[38] Cic. *Leg.* 1.19: 'Quod si ita recte dicitur, ut mihi quidem plerumque videri solet, a lege ducendum est iuris exordium. Ea est enim naturae vis, ea mens ratioque prudentis, ea iuris atque iniuriae regula.'

[39] Idem: 2.8: 'Videamus igitur rursus, priusquam adgrediamur ad leges singulas, vim naturamque legis, ne quom referenda sint ad eam nobis omnia, labamur interdum errore sermonis, ignoremusque vim nominis eius quo iura nobis definienda sint.'

rationality, the law inevitably stands on fragile ground. The legal consequences Cicero derives from the 'evolving character' of the human mind are
illustrated by analysing his theory of tyranny.[40]

Cicero's theory of tyranny is distinctively Roman, and it specifically
reflects the problems that dominate the late Republic during the years of
its crisis from 133 BC onwards. For the Greek world, the idea of tyranny is
inextricably linked with the idea of absolute power. The Greek tyrant does
not merely aim at ruling, but also owns the power to rule. This is the picture
drawn by Plato and Aristotle,[41] and it found its representation in tyrants like
Cypselos, Peisistratos or Hippias. In contrast, the Ciceronian tyrant is less
characterised through his real power, but rather through his intention to
rule: For Cicero, tyrants are those, *qui etiam iam liberata iam civitate domina-
tiones adpetiverunt.*[42] Thus, Cicero's concept marks a shift from the objective
(that is, the real power) to the subjective (that is, the desire to rule): tyranny
becomes detached from the institutions of the state; instead, it is primarily
identified with aberrations of the human mind.[43]

There is strong indication that this concept has to be understood as an
answer to the challenges the late Republic had to face during Cicero's days.
Verres, Catilina nor Clodius – all labelled by Cicero as tyrants[44] – ever
reached a position of absolute power, but as far as Cicero believes, their conspiracies could have successfully subverted the foundations of the *concordia
omnium bonorum*. And indeed: the Republic did not finally fail due to the
revolt of a single powerful man, but because of the weakening of its structure
through a remarkable number of widespread conspiracies and assaults. As
Lintott rightly pointed out, the Republic was especially vulnerable in this
regard because of its lack of a central police power.[45] In addition, its extensive expansions and brutal internal conflicts – in particular in the course of
the *bellum civile* and Sulla's reign – lowered the loyalty of the members of the
ruling class to the republican institutions.

To understand Cicero's 'subjective' approach, this last – moral – aspect
is of specific importance. As not all men succeed in developing reason, not
all men are capable of taking part in legal discourse. Therefore, a community
of men lacking developed reason will fail to exist as a community based on

---

[40] On the following aspects, see B. Forschner 2014: 22f.
[41] Cic. *Rep.* 2.51: 'Quare prima sit haec forma et species et origo tyranni inventa nobis in ea re
publica quam auspicato Romulus condiderit, non in illa quam ut perscripsit Plato sibi ipse
Socrates tripertito illo in sermone depinxerit, ut, quem ad modum Tarquinius non novam
potestatem nactus, sed qua, habebat usus iniuste, totum genus hoc regiae civitatis everterit.'
See also Arist. *Pol.* 1308b20.
[42] Cic. *Rep.* 2.48.
[43] See Büchner 1962: 116–47, 121.
[44] Verres: Cic. *Verr.* 2.1.82, 2.3.71 and 77, 2.5.103; Catilina: Cic. *Cat.* 2.14; Clodius: Cic. *Sest.*
125, 127; Cic. *Mil.* 18 (*usurpator*), 35, 80, 89.
[45] Lintott 2004.

law.[46] Even though these men might adhere to specific laws in a given case, their decision to act lawfully is not driven by the normative power of law, but by its coercive power. They fear the consequences of violating the law, but they are not motivated – as Kant would have put it – 'by duty'. Their ignorance of the intrinsic value of law makes them prone to subvert the stability of the legal order: whenever political institutions break apart or fail to enforce the law, they will take advantage of this situation and ignore the legal provisions for their personal benefit – they only fear, as Cicero puts it, the presence of a witness and a judge, but in the dark they will follow their destructive interests: *Nam quid faciat is homo in tenebris qui nihil timet nisi testem et iudicem?*[47] Law is the substance of human rationality, but human rationality is also a precondition to save the stability of an existing legal order. Thus, a true legal community is not constituted through laws enacted and executed by a political authority, but is based exclusively on the minds of its members.

Given this background, it becomes clear why Cicero's definition of tyranny rather concentrates on the tyrant's *animus* than on his real power. On several occasions, Cicero describes the tyrant as a *belua*, that is, as a wild animal,[48] or – as we will discuss later – as a *furiosus*.[49] One might interpret this use of terminology purely from a rhetorical perspective.[50] However, in Roman law, *furiosus* also appears as a synonym for a mentally disabled person.[51]

It is interesting to observe that Cicero does not only make reference to an established legal terminology here, but that this terminology also reflects the anthropological dimension of his own concept of human nature (and thus of the nature of law). As a result of the evolving character of the human mind, people failing to train their mind and develop rationality differ from animals not by their mental capacity, but only by their human appearance. However, some of them even lack those instincts, which all living creatures equally share, like parental love or the instinct to preserve oneself and one's community.[52] They are ranked below animals; and being monsters in a human disguise, they are excluded from the natural world.[53]

Killing a tyrant differs from killing a man. Just as law contradicting nature must not be called law, men lacking reason and instincts do not count as

---

[46] Cic. *Leg.* 1.42: 'Ita fit ut nulla sit omnino iustitia, si neque natura est[.]'
[47] Idem: 1.42. See also 1.40.
[48] Cf. below fn.53.
[49] Cic. *Mil.* 78.
[50] Cf. Dunkle 1967: 151–71. See also May 1988: 129: 'The speech is transmitted to us in an extraordinary rhetorical composition, often relying upon presentation of character for its effectiveness.'
[51] Cf. D. 27.10.16 pr. (Tryph. 13 disp.). For a comprehensive account cf. Robinson 1996: 8f.
[52] Cic. *Rosc. Am.* 63.
[53] Cf., *inter alia*, Cic. *Rep.* 2.48: 'qui quamquam figura est hominis, morum tamen inmanitate vastissimas vincit beluas'; *Pis. fr.* 5: 'Quae te beluam ex utero, non hominem fudit.'

human beings.[54] Given that law is the highest form of reason, it can exist only among rational human beings. Therefore, the exclusion of the tyrant – be it through death or exile – is a necessary precondition for the existence of human community; otherwise, this community will not be able to survive as a legal order.

4. TYRANNICIDE AND LAW IN CICERO'S FORENSIC SPEECHES

In what follows, it is demonstrated how Cicero applies these abstract theories in specific forensic speeches, in particular in the speech he delivered to defend Milo in early 51 BC against the charge of having murdered Clodius, the tribune of 59/58 BC and arch-enemy of Cicero himself. In contrast to a predominantly rhetorical reading of these speeches, it is shown that especially as an advocate, Cicero – at least in his later days – relied strongly on philosophical foundations. The following short remarks are not aimed at denying Cicero's masterly use of rhetorical tools. But they intend to shift attention to an aspect of Cicero's forensic speeches that often seems to be ignored.[55]

When Cicero, in his speech in defence of Milo, paints his famous picture of Clodius as a tyrant, he has no mighty monarch in mind.[56] Clodius is not a tyrant due to his absolute power, but due to his striving for *dominatio*: his conspiracies never succeed, but he does not stop planning them;[57] he never manages to govern, but he is still starving for power.[58] Thus no successful *usurpationes* make him a tyrant, only his intentions. In *Mil.* 19, Cicero clearly points out that the reason for punishing a tyrant is not grounded in his success, but in his malevolent purpose: 'minus dolendum fuit re non perfecta, sed puniendum certe nihilo minus.'

The anthropological dimension of Cicero's theory of tyranny becomes visible when Cicero calls Clodius not merely a tyrant, but also a *furiosus*.[59] Here, Cicero points at the defective structure of Clodius' mind. Lacking both *ratio* and social instincts, the tyrant is classed below animals; he is a mentally disabled person, detached from the overall community of natural beings. We can find similar patterns in an earlier portrait of Clodius developed by Cicero in his speech for Sestius: Clodius appears as a *homo furibun-*

---

[54] Cic. *Leg.* 2.16: 'hunc hominem omnino numerari qui decet?'; *Rep.* 2.48: 'quis enim hunc hominem rite dixerit[.]'
[55] The philosophically influenced readings of Cicero's speech for Milo by Clark/Ruebel and Dyck are exceptions; cf. Clark and Ruebel 1985: 57–72; Dyck 1998: 228–9.
[56] On the following, see B. Forschner 2015.
[57] Cic. *Mil.* 37.
[58] Idem: 88.
[59] Idem: 78.

dus ac perditus,[60] and finally as a *taetra immanisque belua*.[61] Being a *belua*, he is the opposite of a reasonable man; his character is bad by nature (*natura improbus*) and *furiosus*.[62] Similarly, in his very first forensic speech in a criminal trial delivered in defence of Sextus Roscius in 80 BC, Cicero uses the distinction between those tied together by *vis humanitatis* and those whose bestiality outweighs even that of wild animals: through birth, breeding and the law of nature, wild animals still form some sort of community based on kinship – and thus, one might add, own the community spirit that the bad man lacks. Therefore, the bad man is not truly a man, but only looks like a man due to his human physical appearance.[63] And, as Cicero claims in *Pro Cluentio*, by accusing her own son of having poisoned his father, Cluentius' mother violated *omnia iura hominum*. She proved to be so brainless that she could not be called a human being; so brutal that she could not be called a woman; and so cruel that she could not be called a mother. Apart from her shape, she has totally lost her resemblance to a human creature.[64]

Although the anthropological dimension of tyranny is present in Cicero's speeches even at the beginning of his career, what is still missing is the link between this anthropological aspect and Cicero's concept of the nature of law. It does not seem an accident that this connection finally appears in the *Miloniana*, which was written at the time Cicero started working on the *Laws* and had probably already finished parts of the *Republic*. As outlined in *Leg.* 1.40–2, the wicked man takes law for an external command, and led by self-interest, his decision to obey the law results from a personal cost–benefit analysis. The good man, in contrast, obeys law simply as it is law, that is, he recognises law as an internal command deriving from his own *ratio*. The same argument appears in *Mil.* 43 and 32: Here, Cicero takes the bad man's hope of escaping punishment as the key to his criminal behaviour, with the consequence that, in certain cases, even trivial inducements might make him commit crimes. A virtuous man, by contrast, follows law for its own sake (*non tam praemia sequi solera recte factorum, quam ipsa recte facta*), and thus can overcome any temptation to act illegally, however great the external inducements might be. Clodius' disrespect of the law (*[Clodius], cui iam nulla lex*

---

[60] Cic. *Sest.* 15.

[61] Idem: 16.

[62] Idem: 97.

[63] Cic. *Rosc. Am.* 63: 'Magna est enim vis humanitatis; multum valet communio sanguinis; reclamitat istius modi suspicionibus ipsa natura; portentum atque monstrum certissimum est esse aliquem humana specie et figura qui tantum immanitate bestias vicerit ut, propter quos hanc suavissimam lucem aspexerit, eos indignissime luce privarit, cum etiam feras inter sese partus atque educatio et natura ipsa conciliet.'

[64] Cic. *Clu.* 199: 'at quae mater! [. . .] cuius ea stultitia est ut eam nemo hominem, ea vis ut nemo feminam, ea crudelitas ut nemo matrem appellare possit. atque etiam nomina necessitudinum, non solum naturae nomen et iura mutavit, uxor generi, noverca fili, filiae paelex; eo iam denique adducta est uti sibi praeter formam nihil ad similitudinem hominis reservarit.'

erat, nullum civile ius [. . .])[65] made it impossible for the legal system to deal with him: *eius furores, quos nullis iam legibus, nullis iudiciis frenare poteramus [. . .].*[66] His assassination turns out to be the only way to save the legal – and thus natural – character of the Republic; it is a virtuous act.

As shown above, Cicero, standing in a Stoic tradition, believes that *ratio* is not a pure human trait, but connects human and divine reasoning at its highest level. This theological aspect is the key to understand the subtext underlying Cicero's final remarks in *Mil.* 83–8. Here, Cicero claims that the immortal gods were involved in the assassination of Clodius, who had incurred their hatred many years before, when he attended the festivity of Bona Dea in January 61 BC dressed up as a woman. When the gods noticed Clodius approaching Milo and his entourage on the Via Appia in front of the shrine of Bona Dea, they decided to take advantage of this symbolic situation and put in Clodius' mind the idea to ambush Milo. Clodius, lacking the intellectual capacity to understand the gods' real intentions, attacked Milo and was killed when Milo's slaves defended their *dominus*. Despite its rhetorical implications, this passage also entails the core elements of Cicero's concept of tyrannicide. Being a tyrant, Clodius does not participate in the rational discourse of gods and men. The idea of attacking Milo does not appear as a product of his own reasoning, but was placed in his mind by the gods.

Cicero's much-quoted dictum *silent leges inter arma* (*Mil.* 11) does not neglect the specific legal nature of the problem of tyrannicide. In contrast to its prevalent reading, it does not imply that in a state of emergency legal provisions forfeit their legitimacy and are substituted simply by power and politics. Rather, *silere* is to be understood as deafening silence, as an incorporated part of the law. If Cicero's argument is read within its broader systematic context, the legal implication of *silere* clearly comes to light – the law grants *tacitly* the *potestas defendendi*: *Silent enim leges inter arma [. . .]. Etsi persapienter et quodam modo tacite dat ipsa lex potestatem defendendi.*[67] Given that Clodius' assassination is an act of *summa ratio* and – as Cicero states in *Mil.* 30 – *ratio praescripsit legem*, at least from Cicero's own perspective his arguments to justify Milo must be seen as a *legal* argument: 'if there was no defence in law for what he did, then I have no defence to offer'.[68]

In *Mil.* 88–9, Cicero highlights the responsibility of the *homo privatus* to defend the *res publica* by himself as long as the republic turns out to be incapable of repelling the tyrant 'by its own laws'.[69] Arguing from a positivistic standpoint and therefore identifying 'law' with law as enacted by authorised state institutions, one might assume that Cicero – paradoxically – is putting

---

[65]   Cic. *Mil.* 74.
[66]   Idem: 77.
[67]   Idem: 11.
[68]   Idem: 30: 'Si id iure fieri non potuit, nihil habeo quod defendam' (translation by Berry).
[69]   Idem: 89: 'numquam illum res publica suo iure esset ulta.'

forward the idea of violating the law in order to save it. But for Cicero, law is not an official product of the state, but an individual product of the rational human mind. He rather seems to assert that in cases where state institutions fail to effectively *use* their legal power, the stability of the legal order depends on the commitment of ordinary citizens, who are willing to take advantage of their rights and duties. This reading is backed by the next section, where Cicero deals with the practical – rather than legal – limitations of the power of state institutions: the most crucial problem of keeping Clodius in check is caused not by legal restrictions, but by the consul's lack of courage.[70]

5. PHILOSOPHY AND LEGAL PRACTICE: A FEW SPECULATIVE REMARKS

So far, three questions have been discussed. First: can we find signs of a coherent theory of 'law' in Cicero's writings? Does Cicero's thinking merely reflect a discussion on the relation of different *Rechtsschichten*, like *ius naturale* and *ius civile*, as they are significant in Roman legal thought;[71] or can we observe a more comprehensive approach, dealing with the general question: 'what is law'? Second: given that Cicero developed a theory about the nature of law – how is this theory tied to his understanding of the nature of man? To ask more specifically: does Cicero's concept of law imply any consequences for the subjective character of those constituting a human community based on law? Third: do we have to distinguish sharply between the speeches Cicero delivered as a legal practitioner and his theoretical approach on law developed in writings like the *Laws* and the *Republic*? Or can we find patterns appearing in both practical as well as theoretical contexts alike, suggesting that Cicero made use of his abstract concepts while arguing as an advocate?

The answer to this third question was that Cicero indeed applied arguments in legal practice, which can be understood against the background of his theoretical concept of the nature of law. Focusing on how Cicero deals with the category of the 'tyrant' respectively 'tyranny' in his forensic speeches, one can observe that he makes those references from the very beginning of his legal career onwards. However, the most coherent example of the use of philosophical arguments in legal practice is the speech for Milo, delivered by Cicero as he was gaining political and intellectual consolidation.

It is one thing that Cicero, according to his own concepts, takes his philosophical arguments as essential to his concept of law; it is another thing whether legal practice followed the same path. The general reluctance to

---

[70] Idem: 88–9: 'Senatus credo praetorem eum circumscripsisset. Ne cum solebat quidem id facere, in privato eodem hoc aliquid profecerat. An consules in praetor coercendo fortes fuissent?'

[71] On the role of *Rechtsschichten* as a main trait of Roman law see most recently Babusiaux 2015: 37f. See also Kaser 1986: 90f.

recognise Cicero as a serious lawyer is surely influenced by an understanding of Roman law as an abstract area of elitist discourse, which is seen as
detached from religious and philosophical influences.[72] Nowadays, this
exclusive reading of Roman law is losing support, however strong it may
have been in the past.[73] Starting with Crook's eminent studies in the late
1960s, the social and philosophical rootedness of Roman law has become an
increasingly popular field of study. This does not only apply to the world of
common law, where the burden of a practically relevant 'doctrinal' tradition
of Roman law weighed less than in mainland Europe.

It surely goes too far to believe that from the late Republic onwards,
Roman jurists can be categorised in accordance with specific philosophical
schools. Even Behrends, whose controversial writings promoted this idea in
the past, is currently claiming a rather indirect philosophical influence on
Roman legal thought.[74] But what is true, however, is that Roman jurists had
recourse to terms and argumentative patterns that are equally known from
the discourse of ancient philosophers. They do not make deep philosophical
contributions, and their direct philosophical references seem to be short and
sometimes superficial in comparison with writings like those of Cicero. Nor
do they provide us with coherent theories on the nature of law or the relation between law and human rationality. But it is precisely the partly inhomogeneous character of their writings that demonstrates that legal discourse
was open enough to integrate different strands of philosophical argument.

We will illustrate this assumption by shortly pointing at the use of *natura*
resp. *ius naturale* in early and later classical texts of Roman jurists.[75] Looking
at definitions of the *ius naturale* in texts from the Digest and Gaius' Institutes,
we find the idea of a natural community between men and other animals;[76]
but we also find sources identifying *ius naturale* with *ius gentium*.[77] The *ius
gentium*, again, is (partly) seen as a law common only to all men by nature,
and thus not shared by men and animals alike.[78]

The definition of *ius gentium* as a law *quod vero naturalis ratio inter omnes
homines constituit*[79] seems to be similar to Cicero's understanding of law as the
very essence of human reason. However, the text lacks any deeper explanation of the character of this *ratio*; in particular, it does not clarify how the

---

[72] Cf. Harke 2008: 3: 'für die Gesamtsituation der römischen Reichsbevölkerung ebenso blind
wie für religiöse oder philosophische Vorstellungen unanfällig[.]'

[73] For a short summary of current approaches on Roman law see recently Schermaier 2014:
107–32, 108–10.

[74] Even though he still adheres to his understanding of Roman legal discourse as a discourse of
separate, conflicting schools of thought; cf. Behrends 2013: 432f.; Schermaier 2014: 110.

[75] On the following, see B. Forschner 2015: 61f.

[76] *Iust. Inst.* 1.2 pr.; D. 1.1.1.3–4.

[77] D. 1.1.9 (Gai. 1 inst.).

[78] Gai. *Inst* 1.1.

[79] D. 1.1.9 (Gai. 1 inst.); D. 41.1.1 pr. (Gai. 2 rer. cot.).

ratio became part of the human mind. The *naturalis ratio* might indeed be understood as a Stoic/Ciceronian *nata lex ad quam facti sumus*. But it can also be understood as a reference to the basic ideas of the sceptic Academy, or to no specific philosophical school at all.

Ulpian, by contrast, takes *natura* for a genuine source of law.[80] According to him, understanding the law does not require instinct, but *peritia*, that is, experience; and this experience is not only common to men, but to all animals.[81] However, Ulpian does not draw any consequences from this position: In D. 9.1.1.3 (Ulp. 18 ad ed.), he claims that animals lack *sensus* and thus cannot do any wrong.[82] Here, he seems to distinguish between instinct, experience and reason, and understanding of the law – that is, of the difference between *ius* and *iniura* – is not caused by experience, but by reason.

The inhomogeneous and sometimes superficial use of *natura* in the texts of the Roman jurists becomes particularly relevant when looking at their arguments supporting the right of self-defence. Like Justinian and Cicero, Gaius highlights that this right is grounded on the *ratio naturalis*.[83] However, whereas Cicero develops a broad theory of the anthropological character of this *ratio*, Gaius' texts provide no further hints clarifying his own concept: the *ratio naturalis* is simply taken for granted. Florentinus argues that a man is not allowed to threaten the life or physical integrity of another man, as there exists a natural kinship among all human beings; this, in turn, is the reason why every man has the right to defend himself against those trying to kill or violate him.[84] The idea that *natura inter nos cognationem quandam constituit* reminds one of the wording of Gaius' definition of the *ius gentium* (*[ius], quod vero naturalis ratio inter omnes homines constituit*),[85] but it does not necessarily say the same: whereas the latter takes the *ratio naturalis* as a source of law (which conforms to Gaius' view expressed in D. 9.2.4 pr. that the right of self-defence derives from the *ratio naturalis*), the former does not explicitly discuss the nature of law, but merely points at a specific tie unifying all men. If Florentinus had in mind a concept of the relation of human and legal nature, it did not survive in his text. Ulpian, finally, does not refer

---

[80] D. 1.1.1.3 (Ulp. 1 inst.): 'Ius naturale est, quod natura omnia animalia docuit: nam ius istud non humani generis proprium, sed omnium animalium, quae in terra, quae in mari nascuntur, avium quoque commune est.'

[81] D. 1.1.1.3 (Ulp. 1 inst.): 'Hinc descendit maris atque feminae coniunctio, quam nos matrimonium appellamus, hinc liberorum procreatio, hinc educatio: videmus etenim cetera quoque animalia, feras etiam istius iuris peritia censeri.'

[82] D. 9.1.1.3 (Ulp. 18 ad ed.): 'Pauperies est damnum sine iniuria facientis datum: nec enim potest animal iniuria fecisse, quod sensu caret.'

[83] D. 9.2.4 pr. (Gai. 7 ad ed. prov.): 'nam adversus periculum naturalis ratio permittit se defendere.'

[84] D. 1.1.3 (Florent. 1 inst.): 'Ut vim atque iniuriam propulsemus: nam iure hoc evenit, ut quod quisque ob tutelam corporis sui fecerit, iure fecisse existimetur, et cum inter nos cognationem quandam natura constituit, consequens est hominem homini insidiari nefas esse.'

[85] Cf. D. 1.1.9 (Gai. 1 inst.).

to any philosophical background, but merely states that *natura* grants the *ius defendendi*.[86]

Looking at this selection of legal writings, a negative and a positive assumption can be made. Roman jurists do not, as Cicero did, reflect on the nature of law in a coherent way. Their use of *natura* seems to be much more pragmatic and occasional, and even in writings of one and the same author one finds different – and contradicting – assumptions. They also neither follow Cicero's idea that only law conforming with nature counts as law, nor do they develop a hierarchic understanding of natural law as a law outranking other laws. But what can be said positively is that Roman legal discourse did include philosophical elements; that Roman lawyers seem to believe in the justness of what they perceive as the 'natural quality' of human beings (and animals, to some extent); and that they were concerned with the legal effect of this natural quality. Moreover, they are using a terminology that is also to be found in Cicero's philosophical texts, like *natura*, *naturalis ratio* and *cognatio*.[87]

6. CONCLUSION

Does Cicero's use of philosophical arguments in forensic speeches contradict the legal discourse of his time? The question can only be answered with caution, as republican sources are rare. But with some certainty we can say that Cicero's legal arguments derive from a philosophical background that is more complex and comprehensive than the philosophical splinters found in the texts of classical jurists. This, however, does not necessarily imply that his positions were incompatible with the way in which the Roman jurists argued. Cicero's arguments might have been more grounded, but they were not foreign to Roman law. Like Cicero, the Roman jurists referred to a *ratio* that is inherent in the human mind, and they put forward the idea of a *cognatio* that binds all men (respectively all living creatures) together. And most importantly, they took these philosophical aspects to be legally relevant: *natura* was an established topic in the legal discourse, and it did count as a source of law.

Claiming that Cicero was not a jurist seems to be right and wrong at once. It seems to be right as he does not appear as a *typical* jurist: he shows less interest in the details of the *ius civile*, although he occasionally demonstrates a good knowledge of it; and unlike the jurists, he is strongly concerned with general reflections on the nature of law, the relation between law and society and the human preconditions of a lawful society. However, as the

---

[86] D. 43.16.1.27 (Ulp. 69 ad ed.): 'Vim vi repellere licere Cassius scribit, idque ius natura comparatur.'

[87] For the use of *cognatio* in Ciceronian texts see *Leg.* 1.25, 1.26; for the use of *naturalis ratio* see idem: 1.35.

above analysis of short passages from his forensic speeches demonstrates, Cicero also tries to bridge the gap between his philosophical ideas (that is, his understanding of the nature of law and its relation to human nature) and the rules and structures of legal practice. His theoretical approach does not lack practical relevance, but serves as breeding ground for legal arguments. These arguments accord with arguments found in the jurists' writings, even though they frequently exceed them with regard to their philosophical substance.

BIBLIOGRAPHY

Algra, K. (2003), 'Stoic theology', in B. Inwood, ed., *The Cambridge Companion to the Stoics*. Cambridge. 153–78.

Atkins, J. (2013), *Cicero on Politics and the Limits of Reason: the Republic and Laws*. Cambridge.

Babusiaux, U. (2015), *Wege zur Rechtsgeschichte: Römisches Erbrecht*. Cologne.

Behrends, O. (2013), 'Kontroverse Konjunktionen, oder: War die römische Jurisprudenz eine Wissenschaft?' *Zeitschrift der Savigny-Stiftung für Rechtsgeschichte, romanistische Abteilung* 130: 432–56.

Bees, R. (2004), *Die Oikeiosislehre der Stoa: I. Rekonstruktion ihres Inhalts*. Würzburg.

Büchner, K. (1962), 'Der Tyrann und das Gegenbild in Ciceros Staat', in K. Büchner, *Studien zur römischen Literatur, volume II: Cicero*. Wiesbaden.

Clark, M. and Ruebel, J. (1985), 'Philosophy and rhetoric in Cicero's *Pro Milone*', *Rheinisches Museum für Philologie* 128: 57–72.

Colish, M. (1990), *The Stoic Tradition from Antiquity to the Early Middle Ages, Volume 1: Stoicism in classical Latin literature*. Leiden.

Dunkle, J. R. (1967), 'The Greek tyrant and Roman political invective in the late Republic', *Transactions and Proceedings of the American Philological Association* 98: 151–71.

Dyck, A. (1998), 'Narrative obfuscation, philosophical *topoi* and tragic patterning in Cicero's *Pro Milone*', *Harvard Studies in Classical Philology* 98: 219–41.

Forschner, B. (2014), 'Recht als Vernunft. Bemerkungen zu Ciceros Rechtsmodell in der *Post-Reditum*-Phase', in P. Klausberger, C. Lehne and P. Scheibelreiter, eds, *Disputationes Tirolenses: Tagungsband zum 7. internationalen Treffen der Jungen Romanist(inn)en*. Vienna. 21–38.

Forschner, B. (2015), *Die Einheit der Ordnung. Recht, Philosophie und Gesellschaft in Ciceros Rede* Pro Milone. Munich.

Forschner, M. (1995), *Die stoische Ethik. Über den Zusammenhang von Natur-, Sprach- und Moralphilosophie im altstoischen System*. Darmstadt.

Forschner, M. (2008), 'Oikeiosis. Die stoische Theorie der Selbstaneignung', in B. Neymeyer, J. Schmidt and B. Zimmermann, eds, *Stoizismus in der europäischen Philosophie, Literatur, Kunst und Politik*, volume 1. Berlin. 169–91.

Forschner, M. (2014), 'Die Stoa zur Begründung des natürlichen Gesetzes', *Index* 42: 73–84.

Gagarin, M. (2002), *Antiphon the Athenian: Oratory, law, and justice in the age of the Sophists*. Austin.

Girardet, K. (1983), *Die Ordnung der Welt: Ein Beitrag zur philosophischen und politischen Interpretation von Ciceros Schrift* de legibus. Wiesbaden.

Glucker, J. (1988), 'Cicero's philosophical affiliations', in J. Dillon and A. Long, eds, *The Question of 'Eclecticism'*. Berkeley. 34–69.

Görler, W. (2004), 'Silencing the troublemaker: *De Legibus* 1.39 and the continuity of Cicero's scepticism', in C. Catrein, ed., *Woldemar Görler: Kleine Schriften zur hellenistisch-römischen Philosophie*. Leiden. 240–67.

Harke, J. D. (2008), *Römisches Recht: Von der klassischen Zeit bis zu den modernen Kodifikationen*. Munich.

Heinimann, F. (1965), Nomos und Physis: *Herkunft und Bedeutung einer Antithese im griechischen Denken des 5. Jahrhunderts*. Basel.

Hirzel, R. (1883), *Untersuchungen zu Cicero's philosophischen Schriften*, volume 3. Leipzig.

Hochstrasser, T. J. (2004), *Natural Law Theories in the Early Enlightenment*. Cambridge.

Honsell, H. (1993), 'Nomos und Physis bei den Sophisten', in J. A. Ankum et al., eds, *Mélanges Felix Wubbe*, Fribourg. 179–90.

Kaser, M. (1986), *Römische Rechtsquellen und angewandte Juristenmethode*. Vienna.

Kenter, L. (1972), *A Commentary on Cicero, De Legibus*. Amsterdam.

Kerferd, G. (1981), *The Sophistic Movement*. Cambridge.

Lehoux, D. (2012), *What Did the Romans Know? An inquiry into science and worldmaking*. Chicago.

Lintott, A. (2002), *The Constitution of the Roman Republic*. Oxford.

Lintott, A. (2004), *Violence in Republican Rome*. Oxford.

Long, A. (1996), *Problems in Stoicism*. London.

May, J. (1988), *Trials of Character: The eloquence of Ciceronian ethos*. Chapel Hill.

Nörr, D. (1974), *Rechtskritik in der römischen Antike*. Munich.

Ostwald, M. (2009), 'Nomos and Physis in Antiphon's *Peri Aletheias*', in *Language and History in Ancient Greek Culture*. Philadelphia. 158–74.

Pohlenz, M. (1959), *Die Stoa: Geschichte einer geistigen Bewegung*, volume I. Göttingen.

Powell, J. (2001), 'Were Cicero's laws the laws of Cicero's Republic?', in J. Powell and J. North, eds, *Cicero's Republic*. London. 17–39.

Robinson, D. N. (1996), *Wild Beasts and Idle Humors: The insanity defense from antiquity to the present*. Cambridge, MA.

Schermaier, M. (2014), 'From non-performance to mistake in contracts: the rise of the classical doctrine of consensus', in B. Sirks, ed., Nova Ratione: *Change of paradigms in Roman law*. Wiesbaden. 107–32.

Schofield, M. (1991), *The Stoic Idea of the City*. Cambridge.

Schofield, M. (1995), 'Two Stoic approaches to justice', in A. Laks and M. Schofield, eds, *Justice and Generosity: Studies in Hellenistic social and political philosophy*. Cambridge. 191–212.

Scholten, H. (2003), *Die Sophistik: Eine Bedrohung für die Religion und Politik der Polis?* Berlin.

Spaemann, R. (1987), 'Über den Begriff der Menschenwürde', in E. W. Böckenförde and R. Spaemann, eds, *Menschenrechte und Menschenwürde: Historische Voraussetzungen – säkulare Gewalt – christliches Verständnis.* Stuttgart. 295–313.

Vogt, K. M. (2008), *Law, Reason and the Cosmic City: Political philosophy in the early Stoa.* Oxford.

Part II

On Lawyers

Chapter 5

Cicero and the Small World of Roman Jurists

Yasmina Benferhat

1. INTRODUCTION

What does it take to be number one? What did it take in Rome in the late Republic to be the best among the politicians and senators? How did one go about achieving the most brilliant career? These were questions that the young Cicero had in mind, without any doubt,[1] as he started his *cursus* studying law, rhetoric and philosophy. Similarly, these are questions we need to keep in mind when attempting to understand his judgement of the Roman jurists of his time: Q. Mucius Scaevola, Servius Sulpicius Rufus, Gaius Trebatius Testa. It explains why his testimony, though valuable as can be considering that we do not have that many clues about them, must be considered cautiously: he is not objective, not because of his well-known pride, but because he sees law through the prism of his ambition and determination to achieve immortal glory.

For him it was clear that law was not enough and jurists could not expect to have a brillant career merely because of their knowledge. Cicero was an advocate, the greatest advocate Rome had in the late Republic from 70 BC onwards. He had studied law with the best, but law alone, in his view, was not sufficient to reach the top. Thus modern scholars must apply this filter when attempting to reconstruct the lives of those jurists he knew and assessing their importance in Roman society of the late Republic. The same caveat applies to his views on generals. Cicero considered it useful for the state to have great officers who won battles and wars, but he was convinced that it was not enough to pretend to be the best, and we can assume it was not only because he knew he could never compete with a Pompey or a Caesar. It was also because he believed that a leader had to be more than a victorious general, just as he believed that a jurist could not be a leader with a knowledge only of law.

Once we bear this in mind, we can study the main jurists who lived in or around Cicero's time. Mucius Scaevola was his master in the study of law, until he died; then Cicero had to study with another member of this family. Servius Sulpicius was a colleague, one of the few *consulares* who, alongside

---

[1] Cf. Cic. *QFr.* 3.5.4.

Cicero, were still alive after Caesar's death. The two men grew closer after Caesar's death, shortly before Sulpicius also died. The last one survived Cicero: the young Trebatius was one of his pupils before becoming a friend of Caesar and later of Augustus.

This chapter will not focus on their careers, since much is already well known, thanks to W. Kunkel[2] and Richard Bauman's[3] works. Instead, we will demonstrate how Cicero considered them, and what it tells us about the evolution of the social position of jurists in Rome in the late Republic. We are interested in subjectivity, not in an objective presentation of Mucius Scaevola, Sulpicius Rufus and Trebatius' careers, even if sometimes these themes overlap. The order will be chronological because it reflects the evolution: first Scaevola, then Sulpicius, and last but not least Trebatius.

2. QUINTUS MUCIUS SCAEVOLA AUGUR

The earliest examples of jurists in Cicero's circle were Q. Mucius Scaevola Augur[4] and his cousin the Pontifex,[5] his masters in the study of civil law.[6] The Augur was consul in 117 BC, and died in 88 or 87 BC; his cousin, who was much younger, was consul in 95 BC before going to Asia as proconsul. Cicero had studied around two or three years with the Augur, before briefly studying with the Pontifex, who was killed in 82 BC.

One would expect a positive description of these two figures in Cicero's works harking back to a golden age of the Roman jurists, but the reality is more complex. Indeed Scaevola is praised in *De Republica*: he is a *doctus adulescens*,[7] which likely refers to his studying civil law, even if Cicero, through Laelius, who was Mucius' father-in-law, had already pointed out that law was not enough[8] to solve political crises. His name is the first to appear in the treatise *De Amicitia* where he is praised:

> And so it came to pass that, in my desire to gain greater profit from his legal skill, I made it a practice to commit to memory many of his learned opinions and many, too, of his brief and pointed sayings[.][9]

---

[2] See Kunkel 1967.

[3] See Bauman 1983.

[4] *RE* 21: see Bauman 1983: 312–40; Harries 2006: 41–7; Rawson 1985: 203–11. Bretone 1978: 48–52 believes he was born in 165 BC.

[5] See Harries 2006: 104ff.

[6] Cf. *Amic.* 1. On the teaching of law see Kodrebski 1976 and Liebs 1976.

[7] Cf. *Rep.* 1.18.

[8] Idem: 33.

[9] *Amic.* 1: 'itaque multa ab eo prudenter disputata, multa etiam breviter et commode dicta memoriae mandabam fierique studebam eius prudentia doctior.' All English translations are based on those readily available online at sites such as Lexundria, LacusCurtius, and the Perseus Digital Library.

There is also an allusion to Mucius Scaevola at the beginning of the *De Legibus*,[10] and of course he is one of the main characters of the *De Oratore*, as if he were a kind of totem. Mentioning Scaevola the Augur allowed Cicero to place himself in glorious continuity starting with his political ideal Scipio Aemilianus Africanus, but does it prove he really had a good opinion of his masters?

The answer might seem positive when we read Cicero's judgement of the Augur in the *Brutus*: 'iuris civilis intellegentia atque omni prudentiae genere praestitit'.[11] The Pontifex too is praised as *ingenio et iustitia praestantissimus*.[12] An even better indication may be found in the correspondence when Cicero is sent to Cilicia in 51 BC, since he constantly refers to Mucius' example, and not only because he writes to Atticus, who had been one of his students too. Mucius had been propraetor in Asia, in 115 BC, and could be used as a model to govern a province. Cicero emphasises that he was in charge for only nine months,[13] enough to play the game of the traditional *cursus* but without any excess . . . The proconsul of Cilicia used Mucius' edict[14] in his province:

> I, however, have a proviso in my own edict of equivalent force, but less openly expressed (derived from the Asiatic edict of Q. Mucius, son of Publius) – 'provided that the agreement made is not such as cannot hold good *ex fide bona*', I have followed Scaevola in many points, among others in this – which the Greeks regard as a charta of liberty – that Greeks are to decide controversies between each other according to their own laws.[15]

The problem here was the difficult coexistence between the administration and the merchants in a Roman province. Cicero tried to protect himself, wishing to avoid excesses, but he also wanted to minimise any possible future complaints from the *publicani*. He had not forgotten the problems faced by Mucius Scaevola when he returned from Asia, and he had them in his mind:

> For my part, I shall not cease to defend your decrees: but you know the ways of that class of men; you are aware how bitterly hostile they were to the famous Q. Scaevola himself.[16]

---

[10] *Leg.* 1.13.
[11] *Brut.* 102. See Sumner 1973: 55–6 with the family tree.
[12] *Amic.* 1.
[13] Cf. *Att.* 5.17.6.
[14] See Badian 1956: 104–23; Rawson 1985: 209 and Rigsby 1988.
[15] *Att.* 6.1.15: 'ego tamen habeo ἰσοδυναμοῦσαν sed tectiorem ex Q. Muci P. f. edicto Asiatico, EXTRA QVAM SI ITA NEGOTIVM GESTVM EST VT EO STARI NON OPORTEAT EX FIDE BONA, multaque sum secutus Scaevolae, in iis illud in quo sibi libertatem censent Graeci datam, ut Graeci inter se disceptent suis legibus.'
[16] *Fam.* 1.9.26: 'Equidem non desinam tua decreta defendere, sed nosti consuetudinem hominum: scis, quam graviter inimici ipsi illi Q. Scaevolae fuerint.'

This then is the first serious criticism: being a jurist, and a great one, did not prevent you from having problems in your official career. Scaevola had to defend himself in a trial against Albucius, which he did brilliantly. One could add that the other Scaevola was murdered during the civil war between Marius' partisans and Sulla. This was another example or counter-example that Cicero constantly had in his mind:

> If, on the other hand, I keep my ground and find some footing on this side, I shall have done what L. Philippus did during the tyranny of Cinna, as well as L. Flaccus and Q. Mucius. Though it turned out unhappily in the case of the latter, he used, nevertheless, to say that he foresaw the result (a result which did actually happen), but preferred it to approaching the walls of his native city in arms.[17]

A slight reproach is also visible here, even if Cicero considers Mucius' point of view as *certa quaedam illa Muci ratio atque sententia*: being a specialist in civil law was not enough for political life in Rome. But there were other criticisms too: first, good knowledge of law alone was not enough to win a trial. This does not apply to the Augur who successfully defended himself against Albucius,[18] but to his cousin. Cicero explains that Scaevola eagerly took all the clients who came to him,[19] even if he was not the best person to defend them, and he reminds us of two times where Scaevola was not good enough, though the circumstances would have required it: first when pleading for his close friend Rutilius:

> Q. Mucius too said much in his defence, with his usual accuracy and elegance; but not with that force, and extension, which the mode of trial, and the importance of the cause demanded.[20]

Mucius was not able to save his friend from an unjust exile, because he was not brilliant enough. Cicero is, in effect, indirectly praising his own genius for eloquence, and then his ability to be a great statesman thanks to his eloquence. In another case, the *causa Curiana*,[21] Mucius lost the trial pleading against Crassus, though this kind of case was his speciality:

> For he urged a great variety of arguments in the defence of right and equity, against the literal interpretation of the law; and supported them by such a numerous

---

[17] *Att.* 8.3.6: 'at si restitero et fuerit nobis in hac parte locus, idem fecero quod in Cinnae dominatione (L.) Philippus, quod L. Flaccus, quod Q. Mucius, quoquo modo ea res huic quidem cecidit; qui tamen ita dicere solebat se id fore videre quod factum est sed malle quam armatum ad patriae moenia accedere.'

[18] Cf. *Brut.* 102.

[19] Cf. idem: 155.

[20] Idem: 115: 'et Q. Mucius enucleate ille quidem et polite, ut solebat, nequaquam autem ea vi atque copia, quam genus illud iudici et magnitudo causae postulabat.' On this trial see Gruen 1966: 53ff.

[21] See Harries 2006: 100ff and Harries 2013: 109 – it was a trial in the 90s about a contested will and it involved M. Curius.

series of precedents, that he overpowered Q. Scaevola (a man of uncommon penetration, and the ablest jurist of his time) though the case before them was only a matter of legal right.[22]

It is one thing to know the civil law very well, but another to use it efficiently. Cicero considered Servius a better jurist than Mucius because he not only knew law, he also knew how to use dialectics and was a brillant orator as well.[23] The difference probably lay in the fact that law was a family matter for the Scaevolae: they began acting as lawyers when the civil law was a kind of heirloom reserved for a few families. Cicero never says it clearly but the way he describes another Scaevola, adopted by the Crassi, is quite clear:

> For he had contracted an affinity with that accomplished speaker Servius Galba above-mentioned, by giving his daughter in marriage to Galba's son; and being likewise himself the son of Mucius, and the brother of P. Scaevola, he had a fine opportunity at home (which he made the best use of) to gain a thorough knowledge of the civil law.[24]

In fact, when Cicero criticises Scaevola by praising Servius, one must appreciate that he in effect praising his own model: this is particularly obvious in the *De Oratore* when Crassus affirms that the best jurist will be defeated by the orator who has learned just enough law to seem keen on it. But one must study the way in which Cicero really considered Servius Sulpicius Rufus to prove this.

3. SERVIUS SULPICIUS RUFUS

Servius Sulpicius Rufus[25] comes second in our study, and there is a considerable gap between him and Scaevola. First, they are separated by two generations with all that this implies: Mucius was born around 160 BC, Servius around 105 BC. In second place, Servius' career was far less brillant that that of Scaevola. But why should this be so? The *Pro Murena*, famously delivered in 63 BC, provides valuable explanation. It became tradition in the late Republic to start a trial against another candidate to the consulate who had been elected while you had been defeated. The competition had become all the fiercer after Sulla had increased the numbers of all magistracies, apart from the consulship (though their numbers were eventually increased first

---

[22] *Brut.* 145: 'Ita enim multa tum contra scriptum pro aequo et bono dixit, ut hominem acutissimum Q. Scaevolam et in iure, in quo illa causa vertebatur, paratissimum obrueret argumentorum exemplorumque copia.'

[23] Idem: 151–4.

[24] Idem: 98: 'nam et cum summo illo oratore Ser. Galba, cuius Gaio filio filiam suam conlocaverat, adfinitate sese devinxerat et cum esset P. Muci filius fratremque haberet P. Scaevolam, domi ius civile cognoverat.'

[25] See Harries 2006: 116–26, who sees him as a man of transition.

by Caesar and then through the use of *consules suffecti*). Servius, furious at having been beaten, accused his victorious competitor, Murena, of bribery.

The *Pro Murena* is the speech that Cicero delivered to defend Murena, his main reason being the stability of the state at a risky time with the threat of Catilina never far off. As already known, Cicero never hesitated to caricature his adversaries in a trial: the dancer, the *puer delicatus*, the *meretrix*, the awful mother-in-law, all the stereotypes were good and used if necessary. So, it comes as no surprise when he presents Cato, who then assisted Servius, as a psychorigid Stoic, or Servius as a narrow-minded jurist. But, beyond the exaggerations, Cicero really meant them.

The *Pro Murena* is also a valuable source for us for knowledge of Servius and of Cicero's real view of the jurists. At the outset it should be noted that Servius was never lucky in his career, even if this statement requires greater nuance. In 74 BC he was quaestor in Ostia, which could not have helped him to get many clients.[26] Then as a praetor in 65 he was in charge of the trials *de peculatu*, which was politically pretty embarrassing:

> What department was it that your lot gave you? A disagreeable and odious one. That of inquiry into peculation, pregnant on the one side with the tears and mourning apparel of the accused, full on the other side of imprisonment and informers. In that department of justice judges are forced to act against their will, are retained by force contrary to their inclination. The clerk is hated, the whole body is unpopular. The gratifications given by Sulla are found fault with. Many brave men, – indeed, a considerable portion of the city is offended; damages are assigned with severity. The man who is pleased with the decision soon forgets it; he who loses his cause is sure to remember it.[27]

Was this a matter of chance? We could agree to some extent, even if it is well known that there were special ways to help chance along when balloting for a magistrature or a province. Servius indeed suffered from the political context: he was sacrificed in 63 BC on the altar of the *raison d'état* and it took more than ten years for him finally to be elected consul, because of the Triumvirate. Caesar might have thought of him in 59 BC for a tandem with the Pompeian Gabinius,[28] but he finally chose Calpurnius Piso, which is quite interesting.[29] Piso and Servius had nearly the same profile – they belonged to the Roman aristocracy, even if Servius was a patrician while the

---

[26] Cf. *Mur.* 18.

[27] Idem: 42: 'Quid tua sors? Tristis, atrox, quaestio peculatus ex altera parte lacrimarum et squaloris, ex altera plena accusatorum atque indicum; cogendi iudices inviti, retinendi contra voluntatem; scriba damnatus, ordo totus alienus; Sullana gratificatio reprehensa, multi viri fortes et prope pars civitatis offensa est; lites severe aestimatae; cui placet obliviscitur, cui dolet memini.'

[28] Cf. Cic. *Att.* 2.5.2.

[29] We could also surmise that Servius' connection with Caesar had started much earlier than stated.

Calpurnii Pisones were a plebeian family reaching the consulate for the first time only in 212 BC, and both men were moderate – but Piso was considered a better option politically speaking, and not only because of his daughter.

Nevertheless, as Cicero emphasises, it was not only chance: it was law. Servius chose to be a specialist of civil law[30] and Cicero hints in the *Brutus*[31] he did so after he realised that he could never compete with Cicero himself. We can surmise that he had also understood that he would never be able to compete with a Pompey for military glory, and he refused to be governor of a province after his praetorship. The *Pro Murena* is a speech about the three main ways[32] to reach the top in Rome: Cicero had to glorify the *militia*, for the sake of his client, even if he could not help praising his own choice of eloquence,[33] and the law was the loser of the three.

What were the arguments? Law is hard work with many sources of trouble and not much benefit: so said Cicero. It was not possible to acquire a good network of *clientes* who would vote for you later, by being a legal expert. A second important point would be the recent diffusion of civil law, which allowed everybody to learn it through books, and of course Cicero pretended it was so easy to learn that anyone could quickly become a specialist:

> Nor has any one any right to be considered skillful in law, because there cannot be any difference between men in a branch of knowledge with which they are all acquainted. And a matter is not thought the more difficult for being contained in a very small number of very intelligible documents. Therefore, if you excite my anger, though I am excessively busy, in three days I will profess myself a lawyer.[34]

More seriously, Cicero contested the utility of a science that was limited to the Roman sphere and even caused trouble there: jurists were an obstacle to the good use of law, according to him, because of a mix of tricky ways of changing old laws and the abuse of archaisms. This was indeed a good way to make people laugh at jurists – a long tradition from Aristophanes to Racine's *Les Plaideurs*, not to mention other authors. But we can consider Cicero meant it, as a broader reflection on Rome's history and development.

---

[30] On law and Servius in the *Pro Murena*, see Michel 1975: 95.

[31] Cf. *Brut.* 151. See Sumner 1973: 97 and 155–6 – he speculates that Servius was born in 105 BC.

[32] Cf. Ov. *Her.* 3–6. See Wiseman 1971: 119 on the three ways and 120 on Servius: though a patrician, Servius came from a family that had not given any consul to Rome for probably two generations, since Servius' father remained an *eques*, and his grandfather was *nulla illustri laude illustratus*, cf. Cicero, *Mur.* 16. One might nevertheless surmise that his grandfather had done the *cursus honorum* and been an honourable though an unremarkable magistrate.

[33] Cf. *Mur.* 24 and 29.

[34] Idem: 28: 'Peritus ideo haberi nemo potest quod in eo quod sciunt omnes nullo modo possunt inter se discrepare. Difficilis autem res ideo non putatur quod et perpaucis et minime obscuris litteris continetur. Itaque si mihi, homini vehementer occupato, stomachum moveritis, triduo me iuris consultum esse profitebor.'

To sum it up, the small world of jurists was narrow: their intellectual pursuit was narrow, their activities were narrow, and their lives could only be narrow. And if by chance you were not narrow-minded when you chose to be a specialist of civil law, then law was going to make of you a narrow-minded person: that is what can be inferred from the excellent analysis of Sulpicius' electoral campaign for the consulate. Instead of thinking positively and trying to make people vote for him, as a jurist he reacted by bringing a trial against Murena when he understood he was going to be beaten:

> I often told you, Servius, that you did not know how to stand for the consulship; and, in respect to those very matters which I saw you conducting and advocating in a brave and magnanimous spirit, I often said to you that you appeared to me to be a brave senator rather than a wise candidate. For, in the first place, the terrors and threats of accusations, which you were in the habit of employing every day, are rather the part of a fearless man; but they have an unfavourable effect on the opinion of the people as regards a man's hopes of getting anything from them, and they even disarm the zeal of his friends.[35]

The correspondence is another source for Cicero's view of Servius. Although the judgement is sometimes positive, especially in the months preceding Servius' death, globally the portrait corresponds to what the *Pro Murena* had shown. A first notable phase is around 51–49 BC: eventually Servius was consul in 51 BC, perhaps thanks to Caesar, if we admit that there was a political share not only in the repartition of the censorship that year – Piso was a Caesarian while Appius Claudius was close to Pompey – but also in the choice of the consuls. Then it would suggest that Marcellus was the candidate of Caesar's opponents, while Servius was officially neutral[36] but actually a Caesarian.

Caelius does not hesitate to criticise Servius, even if gently, by calling him a *cunctator*,[37] which, as Fabius' example showed, would not be seen positively in Rome. He probably knew Cicero would agree. In fact, Servius had attempted to preach for peace by delivering an important speech on the past civil wars in Rome, as Cicero recognises much later,[38] without much success.

At the beginning of the civil war, Servius chose to remain in Rome, officially still neutral although his son Servius junior was serving in Caesar's

---

[35] Idem: 43: 'Petere consulatum nescire te, Servi, persaepe tibi dixi; et in eis rebus ipsis quas te magno et forti animo et agere et dicere videbam tibi solitus sum dicere magis te fortem accusatorem mihi videri quam sapientem candidatum. Primum accusandi terrores et minae quibus tu cotidie uti solebas sunt fortis viri, sed et populi opinionem a spe adipiscendi avertunt et amicorum studia debilitant.'

[36] Cf. *Att.* 7.3.3.

[37] Cf. *Fam.* 8.10.3: 'Nosti Marcellum, quam tardus et parum efficax sit, itemque Servius quam cunctator.'

[38] Cf. idem: 4.3.1 (September 46 BC).

armies against Pompey.[39] And he agreed to come to the senate once Caesar had entered Rome, which Cicero could not help criticising, even if indirectly:

> And, in fact, I should myself have written to you before to warn you that your going to the senate – or rather to the convention of senators – would have no result, had I not been afraid of annoying the man who was urging me to imitate you. Him indeed I gave clearly to understand, when he asked me to attend the senate, that I should say precisely what you said about peace, and about the Spains.[40]

Cicero's portrayal of Servius is filled with irony – his colleague prefers his little bed in Rome[41] – and pretty full of contempt. Cicero first considers him to be a coward,[42] then criticised him for being an eternal jurist, evaluating the positive and the negative:

> I never saw anybody so completely beside himself with fear; and yet, by Hercules, he feared nothing that was not a legitimate object of fear: 'Pompey was angry with him, Caesar no friend to him: the victory of either one or the other was alarming, both because of the cruel nature of the one, the unscrupulousness of the other, and also because of the financial embarrassment of both, which could be relieved from no source except that of the property of private persons.' And these remarks were accompanied with such floods of tears, that I wondered they had not run dry from such protracted misery.[43]

Though choosing to go their separate ways, since Cicero found a boat to go to Greece and Servius joined Caesar's side in Italy, the two men kept in touch. When Servius took the charge in Achaia that Caesar had given him, Cicero agreed[44] and never hesitated to send him letters of recommendation. In an interesting letter of September 46 BC, when Servius was in Greece,

---

[39] He joined Caesar's camp in South Italy, cf. *Att.* 10.14.3 ('fili militia Brundisina').

[40] *Fam.* 4.1.1. (21–2 April): 'Atque ipse antea ad te scripsissem te frustra in senatum sive potius in conventum senatorum esse venturum, ni veritus essem, ne eius animum offenderem, qui a me, ut te imitarer, petebat: cui quidem ego, cum me rogaret, ut adessem in senatu, eadem omnia, quae a te de pace et de Hispaniis dicta sunt, ostendi me esse dicturum.'

[41] Cf. *Att.* 10.14.3.

[42] Cf. idem: 'Si vir esse volet . . .' The same negative point of view a bit later beginning of May 49 BC cf. idem: 10.12.4. Cicero wished to convince Servius to sail away with him and join Pompey, which Servius refused to do.

[43] Idem: 10.14.1: 'numquam vidi hominem perturbatiorem metu; neque hercule quicquam timebat quod non esset timendum; illum sibi iratum, hunc non amicum; horribilem utriusque victoriam cum propter alterius crudelitatem, alterius audaciam, tum propter utriusque difficultatem pecuniariam; quae erui nusquam nisi ex privatorum bonis posset. atque haec ita multis cum lacrimis loquebatur ut ego mirarer eas tam diuturna miseria non exaruisse.' Cf. Idem: 10.15.2: 'Servi consilio nihil expeditur. omnes captiones in omni sententia occurrunt.'

[44] Cf. *Fam.* 4.4.2.

Cicero wrote that their two specialisms – eloquence and civil law – were suffering:[45]

> For your professional knowledge – eminent and unrivalled as it is – no sphere much better has been left than for mine. Wherefore, though I do not presume to advise you, I have persuaded myself that you also were engaged in pursuits which, even if they were not exactly profitable, yet served to withdraw the mind from anxiety.[46]

The truth was that Cicero and Servius were among the few surviving *consulares* at that time, and it probably helped Cicero to appreciate Servius' qualities, which he then praised when writing to Torquatus,[47] even if Caesar's death and the necessity to make choices again could reactivate old reproaches. Cicero again criticised Servius' cowardice just after the Ides of March,[48] describing him once more as the eternal jurist:

> Servius, however, the peacemaker, and his young secretary seem to have undertaken a mission and to be on their guard against all possible quibbles of the law. However, what they ought to have been afraid of was not 'the joining hands in legal claim', but what follows[.][49]

Notice the use of the pejorative diminutives – *librariolus* and *captiunculae* – and also the ironic mention of a legal *formula*: Cicero is being very sarcastic here. This did not last: the two men both acted against Antony's abuses, first when Servius obtained from the senate an agreement that Caesar's writings (true or false) should not be used after his death to legitimate Antony's measures. Cicero, missing the absence of Servius in September 44 as he began his battle against Antony in earnest, described him as *summa auctoritate et optime sentiens*.[50] Once back in Rome, Servius helped Cicero in his efforts to promote Octavian[51] against Antony. But a big difference remained between Cicero and Servius, who tried again to play the go-between for peace[52]

---

[45] He writes the same in *Brutus*, also written in 46 BC: cf. *Brut.* 22.

[46] *Fam.* 4.3.4: 'Tuae scientiae excellenti ac singulari non multo plus quam nostrae relictum est loci; qua non equidem te moneo, sed mihi ita persuasi, te quoque in iisdem versari rebus, quae, etiamsi minus prodessent, animum tamen a sollicitudine abducerent.'

[47] Cf. idem: 6.1.6 and 6.4.5. But Cicero never forgets to underline the difference in political choices: cf. idem: 4.6.3 (Caesar is no enemy of Cicero but a friend of Servius).

[48] Cf. *Att.* 14.19. 4: 'Servi orationem cognosco; in qua plus timoris video quam consili.' Compare with idem: 14.18: 'desperatio'.

[49] Idem: 15.7 (end of May 44 BC): 'Servius vero pacificator cum librariolo suo videtur obisse legationem et omnis captiunculas pertimescere. debuerat autem non "ex iure manum consertum" sed quae sequuntur.'

[50] *Fam.* 12.2.3 (letter to Cassius).

[51] Cf. *ad. Brut.* 1.15.7.

[52] Cf. *Phil.* 9.7: Servius Sulpicius Rufus had played a key part in the senate to ensure that an embassy should be sent to Antony, who was besieging Decimus Brutus in Modena in order to negotiate a peace agreement, instead of proclaiming Antony *hostis*, which Cicero would have preferred.

although Cicero did not agree with that policy at all.[53] The ninth *Philippic* contains praise for Servius, who died at the beginning of 43 BC returning from Modena where he had tried to play the go-between between Antony and the senate[54], in order that a statue be obtained for him. This *laudatio funebris* could not of course contain anything negative and so Servius is praised as one of the greatests jurists of Rome:

> The praise of all mortals will forever celebrate his wisdom, his firmness, his loyalty, his admirable vigilance and prudence in upholding the interests of the public. Nor will that admirable, and incredible, and almost godlike skill of his in interpreting the laws and explaining the principles of equity be buried in silence. If all the men of all ages, who have ever had any acquaintance with the law in this city, were got together into one place, they would not deserve to be compared to Servius Sulpicius.[55]

The *Brutus* already had offered the same praise of Servius as the greatest specialist of civil law. But maybe one of Cicero's last remarks was nearer to what he really thought: Servius was a man whose life had been spent *sanctissime honestissimeque*, and he had been often useful to the state as well as a simple citizen than as a magistrate.[56] 'Often' did not mean always, and could remind us of all the times Cicero criticised Servius . . .

4. GAIUS TREBATIUS TESTA

Our third case is Gaius Trebatius Testa[57] who we meet mostly in Cicero's letters, first in 54–3 BC when the young jurist was sent to Gaul to Caesar's headquarters, then during the civil war. It is a difficult case because Cicero's presentation is far from being complete: a short time in a long life, first, since Trebatius was born around 75 BC if not around 80 BC, and died after AD 4 under Augustus, whom he assisted. A second problem is connected with politics: Trebatius was a Caesarian, which we know thanks to other authors, but Cicero does not seem to be willing to see or to appreciate it.

---

[53] Cf. idem: 8. 20–1. The whole sixth and seventh *Philippics* are a criticism of the embassy.

[54] Cf. idem: 9. 5–9, 13. 20 and 29, 14.4.

[55] Idem: 9.10: 'Semper illius gravitatem, constantiam, fidem, praestantem in re publica tuenda curam atque prudentiam omnium mortalium fama celebrabit. Nec vero silebitur admirabilis quaedam et incredibilis ac paene divina eius in legibus interpretandis, aequitate explicanda scientia. Omnes ex omni aetate, qui in hac civitate intellegentiam iuris habuerunt, si unum in locum conferantur, cum Ser. Sulpicio non sint comparandi.'

[56] Idem: 15.

[57] Trebatius has not been studied extensively: we have first Sonnet, who wrote the entry for the Pauly–Wissowa (*RE* 7), around 1930. See Kunkel 1967: 28 fn.44 and Bauman 1983: vol. 2, 125ff; and D'Orta has published several studies (1984–5, 1987, 1990, 1991). Recently Harries 2006 has studied Trebatius among other Roman jurists. See also Benferhat 2005: 274–81. Sources for Trebatius' legal works are to be found in Bremer 1896: 376–424.

But at the same time it is a very interesting case because Trebatius was a young thing and Cicero at his peak when he wrote: so he did not have to hide what he really thought about lawyers, and thus we have a frank point of view without the respect due to a master – Scaevola – or the politeness due to a colleague, Sulpicius. When Cicero recommends him to Caesar, in April 54, Trebatius has already studied law with his master Cornelius Maximus:[58] *familiam ducit in iure civili singulari memoria, summa scientia.*[59] These qualities are listed second after personal virtues: honesty, a sense of duty. This might be the first evidence of Cicero's view about a good knowledge of law: it was not enough to win the favour of Caesar, who was in need of men he could trust. At the same time we can assume that this presentation was also tactical, since Cicero knew that Trebatius' big advantage was his legal education.[60]

The initial reactions of Trebatius, as Cicero criticised the jurists – *ineptias istas et desideria urbis et urbanitatis*[61] – are interesting because they are a sign of an evolution: the young jurist does not want to leave Rome and the city life, where he knows he is at his best. It is very amusing to see Cicero trying to give Trebatius the traditional *cursus*[62] with a mission in a general's staff, just like he had done in his youth in Pompeius Strabo's *castra*,[63] though we know Cicero himself did not like this at all. But Trebatius decided to refuse to play the game: Cicero hints at this with the expressive verb *extrudere*[64] to remind the young man of his own efforts to convince him.

Trebatius kept on refusing to play the game by declining first the offer to be a *tribunus militaris*, though Caesar had made it comfortable (this post usually allowed an individual to have their first experience of commanding men in the army and being a member of the *consilium* where the decisions were taken[65]):

> and at the same time I wondered why you despised the profits of a military trib-uneship, especially as you are exempted from the labour of military duty.[66]

Then he refused to go to Britain with Caesar.[67] What could seem bold and was indeed interpreted this way by Cicero might have been mere realism:

---

58 *RE* 264. See Kunkel 1967: 24 n°39.

59 Cic. *Fam.* 7.5.3.

60 Cf. Cic. *QFr.* 2.13.3: Cicero mentions Caesar's remark on the lack of good lawyers in his staff. The same in *Fam.* 7.16.3: 'constat enim inter omnis neminem te uno Samarobrivae iuris peritiorem esse'.

61 Cic. *Fam.* 7.6.1. Same reproach some months later in October 54, cf. idem: 7.17.1: 'levis in urbis urbanitatisque desiderio'.

62 Cf. idem: 7.17.2.

63 See Benferhat 2014: 183–97.

64 Cic. *Fam.* 7.6.1.

65 See Le Bohec 2001: 92–4.

66 Cic. *Fam.* 7.8.1: 'et simul sum admiratus cur tribunatus commoda, dempto praesertim labore militiae, contempseris.'

67 Cf. idem: 7.17.3; 7.16.1; 7.10.1–2.

Trebatius was aware that his best way to serve Caesar was his competence in civil law. But the problem was spring and summer were commonly used for military expeditions: so it took many months (too many according to Trebatius who seems to have been a bit impatient at the beginning) and the coming of winter usually devoted to civil affairs before the mission began to look attractive.

We can observe then a serious misunderstanding between Cicero and his 'protégé'. Cicero, faithful to tradition, thought it was better for Trebatius to leave Rome and Italy, in order first to get some money,[68] and second to be on good terms with Caesar, probably not only for his own sake: in the usual game of *beneficia*, or the exchange of mutual favours/services, Trebatius could play the part of go-between between Caesar and Cicero, who could also get some news this way about the situation in Gaul. But sending Trebatius to Caesar had another consequence: the perfect match between the general and a good jurist, which prefigures the monarchic system under the Empire.

Cicero didn't realise it: when he describes Trebatius under the charm of Caesar,[69] he was not surprised since Caesar was intellectually a most seductive man. The brothers Cicero could have attested it.[70] He was even a bit jealous, pretending Trebatius seemed all the more good at law since he had no real competition in Gaul.[71] Actually the young man was sent to the *Tresviri*[72] with Labienus, at the end of the winter 54–3 BC to solve legal problems, which Cicero hints at in his famous letter about Trebatius' conversion to Epicureanism:[73] his main activities were a mix of law and war.

This letter is also interesting because of the mention of Pansa. Later we see Matius mentioned as a new close friend of Trebatius,[74] but we must not forget the most important event: after fourteen months in Gaul, Trebatius was close to Caesar himself.[75] To sum it up, as a friend of Pansa, Matius and Balbus,[76] too, Trebatius was at the very core of the Caesarian system.

This should be on our mind when we read letters written during the civil war: Trebatius appears always as a go-between, alone or with another Caesarian, between Cicero and Caesar. It starts in February 49 BC, as we can

---

[68] The hints are pretty numerous: cf. idem: 7.7.1; 7.9.2; 7.16.3; 7.11.2–3; 7.13.2.

[69] Cf. idem: 7.16.1: *inlectus*. The change was obvious since Trebatius started to make jokes, being in a much better mood. cf. idem: 7.11.2.

[70] Cf. Cic. *QFr.* 3.1 for example.

[71] Cf. Cic. *Fam.* 7.10.1.

[72] Cf. idem: 7.13.2.

[73] See D'Orta 1991 and Benferhat 2005: 274–7.

[74] Cf. Cic. *Fam.* 7.15.2: 'in C. matii, suavissimi doctissimique hominis familiaritatem venisti.'

[75] Ibidem: 'te esse Caesari familiarem.'

[76] He might have noticed the young man already in Rome since he was there when Cicero chose to send Trebatius to Caesar proposing to take one of his friends onto his staff, cf. Cic. *Fam.* 7.5.2, and he kept an eye on him for the whole year (54 BC).

see in a letter to Atticus:[77] Caesar used Trebatius to try to convince Cicero
to stay in Rome when Pompey was leaving with almost all the senators.
For Cicero Trebatius was no Caesarian: he described him twice as a good
citizen,[78] *bonus vir et civis*, which means a Republican. It seems it was an
illusion: Trebatius was one of Caesar's go-betweens and it is not surprising
to find him in Rome with Sulpicius Rufus[79] with whom he shared an interest in law but he was also a *consularis* that Caesar needed badly in the city.
Trebatius as a jurist could be useful to convince Sulpicius as well as Cicero
to stay in Italy and maybe even help Caesar.

He was probably also useful in coming up with solutions to the economic
situation in Italy with the debt problem,[80] and he also played the part of
political advisor as well, as Suetonius tells us when relating how Caesar did
not get up for senators as they were arriving:

> Some think that when he attempted to get up, he was held back by Cornelius
> Balbus; others, that he made no such move at all, but on the contrary frowned
> angrily on Gaius Trebatius when he suggested that he should rise.[81]

But we do not see it in Cicero's letters: nevertheless his testimony is important because it shows us a Trebatius who was then an important piece of
Caesar's strategic team: the men who played their part in the shadows, with
technical competences and a real ability to serve as intermediaries. They
actually often worked in tandem: Oppius with Balbus, Hirtius with Pansa,
Trebatius with Matius.

After Caesar's murder, Trebatius appears again in Cicero's letters from
the year 44 BC. It seems he had a house in Rome on the Lupercal, but also
some properties in Velia thanks to his father.[82] Cicero keeps on juxtaposing
his own model – eloquence over all – with that of Trebatius' specialisation in
civil law: he offers him the *Topica*,[83] written at the beginning of the summer,
trying to convert him to rhetoric. Law appears to be something hard to learn:

> I send you this book from Rhegium written in as clear a style as the subject admit-
> ted. But if certain parts appear to you to be somewhat obscure, you must reflect
> that no art can be learnt out of books without some one to explain it and without

---

[77] Cf. Cic. *Att.* 7.17.3.
[78] Cf. idem: 10.1.3 and 10.11.4: 'vir plane et civis bonus.' Nevertheless Atticus has a curious
expression (cf. 9.9.4): 'nihil bene sperat'. That could mean Trebatius had no good hope about
the situation, at a time when Pompey was leaving Italy for Greece, or if we consider the
adverb *bene* as a political code refering to the *boni*, it could mean Trebatius was a Caesarian
from Atticus' point of view.
[79] Cf. Cic. *Fam.* 4.1.1.
[80] Cf. Cic. *Att.* 13.23.3.(?)
[81] Cf. Suet. *Caes.* 78.
[82] Cf. Cic. *Fam.* 7.20.1.
[83] See Harries 2006: 126–32. There are two main studies on the *Topica*: see Riposati 1947 and
Reinhardt 2003.

some practical exercise in it. You will not have to go far for an instance. Can the art of you jurisconsults be learnt out of books? Though there are a great number of them, they yet require a teacher and actual practice.[84]

But in fact Trebatius was already far too advanced on his own path: as a close friend of Matius, he was probably helping the young Octavian. He plays once more the role of an intermediary between Matius and Cicero in October 44 BC, that is not only between two men but also between two political camps: Cicero supports the Republicans around Brutus and Cassius, while Matius remains faithful to Caesar and has started to support his legal heir Octavian[85] with the organisation of the *Ludi Victoriae*. He was then already a first-class jurist, as Cicero admits, in a joke about a discussion over dinner:

> Accordingly, though I returned home full of wine and late in the evening, I marked the section in which that question is treated and caused it to be copied out and sent to you. I wanted to convince you that the doctrine which you said was held by no one was maintained by Sextus Aelius, Manius Manilius, Marcus Brutus. Nevertheless, I concur with Scaevola and Testa.[86]

To be put at the same level as Quintus Mucius Scaevola Augur was indeed an accomplishment.

5. CONCLUSION

What did it take to be number one in Rome? That was our primary question and the answer is this: from Caesar to at least Theodosius it took a general assisted by jurists. There were three ways in the *Pro Murena*: the *militia* kept playing the most important part, since armies were used not only against external enemies to obtain power, but also against citizens. Whatever Servius and Cicero might have hoped, and they were like twins (as said in the *Brutus*)[87] united in the thought that the time of civil lawyers had finally come, the generals never lost their power and influence.

Cicero's eloquence and Servius' civil law both needed peace to flourish: nevertheless, eloquence died the day peace was ensured by the victory of one man and the advent of the Principate. Tacitus[88] in his *Dialogue* clearly states this after a century of monarchy in Rome. Meanwhile, the jurists, by adapting their careers to the new deal, maintained real importance in the exercise of political power. What Cicero had said to defend Murena about the civil law being of no use except in Rome proved wrong with the advent of the

---

[84] *Fam.* 7.19.1.
[85] Cf. idem: 11.28.6.
[86] Idem: 7.22 (possibly written in 46 or 44 BC). See Fraenkel 1957: 67–8.
[87] *Brut.* 150.
[88] *Dial.* 36–41.

Roman Empire. Roman civil law became the civil law of an Empire and then the matrix of European laws much later.

What emerges here is a time in the late Republic when there were various experiments to try to answer to the need for changes that the Romans could feel: some tried to get power using civil law as a speciality, some tried to be number one by intellectual genius and eloquence, some solved the problem with their armies. Cicero unwittingly helped the real revolution, that is to say the coming of the Principate and the end of the Republic: he did not see Trebatius and Caesar as precursors of a new way to exercise power. And so came the result towards the end of 43 BC first with his own execution, then in the following centuries: game over . . .

BIBLIOGRAPHY

Badian, E. (1956), 'Q. Mucius Scaevola and the province of Asia', *Athenaeum* 34: 104–23.

Bauman, R. (1983), *Lawyers in Roman Republican Politics: A study of the Roman jurists in their political setting*. Munich.

Benferhat, Y. (2005), Cives Epicurei: *Les épicuriens et l'idée de monarchie à Rome et en Italie de Sylla à Octave*. Brussels.

Benferhat, Y. (2014), 'Marcus s'en va-t-en guerre', in Ph. Guisard and Ch. Laizé, eds, *La guerre et la paix*. Paris. 183–97.

Bremer, P. (1896), *Iurisprudentiae antehadrianae quae supersunt*, volume 1. Leipzig.

Bretone, M. (1978), 'Cicerone e i giuristi del suo tempo', in *Ciceroniana: atti del III colloquium tullianum*. Rome. 47–68.

D'Orta, M. (1984–5). 'Inquietudini di Trebazio Testa cavaliere', in *Sodalitas. Scritti in onore di Antonio Guarino*, volume 2. Naples. 942–61.

D'Orta M. (1987), 'Per una storia della cultura dei giuristi reppublicani', *Bullettino dell'Istituto di Diritto Romano* 90: 221–84.

D'Orta, M. (1990), *La giurisprudenza tra Repubblica e Principato: Primi Studi su Gaio Trebazio Testa*. Naples.

D'Orta, M. (1991), 'Giurisprudenza e Epicureismo (Nota su Cic. 'ad fam', 7.12.1–2)', *Iura* 42: 123–45.

Fraenkel, E. (1957), 'Some notes on Cicero's letters to Trebatius', *Journal of Roman Studies* 47: 66–70.

Gruen, E. (1966), 'Political prosecutions in the 90s BC', *Historia* 15: 32–64.

Harries, J. (2006), *Cicero and the Jurists: From citizens' law to the lawful state*. London.

Harries, J. (2013), 'The law in Cicero's writings', in C. Steel, ed., *The Cambridge Companion to Cicero*. Cambridge. 107–21.

Kodrebski, J. (1976), 'Der Rechtsunterricht am Ausgang der Republik und zu Beginn des Prinzipats', *Aufstieg und Niedergang der Römischen Welt* 2.15: 177–96.

Kunkel, W. (1967), *Herkunft und soziale Stellung der römischen Juristen*, 2nd improved edition. Graz.

Le Bohec, Y. (2001), *César chef de guerre*. Paris.

Liebs, D. (1976), 'Rechtsschulen und Rechtsunterricht im Prinzipat', *Aufstieg und Niedergang der Römischen Welt* 2.15. 197–286.

Michel, J. H. (1975), 'Le droit romain dans le *Pro Murena* et l'oeuvre de Servius Sulpicius Rufus', in A. Michel and R. Verdière, eds, *Ciceroniana. Hommages à Kazimierz Kumaniecki.* Leiden. 181–95.

Rawson, E. (1985), *Intellectual Life in the Late Roman Republic.* London.

Reinhardt, T. (2006 [2003]), *Marcus Tullius Cicero's* Topica. Oxford.

Rigsby, J. (1988), '*Provincia Asia*', in *Transactions of the American Philological Association* 118: 123–53.

Riposati, B. (1947), *Studi sui* Topica *di Cicerone.* Milan.

Sumner, G. (1973), *The Orators in Cicero's* Brutus: *Prosopography and chronology.* Toronto.

Wiseman, T. P. (1971), *New Men in the Roman Senate: 139* BC–AD *14.* Oxford.

Chapter 6

'Jurists in the Shadows': The Everyday Business of the Jurists of Cicero's Time

Christine Lehne-Gstreinthaler

1. INTRODUCTION: WHO WAS A JURIST?

It is a matter of dispute whether the Roman jurists of the Republic can be aptly described as such. There was no formalised training for the legal profession nor is it clear how much time the Roman jurists devoted to their profession. Indeed, the jurists of Cicero's time were amateurs compared to modern jurists. The Roman jurists active during that time could be described most accurately as 'gentlemen', men from higher classes who engaged in giving legal advice and representing parties in court due to favours owed to their clients, acquaintances and family members. Legal services were not paid for but nor were they free of charge. Rewards were often made in the form of gifts, bequests or other services. Monetary reward, even the prospect of financial gain, was, although undoubtedly present, looked down upon by the Roman aristocracy. For them, giving legal advice, making accusations, litigating on behalf of others and arbitrating was part of the duties of a *vir bonus*. Moreover, it was considered necessary to legally assist friends and acquaintances to spread favours before and for elections.[1]

2. SOCIETY AND THE LAW

In earlier works[2] I used to define as jurists men (1) who identified as such, (2) who were called jurists, (3) to whom considerable legal knowledge was attributed and (4) who had left *responsa*. For the purpose of this chapter I would like to supplement a fifth category: men of whom legal knowledge can be presumed on the basis of their legal work.

I want to define as jurists in the shadows men from a lower social background, who devoted themselves to less illustrious legal work and were therefore, when consulted, seldom mentioned by name. Their activities can be attributed to the following categories: legal representatives, the staff

---

[1] Cf. Cicero's remarks on Hirrus in *Fam.* 8.6 after he lost an important election: 'Moreover, he, who never appeared in the forum and hardly had anything to do with litigation, is representing generously, though seldom past noon.'

[2] Lehne (unpublished, 2011): 5. See also Lehne 2014: 232 fn.66.

and other advisors of the magistrates, businessmen, and conveyancers. It should be stressed, however, that these categories are neither exhaustive nor exclusive. For example several *negotiatores* served as *procuratores*,[3] Atticus, a respected businessman, drafted at least two last wills[4] and private secretaries had official duties when their patron became a magistrate.

2.1 Legal representatives: *procuratores* and *cognitores*, advocates and sycophants

Procuratores/cognitores and advocates are generally seen as separate entities. This may be partly due to the fact that according to the prevailing view, lawyers stemmed mostly from Rome's leading classes, while *procuratores* and *cognitores* are assumed to have belonged to the lower classes. Another assumption is that neither *procuratores/cognitores* nor advocates needed legal knowledge, because legal questions were already accounted for *in iure*.

Both assumptions are untrue: *procuratores* especially, who represented others in lawsuits, had to have sufficient legal knowledge.[5] Sext. Alfenus, *procurator* of P. Quinctius, who, incidentally, had a higher social status than both Quinctius and Naevius,[6] showed his knowledge of legal proceedings when he defended P. Quinctius. The *negotiator* Herennius, a *procurator* to C. Matrinius, defended Matrinius' *vilici* and *pastores* when they were accused by Verres.[7] Last but not least, Cicero himself was asked to manage the assets of Sittius *tamquam procurator*.[8] Often, though, the terms *procurator* and *cognitor* were used as invectives by Cicero against his enemies.[9] This leads me to believe that, while not all *procuratores* and *cognitores* had low social status or a bad reputation, the image of the profession prevented men from the senatorial or equestrian order from declaring themselves as *procuratores*, even though they fulfilled this duty. A case in point is T. Pomponius Atticus, who managed Cicero's assets – however, in the *Letters to Atticus* the term *procurator* is never mentioned in his regard.

Cognitores, too, possessed considerable legal knowledge. In Satire II.5 Horace advises his reader to act as a *defensor* and *cognitor* while advertising legal knowledge.[10] Similarly, Cicero addresses Aebutius as *cognitor viduarum*, who is learned in law but is considered a jurist only among women.[11] If we

---

[3] Treggiari 1969: 104.
[4] The wills of Terentia and Cicero.
[5] Frier 1985: 67.
[6] Schaefer 1998: 90.
[7] Cic. *Verr.* 2.5.15, 2.5.155. Schulz 1997: 264.
[8] Cic. *Fam.* 8.11.4.
[9] Cic. *Caecin.* 14; Cic. *Rosc. Am.* 23; *Verr.* 2.3.78, 178; *Phil.* 12.18.
[10] Hor. *Sat.* 2.5.30–8.
[11] Cic. *Caecin.* 14.

put Cicero's invective against the social climber Aebutius aside,[12] we can clearly deduce from this passage that Aebutius had decent knowledge of law. He interfered in litigation on behalf of others and was actually quite successful, a fact Cicero himself grudgingly concedes.[13] Cicero had an equally low opinion of C. Claudius Palatina, the *cognitor* appointed by Verres for Sthenius.[14] However, the list of occupations listed for Claudius – *sequester, interpres, confector negotiorum, prope conlega Timarchidi*[15] – implies forensic experience and probably also legal knowledge.

Cicero's views on the social background of his adversaries also influenced Roman linguistic usage regarding lawyers. While men from the senatorial order were addressed with the reverential term *patronus, advocatus* or *causidicus* was often used for lawyers who had legal knowledge[16] or who stemmed from a lower social background.[17] *Advocati* who were freedmen were not uncommon,[18] as is illustrated by the examples of L. Aelius, a freedman who accused T. Quinctius Mutto (*Scaur.* 23), an enemy of his *patronus*,[19] and Voltacilius Plotus, a *libertus* who defended his *patronus* and taught oratory.[20] Another freedman who acted as advocate did not concern Cicero: 'Selius may be eloquent enough to prove himself freeborn, I do not worry'.[21] Last but not least, the freedman Trimalchio mentions advocacy or acting as a *praeco* as a possible career for his son.[22]

Similarly, sycophants (*quadruplatores, calumniatores*), men who accused others on a professional basis, were not worthy to be called jurists, although serial accusers like Naevius Turpio[23] or Aelius Ligus, whom Cicero coined a *venalis adscriptor*,[24] often had legal knowledge. Indeed, Cicero himself acknowledges the legal knowledge of the unknown accuser in his defence of L. Cornelius Balbus.[25]

2.2 The staff of the magistrates and the magistrate's helpers

The staff who helped Roman officials has often been overlooked. The duties of these men (*scribae, accensi, praecones, lictores, accensi, interpretes*)

---

[12] He was probably an *eques* anyway, see Frier 1985: 35.
[13] Cic. *Caecin.* 14.
[14] Cic. *Verr.* 2.6.106
[15] Idem: 2.6.108.
[16] Cic. *Off.* 1.32
[17] Cic. *Verr.* 2.3.184; *Rosc.* 28; *Att.* 1.16.2; *De or.* 2.283; *Brut.* 289; *De or.* 1.202; *Orat.* 30.
[18] Freedmen who acted as *advocati* had been mentioned in Plautus' *Poenulus*.
[19] Cic. *Scaur.* 23.
[20] Treggiari 1969: 118.
[21] Cic. *Fam.* 7.32.3.
[22] Petron. *Sat.* 46.
[23] *Verr.* 2.3.90; 2.5.108. See also Schulz 1997: 137.
[24] Cic. *Dom.* 49. He is also mentioned in *Sest.* 69 and *Har. resp.* 5, although not by name.
[25] Cic. *Balb.* 20, 27.

included helping in drafting edicts, laws and *senatus consulta*; drafting contracts for the publicans and providing assistance in comprehending and following the numerous laws regulating the duties of the Roman officials. Indeed, Cicero points out, the *apparitores* often knew best where you could find the laws[26] and that most of the magistrates only knew as much as the *apparitores* allowed them to know.[27] Cicero was not alone in his opinion: the younger Cato, according to Plutarch, tried to curb their influence[28] and Philo of Alexandria mentions that Aulus Flaccus Avillius was so knowledgeable as prefect of Egypt that his scribes became redundant.[29] Schulz has correctly pointed out that the personnel had a great deal of routine and assisted their magistrate, even more so in the provinces where news and help from Rome needed considerable time.[30] Among the *apparitores*, the *accensi*, the scribes and the *praecones* were most closely involved with legal affairs.

The *accensi*, stewards to the higher magistrates, were personally appointed for the magistrate's term of office and could gain considerable influence on the decision-making processes.[31] More often than not they controlled who had access to the governor. [32] These men usually had a lower social status. Many of them were freedmen (sometimes even slaves acted as *apparitores*) and it was not unusual for a magistrate to bring his own freedman with him.[33] An extraordinary example for such a freedman is Q. Tullius Statius, the *accensus* of Cicero's brother Quintus:[34] Cicero, who apparently disliked Statius,[35] complains that due to Statius' influence Quintus was less accessible and felt that Statius had more responsibility than he was due. Cicero illustrates this impression with an example, namely, when Statius handled his *patronus*' official correspondence.[36] Similarly, Verres' *accensus*, Timarchides, was infamous for acquiring money for Verres, be it by collecting tax money[37] or buying art for a low price.[38] Additionally, Timarchides was also involved in trials.[39] To stress the influence of the *apparitores*, Cicero cites a letter in

---

[26] See for example *Leg. agr.* 2.13: The public scribes brought Cicero a copy of Rullus' draft.
[27] Cic. *Leg.* 3.46, 48. See also Treggiari 1969: 158.
[28] Plut. *Cat. Min.* 16.2–5.
[29] Philo. *In Flaccum* 3.
[30] Schulz 1997: 128.
[31] Kunkel and Wittmann 1995: 126f, Treggiari 1969: 154–6.
[32] Schulz 1997: 105, 143–5.
[33] See also Treggiari 1969: 153.
[34] Treggiari 1969: 158 thinks that Statius was a private secretary, not an *accensus*, but one who performed public duties.
[35] Cf. *Att.* 2.18.4, 2.19.1.
[36] QFr. 1.2.1–3, 8. See also Treggiari 1969: 149, 158, 181 and Schulz 1997: 151–3.
[37] Cic. *Verr.* 2.3.171, 175.
[38] Idem: 2.4.35. See also Classen 1998: 127f and Schulz 1997: 243.
[39] Cic. *Verr.* 2.2.74, 2.3.69.

which Timarchides advises Apronius to acquire influence with the new scribes and *apparitores* to gain the praetor's respect.[40]

In contrast to the *accensi*, scribes were often freeborn, especially those who had more reputable positions like the *scribae quaestorii*. In *Verr.* 2.3.184 Cicero portrays the scribes as honourable but socially low-standing people, although some of them used this *ordo* as a means of social climbing (this is also alluded to by Horace).[41] Their miscellaneous duties included writing protocols,[42] managing the public funds[43] (which also gave them the opportunity to appropriate them),[44] maintaining the *tabulae publicae*[45] and participating in trials and lawsuits.[46] Especially for the latter, legal knowledge proved to be useful (one only has to keep in mind the *scriba* Cn. Flavius who published the *fasti*) and some scribes bragged about their legal skills in their funerary inscriptions.[47]

Among those with extensive legal expertise was the scribe Sext. Clodius (sometimes referred to as Sext. Cloelius). He assisted Clodius in drafting contracts and laws, for example the contracts with exiles from Byzantium[48] and the *lex Clodia de exilio Ciceronis*.[49] Others are mentioned by Cicero but it is not clear which proposals and laws he meant.[50] Generally, drafting laws was considered a task for the nobility,[51] which is why Cicero vehemently attacked Clodius for breaking this noble tradition.[52] M. Aemilius Scaurus and L. Licinius Crassus, who descended from established families, helped Drusus in drafting his laws.[53] P. Sestius and Visellius both prepared a draft of the law that should have restored Cicero's rights:[54] Cicero himself much preferred the draft that Visellius made for T. Fadius to the draft of Sestius, whom he considered incapable.[55] Politicians regularly used jurists to draft

---

[40] Idem: 2.3.154–7.
[41] Hor. *Sat.* 2.5.56–7. It is important to note that Horace was also a *scriba quaestorius* (Suet. *Hor.*).
[42] *Verr.* 2.5.54. See Schulz 1997: 105.
[43] Cic. *Dom.* 74.
[44] Cic. *Pis.* 61.
[45] Cic. *Verr.* 2.3.184; Cic. *Dom.* 74.
[46] See Kunkel and Wittmann 1995: 111 fn.28 and Purcell 1983: 130.
[47] *CIL* VI 1853; *CIL* VI 1819. See Damon 1992: 236 fn.22 and Purcell 1983: 130 fn.22.
[48] Cic *Dom.* 83.
[49] Idem: 47f, 83; *Sest.* 133.
[50] Cic. *Dom.* 129; Cic. *Har. resp.* 11; Cic. *Mil.* 33. See also Damon 1992.
[51] Cic. *Dom.* 48.
[52] Apart from Sext. Clodius, Clodius (Cicero's adversary) used a certain Decimus for drafting laws (Cic. *Dom.* 50).
[53] Cic. *Dom.* 50.
[54] Cic. *Att.* 3.30.3; 3.23.4.
[55] Cic. *Att.* 7.17.2.

laws.[56] P. Sestius helped Pompey in drafting laws,[57] while Balbus helped Caesar in drafting the *lex Iulia municipalis*.[58] Those who drafted their own laws, like Vatinius, emphasised their achievements.[59] Other drafters of the laws were known to Cicero's audience but are unknown to modern readers such as the unnamed *iure consultus* called out in the *Philippicae*[60] or the *auctores* responsible for the draft of P. Servilius Rullus.[61]

Verres' scribes, M. Papirius Potamo and Maevius,[62] also exerted their influence on Sicily. While M. Papirius Potamo, an *eques Romanus*, who had previously served Caecilius, participated in Verres' *consilium*,[63] Maevius had a far more important role in Verres' dealings. He assisted Verres in bringing in tax money and the delivery of grain[64] and was rewarded for his services with a gold ring, which made him an *eques*.[65] Last but not least there was Cicero's own scribe, M. Tullius, who handled his official correspondence and assisted him in preparing his accounts before he left his province.[66]

Other helpers of Verres who had legal responsibility and (presumably) legal knowledge were his *praeco* Valerius, who was among the judges who decided the lawsuit of Nympho,[67] C. Claudius, an *interpres* who was already mentioned above,[68] A. Valentius, another *interpres*, who also acted as *publicanus*[69] and M. Petilius, a personal advisor of Verres, who functioned as a *iudex* and participated in another judge's *consilium*.[70]

Generally, because of their involvement in public and private auctions,[71] *praecones* were not held in high esteem by Roman society.[72] However, their influence was substantial, and the function of a *praeco* represented a chance for social advancement.[73] Sext. Naevius, a *praeco* and Cicero's adversary

---

[56] The *scriptor*'s intentions were a major point in interpreting the law, too (Cic. *Part. or.* 134, 136; Cic. *Inv. rhet.* 2.137, 139), which probably explains why the *auctor* of a law is quite often named.

[57] Cic. *Att.* 7.17.2.

[58] Cic. *Fam* 6.18. See also Simshäuser 1973: 137–9.

[59] Cic. *Vat.* 27.

[60] Cic. *Phil.* 2.96.

[61] Cic. *Leg. agr.* 2.98.

[62] *Verr.* 2.3.168.

[63] *Div. Caecin.* 29; *Verr.* 2.3.137.

[64] Cic. *Verr.* 2.3.171, 175. He also kept some money for himself (*Verr.* 2.2.170, 2.3.181–7).

[65] Idem: 2.3.185. See also Bleicken 1995: 51.

[66] Cic. *Fam.* 5.20.1. On Tullius see Treggiari 1969: 258.

[67] Cic. *Verr.* 2.3.54.

[68] See 90.

[69] Cic. *Verr.* 2.3.84; 2.4.58.

[70] Idem: 2.2.71, 73.

[71] See Thielmann 1961: 42, 53f.

[72] Kunkel and Wittmann 1995: 126. cf. Catull. 106.

[73] The father of L. Aelius Stilo Praeconinus was a *praeco* (Plin. *NH* 33.29). Horace, too mentions being a *praeco* as a possible career for himself (*Sat.* I.6.86). On *praecones* see also Treggiari 1969: 99–101.

in *Pro Quinctio*, is painted in a harsh light by Cicero.[74] At the same time, Bannon has pointed out that Naevius, who had learned to use the legal system to his advantage over the course of his career, is also a good example of a *praeco*.[75]

At this point, it is interesting to note that Cicero used terms applicable to the support staff of a magistrate and other less reputable professions to ridicule jurists: *praeco actionum*,[76] *interpres iuris*,[77] *interpres legum*,[78] *cantor formularum*,[79] *auceps syllabarum*,[80] *ministrator*.[81] However, different factors might be at work. On the one hand, *praecones* and *interpretes* dealt, among other things, with legal affairs. On the other hand, jurisprudence was in Cicero's view all but an ancillary discipline to oratory,[82] a necessary evil an orator had to resort to, if he wanted to win a lawsuit.[83]

A magistrate did not depend solely on his staff. To a certain degree – and this was especially true of governors – he also needed to rely on his subordinates (*tribuni militum, praefecti fabrum, legati*) and advisors (the so-called *cohors amicorum*).

The *praefecti fabrum* in particular gathered considerable influence.[84] A representative of this group was L. Cornelius Balbus, who served as a *praefectus fabrum* to Caesar in Hispania and Gallia. After Caesar's governorship he remained his chief advisor, advising him on political and financial matters and helping him to draft laws.[85] More importantly, during the civil war, he and C. Oppius remained in the city and acted as intermediaries between him and his allies. Their power was so great that Cicero bitterly called them 'kings of Rome'.[86] After Caesar's death, both transferred their loyalties to Octavian.

Another group of men who had considerable impact on legal and politi-

---

[74] See also Damon 1997: 197. However, not all *praecones* were held in such low esteem by Cicero. Q. Granius, a *praeco*, who was famed for his wit, was held in high regard by him (see for example Cic. *Planc.* 33).

[75] Bannon 2000: 75, 82.

[76] Cic. *De orat.* 1.236.

[77] Cic. *Top.* 4.

[78] Cic. *Tusc.* 5.105.

[79] Cic. *De orat.* 1.236

[80] Idem: 1.236

[81] Idem: 2.305

[82] Cic. *Orat.* 141; *De orat.* 2.142–4.

[83] Of course this is only a simplified version of Cicero's view, albeit one he promoted in most of his orations and theoretical writings. Taking into account his letters to Trebatius, Cicero portrays himself as a man with solid legal knowledge who seems to covet their shared interest in jurisprudence. However, Cicero was a self-conscious man who yearned for the acceptance of the *boni viri* and therefore never declared himself as a jurist (although he could be considered to be one).

[84] Schulz 1997: 160f.

[85] Tac. *Ann.* 12.60.

[86] Cic. *Att.* 12.12.1; *Fam.* 9.19.

cal matters were the *legati*. Often they were recruited from family, friends or business associates.[87] One of their duties involved the exercise of judicial functions, either exercising jurisdiction themselves[88] or participating in the *consilium* of the magistrate.[89] Men like Trebatius and C. Matius, a friend of both Cicero and Trebatius,[90] acted as legal advisors to Caesar. Another friend of Cicero, the jurist Valerius, was employed by both P. Cornelius Lentulus Spinther[91] and Appius Claudius Pulcher.[92] At other times the *legati* assisted in drafting enactments and decrees, for example Gaius Longus and Publius who helped L. Sempronius Asellio in drafting his edict.[93]

Influence on the edict was not limited to *legati*. Verres' *familiaris* Q. Apronius, a *publicanus*, initiated the edict on *pactiones*[94] and it is probable that he influenced other portions of the edict[95] as well as the jurisdiction,[96] and Cicero often mentions the power Apronius exerted on Verres and the province as a whole.[97]

2.3 *Negotiatores* and *publicani*

Another group of men whose legal knowledge is rarely recognised were the *negotiatores*, merchants who belonged to the *equites* and who engaged in banking, auctions and (the slave) trade. Most of Rome's leading class was involved in making money[98] but since the senatorial class was forbidden to engage in certain activities, they depended on the *equites* for most of their financial affairs.[99] The *negotiatores* differed from the *publicani* whose association Cicero sought and emphasised,[100] insofar as Cicero called *negotiatores* those who could or would not accept the lease of taxes.[101] Since the *equites* and the *tribuni aerarii* were often called upon as judges in trials and took part in the *conventus civium*,[102] they acquired quite a bit of forensic experience and Cicero could single out men like Q. Considius, and M. Iuventius Pedo for

---

[87] Schulz 1997: 173f.
[88] Behrends 1970: 31.
[89] Brennan 2000: 443, 480, 539.
[90] Cic. *Att.* 9.1.12, 14.1, 14.2; *Fam.* 7.15.
[91] Cic. *Fam.* 1.10.
[92] Idem: 3.1.
[93] Diod. Sic. 37.8.
[94] Cic. *Verr.* 2.3.36. See also Schulz 1997: 224.
[95] Cic. *Verr.* 2.3.25, 28, 70.
[96] Idem: 2.3.23.
[97] For example, idem: 2.3.22, 32, 40, 60–2, 106, 178, 228.
[98] See Cic. *Att.* 9.13.
[99] Cf. the praise for Rabirius Postumus because he strove to enlarge his friends' assets (*Rab. Post.* 4).
[100] On this topic see Bleicken 1995 and Treggiari 1969: 103.
[101] Bleicken 1995: 30.
[102] See also Idem: 1995: 32–43.

their experience, their legal knowledge and their fairness in judging.[103] A less than stellar example of this *ordo* was the promagister L. Carpinatius, who assisted Verres in making and selling judgements.[104]

A man whose legal qualifications are often overlooked is T. Pomponius Atticus, Cicero's most trusted friend, who not only advised him in personal matters but whose duties also included the management of Cicero's funds. Additionally, he managed the funds of Q. Tullius Cicero, M. Porcius Cato, Q. Hortensius, Aulus Manlius Torquatus and many more.[105]

An area of law he was very often involved in was auctions, since he administered the auctions of Cicero's various inheritances. He advised Cicero on whether to accept or deny an inheritance, and handled the actual auction.[106] However, he did not take part in public auctions[107] and while he had good contact with the publicans and acted as an intermediary, he never acted as a *praes* or *manceps*.[108] Further legal duties of Atticus included collecting and accepting Cicero's debts,[109] paying and enforcing the repayment of Tullia's dowries,[110] and repaying the dowries of Terentia and Publilia.[111] Several letters of Cicero to Atticus are dedicated to the acquisition of some gardens where Cicero wanted to build a monument for his daughter Tullia.[112]

Financial law was but one area in which Atticus' expertise was visible, however, he had knowledge of inheritance law as well. Cicero asked Camillus and Atticus to assist Terentia in drafting her last will[113] and it is obvious from *Att.* 12.18a.2 that he also had a hand in formulating Cicero's will. Interestingly enough, he also handled property law: Cicero instructed Atticus to waive a servitude regarding one of his neighbours.[114] Although Nepos mentions that Atticus never filed a suit on his own account, this does not mean that he never litigated. While he was neither an *accusator* nor a *subscriptor*, he was involved in several lawsuits and assisted Antonius' wife Fulvia in her lawsuits.[115]

Another jurist whose expertise Cicero often sought was C. Furius Camillus, who specialised in the *ius praediatorium*.[116] Cicero consulted him among other jurists in reference to the debts of Valerius, which he wanted to transfer to his

---

[103] Cic. *Clu.* 107.
[104] Cic. *Verr.* 2.2.169–73.
[105] Nep. *Att.* 15.3.
[106] See e.g. Cic. *Att.* 11.13, 11.14, 11.15, 11.16, 12.1, 12.21; 12.23; Cic. *Fam.* 14.5.
[107] Nep. *Att.* 6.3.
[108] Idem: 6.3.
[109] Cic. *Att.* 12.1, 12.6.
[110] Idem: 11.2, 11.3, 11.4a, 11.25.
[111] Idem: 14.13, 16.2; Plut. *Cic.* 41.3.
[112] Cic. *Att.* 12.24, 12.25, 12.27, 12.28, 12.29, 12.30, 12.31, 12.33.
[113] Idem: 11.16.5.
[114] Idem: 15.26.4.
[115] Nep. *Att.* 9.4.
[116] Cic. *Balb.* 45.

legatus Q. Volusius.[117] Camillus was involved in the sale of Milo's assets.[118] Together with Atticus he helped Terentia when she drafted her last will.[119] Similarly, he helped Cicero in drafting his own will.[120] Like Atticus, he was involved in auctions and accepted payments on Cicero's behalf.

Bankers, too, had extensive legal knowledge. Horace mentions three *faeneratores*, Nerius, Parellius and Cicuta, in *Sat.* 2.3,[121] and makes reference to the 'knotty contracts' (*nodosae tabulae*) of Cicuta, from which few can escape. Taking into account that Porphyrio calls Parellius and Cicuta jurists,[122] we can reasonably assume that they were not the only bankers who had legal knowledge and used it to the detriment of their clients.

2.4 Legal advisors and conveyancers

Legal advisors and conveyancers were jurists who specialised in giving legal advice or drafting contracts autonomously, but who for some reason or other were not viewed as jurists. One relevant factor was the area of law with which these men occupied themselves. If a man was involved in a less distinguished area of law, it soiled his reputation. This is especially true of *ius praediatorium*, because it dealt with the assets of debtors who could not repay their debts. In fact, auctions for indebted persons were so frequent that although they did not deal exclusively with such cases, they were identified with indebtedness.[123] This also might account for the lack of sources on auctions in the Digest.[124]

Apart from the men mentioned above there were also those who assisted private men in drafting contracts (for example for dowries, sales or contracts for work); often these men were secretaries and their legal work was just one aspect of their occupation. Others were small town officials and priests.[125] Many of them were experts in less distinguished areas of the law: Cascellius (father of the famous jurist A. Cascellius) and Furius, who specialised in the *ius praediatorium*,[126] could not expect much respect from their fellow citizens. This did not mean, however, that they had no work. Similarly, areas of law that were deemed too exotic or too useless did not command respect.[127]

---

[117] Cic. *Fam* 5.20.3
[118] Cic. *Att.* 5.8, 6.1.19, 6.5.2.
[119] Idem: 11.17, 11.21, 11.22, 11.24, 11.26, 11.27, 12.16.
[120] Idem: 12.16.
[121] Hor. *Sat.* 2.3.69, 75.
[122] Porph. In idem: 2.69, 75.
[123] Thielmann 1961: 47f.
[124] Cf. idem: 81.
[125] For examples see Schulz 1997: 136.
[126] Cic. *Balb.* 45.
[127] A similar problem seems to exist in German scholarship on Roman jurists who devoted themselves to public law.

Things were different with inheritance law. Although 'normal' jurists were often asked for *responsa* in inheritance law, drafting the actual testament was often (not always) the task of freedmen: Polybius and Hilarion, Augustus' freedmen, are mentioned as helping him write his will.[128] Later this task fell to the *tabelliones*.

Another aspect that almost certainly played a role was the social status. Freedmen who gave legal advice (like the title-giving parasite Phormio in Terence's comedy) or drafted contracts were not considered jurists due to their low social status. Most of these were former scribes, or *librarii*, who continued to do the same work they had performed as slaves. [129]

3. CONCLUSION

Who was considered a jurist did not necessarily depend on the legal knowledge of those concerned: Quite contrary to modern perceptions, many factors played a role: The bad reputation of some professions (for example *procuratores* and *cognitores*) obscured the forensic experience of those fulfilling these duties. Other men (for example Cicero) may have baulked from declaring themselves as jurists, since for them jurisprudence was always second to oratory. Some were impeded by their origins from being perceived as jurists, others were hindered by their chosen area of law. In sum, the jurists of the late Roman Republic were a very heterogeneous group on which future research is much needed.

BIBLIOGRAPHY

Bannon, C. J. (2000), 'Self-help and social status in Cicero's *pro Quinctio*', *Ancient Society* 30: 71–94.

Brennan, C. (2000), *The Praetorship in the Roman Republic*, volumes I–II. Oxford.

Behrends, O. (1970), '*Ius* und *Ius civile*: Untersuchungen zur Herkunft des *ius*-Begriffs im Zivilrecht', in *Sympotica Franz Wieacker*. Göttingen. 11–58.

Bleicken, J. (1995), *Cicero und die Ritter*. Göttingen.

Classen, C. J. (1998), *Zur Literatur und Gesellschaft der Römer*. Stuttgart.

Damon, C. (1992), 'Sex: Cloelius, scriba', *Harvard Studies in Classical Philology* 94: 227–50.

Damon, C. (1997), *The Mask of the Parasite: A pathology of Roman patronage*. Ann Arbor.

Frier, B. W. (1985), *The Rise of the Roman Jurists: Studies in Cicero's Pro Caecina*. Princeton.

Kunkel, W. and Wittmann, R. (1995), *Staatsordnung und Staatspraxis der Römischen Republik*. Munich.

---

[128] Suet., *Aug.* 101.
[129] Treggiari 1969: 148.

Lehne, C. (unpublished, 2011), Sententiae et Opiniones: *Eine Untersuchung zur römischen Rechtswissenschaft der Republik*. Dissertation. Innsbruck.

Lehne, C. (2014) 'Die Stellung der Juristen im Formularverfahren', *Zeitschrift der Savigny-Stiftung für Rechtsgeschichte, romanistische Abteilung* 131: 216–312.

Purcell, N. (1983), 'The *apparitores*: a study in social mobility', *Papers of the British School at Rome* 51: 125–73.

Schäfer, C. (1998), *Spitzenmanagement in Republik und Kaiserzeit: die Prokuratoren von Privatpersonen im* Imperium Romanum *vom 2. Jh. v.Chr. bis zum 3. Jh. n.Chr*. St. Katharinen.

Schulz, R. (1997), *Herrschaft und Regierung: Roms Regiment in den Provinzen in der Zeit der Republik*. Paderborn.

Simshäuser, W. (1973), Iuridici *und Munizipalgerichtsbarkeit in Italien*. Munich.

Thielmann, G. (1961), *Die Römische Privatauktion: zugleich ein Beitrag zum römischen Bankierrecht*. Berlin.

Treggiari, S. (1969), *Roman Freedmen During the Late Republic*. Oxford.

Chapter 7

Cicero's Reception in the Juristic Tradition of the Early Empire

Matthijs Wibier

1. INTRODUCTION

Anyone interested in Cicero as a legal thinker and his importance in the development of Roman law will find herself facing a somewhat paradoxical situation. On the one hand, Cicero is often counted among the greatest ancient thinkers on law, while on the other his name and writings are largely absent from ancient Roman legal scholarship. A quick glance reveals that the Institutes of Gaius, a text from the second century AD, do not cite Cicero by name. Likewise, the fifty books of Justinian's Digest, our most important source for juristic writings, mention Cicero only a handful of times.[1] Even when it comes to the reception of ideas, Cicero's presence seems limited; it is at least sufficiently elusive as to create ample scholarly disagreement.[2] Yet Cicero undeniably had an extensive interest in legal matters, ranging from the wording of wills to questions about natural justice, and there is every indication that much of his œuvre has circulated widely since his lifetime. For these reasons, it is worth considering how Cicero and his works were received by the jurists and how we should understand his relatively marginal presence in Roman legal thought.

The relation between Cicero and the Roman jurists has undergone thorough scholarly scrutiny, albeit mostly from a Ciceronian perspective.[3] Designated by Latin words such as *iure consultus* or *iuris peritus* or simply *prudens*,[4] a jurist functioned as a legal advisor to individuals with questions about the 'proper' interpretation of the law, which could involve written as well as unwritten law.[5] A jurist's answer, specific to the case at hand and known as a *responsum*, could be cited in court in support of one's case. The

---

[1] For a discussion of some of the complications involved in using the Digest as a source, see the next section.
[2] See for example Nörr 1978; Atkins 2013; MacCormack 2014, for widely different analyses and appraisals.
[3] Seminal studies are Frier 1985 and Harries 2006.
[4] Although generally accompanied by *iuris* or *iure*, all three adjectives do occur alone to refer to jurists (see OLD s.vv).
[5] *Interpretatio* is in fact used by jurists as a technical term to describe their activities. See Pomp. D. 1.2.2.6 (cf. Cic. *Off*. 2.65).

authority of *responsa* was a function of the authority of their authors, who needed to be experts on customary practices in order to find a solution that could be considered 'right' – that is, a solution in line with traditional interpretations of statutes, or customary law, or, in lack thereof, Roman traditions. We should note at the outset that Cicero is generally not considered a jurist, either by the ancients or by modern scholars. The main reason is that Cicero, when pleading a case in the courtroom, is out primarily to win the suit for his client and as such acts as an advocate, not a jurist.[6] This image is strengthened by Cicero's own writings: he regularly portrays jurists as a group to which he himself does not belong.[7] As recent studies have pointed out, however, it is crucial to keep in mind that Cicero is often trying to construct an authoritative *persona* at the expense of the jurists.[8] The late Republic was a world that lacked a single ultimate legal authority and as such ownership of the law was diffused.[9] The result was that many individuals staked claims to legal expertise. Since it was his business to persuade others of his views, it served *Cicero the Advocate* to marginalise rival lawyers by relegating them to the ranks of the jurists, who he tends to construct as a class of inferior and somewhat pedantic students of the law. Hammering home the idea that he himself outclassed the jurists proved to be one of Cicero's favourite rhetorical ploys in a context in which the boundaries between different types of lawyers (including jurists and forensic orators) were not as clear as Cicero claimed them to be.[10]

In this chapter, I explore Cicero's relation to the jurists from the opposite perspective by studying how jurists viewed and read Cicero. Since only very little juristic material survives that dates to Cicero's lifetime, I will be focusing chiefly on jurists from the early Empire. On the one hand, this allows us to get as close as possible to the views of Cicero's contemporaries. On the other hand, and more importantly so, we should realise that intellectual legacies take shape over several generations and may display a multiplicity of appraisals. This is certainly the picture we get from several recent studies on Cicero's early reception outside the juristic sphere. Thus we should note that Cicero's actions as a politician received a mixed press. While executing some of Catiline's fellow conspirators provoked intensely hostile reactions for centuries after his death, Cicero's verbal attacks on Antony earned him superlative and universal praise. Yet in contrast to his equivocal reception as

---

[6] See Crook 1995 for an excellent discussion of legal advocacy in the Roman world.

[7] For example at *Brut.* 150–7; *Mur.* 19–30.

[8] Harries 2006.

[9] See Harries 2002.

[10] Even though by the second century AD jurisprudence had grown into a more specialist discipline, gentlemen scholars such as Gellius were reading legal works and discussing legal problems. This suggests that law was far from being isolated from mainstream culture, as was held by scholars of previous generations. For an excellent discussion of Gellius and the jurists, see Howley 2013.

a politician, Cicero's reputation as a speaker and stylist was never seriously criticised; his eloquence (in writing) formed the gold standard for every orator who came after him.[11] These observations indicate that the reception of the author-as-person may be different from the reception of his writings. This distinction will prove relevant for the jurists as well, since some of their most polemical passages involve the name of Cicero rather than an engagement with his contributions to law. It should be clear that my reception-based approach has a major advantage over the traditional *Quellenforschung* approach. Where an earlier survey tried to establish the mechanics of quotation and misquotation,[12] this chapter takes as a starting point that quotation, and especially paraphrase and adaptation, presuppose a selection process on the part of the receiving author, which raises acute questions about underlying agendas. Similarly the reception perspective opens our eyes to how jurists construct the figure of Cicero in (sometimes, very) particular ways.

In mapping Cicero's legacy, I will proceed in three steps, which correspond roughly to his reception in juristic, rhetorical and philosophical terms. The next section discusses a number of quotations from Cicero's works in the Digest that are cited and used in the way jurists engage with the works of other jurists. This suggests that Cicero must occasionally have acted like a jurist, and that jurists mined his works to some extent for useful materials. The subsequent section studies juristic attitudes towards Cicero's place in legal history by focusing on the famous history of jurisprudence by Pomponius. Against the background of the polemical use of Cicero in the rhetorical tradition, we can see how Pomponius' narrative uses the figure of Cicero and rewrites some of his most hostile passages in order to push back on his attacks on the jurists. The final section addresses Cicero's importance as a legal philosopher. Arguing first that Cicero's philosophical reception in the juristic tradition cannot be proven, I show that the jurists avoid crediting the figure Cicero for any philosophical contributions at all. In his stead, they project and construct the jurist Labeo (Augustan Age) as the all-eclipsing legal philosopher of Rome – and it seems that polemical considerations once more play a role here.

2. THE JURISTIC TRADITION AND THE DEFINITIONS OF MARCUS TULLIUS

This section surveys the quotations that the Digest ascribes to Cicero. I argue that they are well at place in, and should hence be understood within,

---

[11] A recent survey is Gowing 2014; older surveys are Kennedy 2002 and Winterbottom 1982. See MacCormack 2014 for late antiquity, Bishop 2015 for Cicero's pairing with Demosthenes and Plato, Kaster 1998 on Cicero in the rhetorical schools (cf. La Bua 2006), and Dressler 2015 on the figure of Cicero.

[12] Nörr 1978 (a slightly expanded version of Nörr 1977).

a book culture that is characterised by jurists who excerpt other jurists and compile collections of legal opinions. Before turning to Cicero, then, I will first discuss briefly the juristic tradition and point out some of the peculiarities involved in working with excerpts.

The introduction above has mentioned that legal opinions were typically given in response to specific queries. From scattered remarks in Cicero's œuvre, it appears that for the middle and late Republic the standard scenario involved individuals approaching a fellow citizen with a certain authority in legal affairs.[13] But it is important to stress that questions could come up and might need addressing in many situations: while court cases obviously often revolved around legal technicalities, issues could also arise with officials in exercising their office as well as during discussions in an educational setting.[14] Legal opinions given in response to such problems were treated as interpretations of the law with a certain authority, although this varied somewhat depending on the status of the issuing jurist. Since they clarified problematic aspects of the law, *responsa* along with case descriptions (occasionally including case decisions) were preserved for future reference, which in addition to legal disputes included legal education. According to Cicero, in educating the next generation some prominent jurists allowed students merely to observe their giving of *responsa*, while others invited students to their houses for question-and-answer sessions that went over old cases and sometimes developed hypothetical problems as well. For the specific legal cases we hear about in the sources, it is often impossible to establish in what form their dossiers reached the jurist–teacher who discussed them with his students; but generally speaking it must have involved a mixture of the senior jurist's personal recollection, of documents preserved in the family archive, and increasingly also of material found in opinion collections in book form. Cicero's œuvre once more makes it clear that by his time opinion collections circulated that contained the views of more than one older generation of jurists. For example, we learn from one of Cicero's letters that the work *De iure civili* of Quintus Mucius Scaevola the Pontifex (consul 95 BC) listed the opinions of different jurists organised by topic.[15]

The same letter from Cicero indicates that Mucius' work made it easy to look up what others had said about a certain topic. From the excerpts of juristic works preserved by Justinian, we can see that as time evolves jurists increasingly cite and refer to other jurists. While commentaries and polemical works were being produced and survive in small fragments,

---

[13] The following short overview intends to present the standard narrative; for an overview with ample source references, see for example Wibier 2014: 361–3.

[14] See for example Gell. *NA* 13.13 (a *quaestio* concerning jurisdiction) and Alfenus Varus, D. 38.1.26.1 (for a question of a student to his teacher).

[15] Cic. *Fam.* 7.22 (= SB 331). The letter does not explicitly say that Mucius' work was consulted, but scholars generally assume so (e.g. Shackleton Bailey 2001).

much effort was devoted to producing selections from previous literature, so-called digests, in order to keep track of legal opinions and arguments that had been circulated, and to keep consultation of a variety of views manageable.[16] In effect, Mucius' work constitutes the earliest such digest of which we know. Alfenus Varus (cos. suf. 39 BC) was the first to use the title *Digesta* for his work, which was probably a collection of both his own opinions and those of his teacher Servius Sulpicius Rufus. The second-century AD jurist Pomponius tells us that a certain Aufidius Namusa, a student of the same Servius Sulpicius, 'digested' the works of his fellow students in a massive work spanning 140 books (*digesti sunt*, D. 1.2.2.44). Even introductory legal textbooks could take the form of digests: Gaius' Institutes, one of the few legal texts from the early Empire that survive independently from Justinian's project, is a handbook that credits points of legal doctrine to individual jurists. Standing at the end of a long tradition of legal digests, the fifty books of Justinian's Digest (brought into circulation in AD 533) present the opinions mainly of jurists dating to the first through third centuries AD, although the views of older jurists are regularly quoted directly or indirectly. For example, while Q. Mucius Scaevola himself features occasionally in the Digest, in practically all cases his opinions occur as quoted or paraphrased by other jurists.[17]

Once we realise that excerpting and paraphrasing are central technologies of the Digest and its forerunners, questions arise in terms of textual and source criticism: what does it mean for the text, and the ideas presented therein, that we are dealing with an excerpt or even a paraphrase? How accurate are the texts? How much have the excerpted texts been edited? These questions in combination with worries about poor syntax gave rise to a hunt for 'interpolations' in the Digest among earlier generations of scholars. While the problem is real, recent studies of passages in the Digest that are also attested via independent channels have shown that syntactical and stylistic considerations are often misleading and highly subjective, and that the interventions of excerptors appear to be primarily stylistic rather than substantive.[18] As such, most scholars now work on the hypothesis that the Digest gives a fair rendering of the words of the authors it is quoting, while remaining open to the possibility that new evidence might prove otherwise for the particular excerpt under scrutiny.

The following passage gives a flavour of juristic excerpt collections and brings us back to the issue of quotations from Cicero in the Digest:

---

[16] To be sure, I am using the term 'digest' here fairly widely to refer to a type of text that brings together and organises legal opinions on certain topics. My usage here is not limited to works entitled *Digesta*.

[17] See Lenel *Paling.* 2.757–62.

[18] See Nelson 1981 for a collation of quoted passages from Gaius' Institutes in the Digest against the MS of Gaius. See in general Honoré 2010.

CELSUS libro vicensimo quinto digestorum. litus est, quousque maximus fluctus a mari pervenit: idque Marcum Tullium aiunt, cum arbiter esset, primum constituisse. [1.] praedia dicimus aliquorum esse non utique communiter habentium ea, sed vel alio aliud habente. (D. 50.16.96 pr. – 1.)

CELSUS, *in the twenty-fifth book of the Digesta*: the 'shore' is as far as the highest tide reaches from the sea: and they say that Marcus Tullius first established this, when he was deciding a case. Of 'estates' we surely do not say that they belong to those holding them in common, but rather when everyone has their own.

The passage gives us two definitions, suggesting that it was excised from a longer list of legal definitions. Note further that this excerpt is a digest at several levels: being part of Justinian's Digest, it quotes Book 25 of a work rather aptly entitled *Digesta* by the jurist Celsus, who was active in the reigns of Trajan and Hadrian. Celsus himself excerpts and summarises further, mentioning unnamed others who quote or paraphrase Cicero. The term *aiunt* is conventional language among the jurists, which generally indicates that they found something in a written source.[19] Furthermore, the fact that Celsus mentions Cicero's capacity as an *arbiter* suggests that Cicero (supposedly) formulated this view during a legal proceeding when a question about the exact boundaries of the shore came up. Expressed in a practical situation in response to a specific query, the opinion was apparently appreciated, and it entered the juristic tradition for that reason. Celsus' *aiunt* indicates that by his time the definition was generally accepted and could be found in many legal works, which is confirmed by Quintilian's report that 'jurists' (*iuris consulti*), as a group it seems, define the shore as 'as far as the tide rolls' (*qua fluctus eludit*, 5.14.34–5).

While Celsus and Quintilian both point out that the definition circulated widely, the difference in wording between them opens up the source question. It has long been pointed out that both authors take up a passage from Cicero's *Topica*:[20]

solebat igitur Aquilius collega et familiaris meus cum de litoribus ageretur, quae omnia publica esse voltis, quaerentibus iis quos ad id pertinebat quid esse litus, ita definire: *qua fluctus eluderet*.

For, when there was a case about shores, which you [jurists] want to be all communal, my colleague and friend Aquilius used to give the following definition when those whom this concerned asked what a shore was: 'as far as the tide rolls'.

It should be clear from this passage that Quintilian stays closest to the Ciceronian text. Celsus, on the other hand, not only reformulates the

---

[19] For example in Pomponius, who introduces a paraphrase of Cicero's *Brutus* with the words *Cicero ait* (D. 1.2.2.40). See below.
[20] *Top.* 32. See Nörr 1978: 126.

definition, he also ascribes the definition to Cicero himself rather than to Aquilius Gallus. Regarding the reformulation, we should note that it cannot really be considered a corruption of Cicero: while the Ciceronian–Aquilian concept of 'shore' is preserved, the tweaking of the phrasing makes the expression even clearer, which should be no problem in a legal context. We may thus take Celsus to be paraphrasing a definition found in the Ciceronian *corpus*. Furthermore, the attribution to Cicero instead of Aquilius suggests that Celsus (or his source) quoted from memory, and then put the definition down in much the same words as before and tagged it with Cicero's name.[21] Yet even if this seems a straightforward account of the divergence between Celsus and the text of the *Topica*, the present state of evidence does not allow us to rule out at least two further interpretations. On the one hand, it is not impossible that Cicero actually used Aquilius' definition in a case in which he was an *arbiter*, and that the version found in the case dossier somehow entered the juristic tradition. On the other hand, we will see in more detail in the next section that the jurists of the early Empire operated in an intellectual setting that was rife with polemic against them. These attacks were themselves a self-conscious form of Ciceronian reception, projecting Cicero, and with him oratory, as superior to jurisprudence. Within this context, we may read Celsus' elision of Cicero and Aquilius as a deliberate attempt to co-opt Cicero for the juristic tradition and to show that he at times wore a jurist's hat, thus erasing to some extent the boundaries between types of lawyers as found in the Ciceronian *corpus*.[22] No matter which of these views we prefer, the key point to note is that Cicero is presented as an authority of legal definition and is treated as a fellow jurist by Celsus (and perhaps already his source), and later by Justinian's compilers, without hesitation or justification. All this indicates that Cicero and his writings could be taken seriously as contributing to juristic debates in the first centuries after his death.

A similar argument about Cicero's potential value to juristic discussions can be made on the basis of a definition of *latitare* ascribed to him by the third-century AD jurist Ulpian. The following quotation is a passage taken from Ulpian's commentary on the praetor's edict:

> quid sit autem latitare, videamus. latitare est non, ut Cicero definit, turpis occulta-
> tio sui: potest enim quis latitare non turpi de causa, veluti qui tyranni crudelitatem
> timet aut vim hostium aut domesticas seditiones. [5.] sed is, qui fraudationis causa
> latitet, non tamen propter creditores, etsi haec latitatio creditores fraudet . . . (D.
> 42.4.7.4–5)

---

[21] Cf. also the reformulation of *cum … ageretur* as *cum arbiter esset*. This is along the lines of the explanation given by Nörr 1978: 126–31, although I do not think that Celsus' reformulation necessarily means that the text of the *Topica* was only transmitted orally, which Nörr contends.

[22] See below. We will see that jurists generally try to exclude Cicero from their ranks, but there is no need to assume that all jurists had the same ideas about how to handle Cicero and Ciceronian polemics.

But let us see what constitutes 'hiding'. 'Hiding' is not, as Cicero defines it, a shameful concealment of oneself: for someone can hide due to a cause that is not shameful, such as when someone fears the cruelty of a tyrant or the strength of the enemy or uprisings at home. However the person who hides in order to deceive, yet not because of his creditors, although this hiding deceives the creditors . . .

This discussion about the meaning of 'hiding' comes up in the context of a praetorian provision known as *missio in possessionem* ('seizure of property'), which could be used, for example, against someone who was in debt. Ulpian informs us that the praetor will grant an action against a person hiding out of fraudulence (*praetor ait: qui fraudationis causa latitabit . . .* 42.4.7.1). After a few introductory points, the question about the technical legal meaning of *latitare* is raised. Several definitions are reviewed. The first of these, which is rejected, is explicitly attributed to Cicero. This definition was long considered a fragment from a lost work of Cicero until Jane Crawford demonstrated that it forms a paraphrase of *De domo sua* 83.[23] Furthermore, Crawford has suggested that Ulpian's subsequent discussion of the technical juristic definition may evoke Cicero's *Pro Quinctio*, which features the phrase *qui fraudationis causa* and a form of *latitare* at two points (60, 74). Even though both Ulpian's text and the *Pro Quinctio* indicate that this clause occurred in the praetor's edict and must as such have been fairly widespread,[24] the activation of the Ciceronian connection in the preceding sentence invites us to consider Cicero's more technical discussion of *latitare* in the *Pro Quinctio*, which is in line with technical juristic conception of the term. On this reading of the passage quoted above, Ulpian's text engages with the Ciceronian *corpus* in a complex way. First and foremost, it signals the value for a jurist of comparing and contrasting different speeches of Cicero, and the legal knowledge that can be harvested from this process if done in the right way. In addition, by showing off knowledge of Cicero's works, the text casts Ulpian as a jurist exemplary for his learnedness and the acumen required for properly assessing the writings of others.[25]

The final explicit reference to Cicero's writings in a discussion of legal doctrine can be found in a passage by the jurist Tryphoninus (active around/

---

[23] Crawford 1994: 311–12, '*turpis occultatio sui ~ latitat omnino, sed, si requiri iusseris, invenient hominem apud sororem tuam occultantem se capite demisso.*'

[24] This is indicated by Ulpian's *praetor ait* and Cicero's *recita edictum* (*Quinct.* 60). See Lenel 1927: 405 (= 38.205). The fact that Probus included FCL (= *fraudationis causa latitat*) in a list of legal abbreviations indicates that the phrase was ubiquitous (*Not. iur.* 6.66.1). However, it appears hardly attested outside juristic texts except in Cicero's *Pro Quinctio*.

[25] Even if we do not accept that the passage may call to mind the *Pro Quinctio*, it still suggests that jurists may profit from reading Cicero. A favourite rhetorical strategy among jurists is to take someone's legal definition in order to sharpen one's own. As Gai. *Inst.* 3.183 shows, this does not necessarily imply a generally negative attitude towards the criticised author in question, as Nörr proposed for Ulpian in relation to Cicero on a tenuous parallel (1978: 134–6).

after 200 AD). The Digest features the following excerpt discussing the deliberate abortion of pregnancies:

> Cicero in oratione pro Cluentio habito scripsit Milesiam quandam mulierem, cum esset in Asia, quod ab heredibus secundis accepta pecunia partum sibi medicamentis ipsa abegisset, rei capitalis esse damnatam. sed et si qua visceribus suis post divortium, quod praegnas fuit, vim intulerit, ne iam inimico marito filium procrearet, ut temporali exilio coerceatur, ab optimis imperatoribus nostris rescriptum est.[26]

> Cicero in the speech *Pro Cluentio* wrote that, when he was in Asia, some woman from Miletus had been condemned on a capital charge because she herself had driven off her own foetus by means of drugs after having taken money from the substituted heirs. But also if a woman after a divorce applies violence to her womb because she is pregnant, in order not to produce a child for her now hateful husband, it has been ordered in an imperial rescript by our very best emperors that she be punished with temporary exile.

The second half of this passage tells us that the emperors of Tryphoninus' day, probably Septimius Severus and Caracalla,[27] affirmed that a woman who aborted her pregnancy after a divorce would be liable to penalty. That they did so in a rescript, which is an official communication in response to a petition, suggests that Roman law did not punish the abortion, or at least that the legal situation needed clarification. This impression is substantiated by Dieter Nörr's discussion of the passage, which argues that, while Roman attitudes towards abortion were generally hostile, it only became punishable in the Severan Age.[28] The near-quotation from the *Pro Cluentio* in the first sentence seems to point in a similar direction: not only did Tryphoninus apparently find no juristic authorities who had formulated a view in line with the rescript before, he referred to a peregrine (not Roman) case found in a by-then centuries-old courtroom speech. That is to say, the reference to Cicero must have served to create some sort of precedent or parallel for the opinion expressed in the rescript, and we should note that Tryphoninus apparently considered Cicero sufficiently authoritative as to make the rescript more palatable to a wider juristic audience.[29]

All in all, then, we have seen that Cicero's writings were read by jurists and were referenced in the juristic tradition, even though his occurrence is

---

[26] D. 48.19.39 pr.
[27] See the jurist Marcian at D. 47.11.4.
[28] Nörr 1978: 122–5, with Ulpian (D. 48.8.8) and Marcian (D. 47.11.4).
[29] See also Nörr 1978: 124–6, who entertains the idea that Tryphoninus may have circulated his rendering of the *Pro Cluentio* already before the rescript was issued and may as such have influenced policy change. This must remain speculative. I also see no reason to suppose that the second sentence in the block quote above is a later addition.

relatively marginal.[30] Furthermore, it should be noted that whenever Cicero is cited, he is cited for a detailed piece of legal doctrine, which is used by later jurists to support or sharpen their own views. Crucially, then, while the jurists quote Cicero only sparsely, they do quote him as if he is a jurist. Nörr emphasised that these quotations do not support the claim that the jurists considered Cicero a professional colleague, but this is once more to perpetuate Cicero's own rhetorical and somewhat disingenuous dichotomy.[31] Rather, the passages discussed suggest that Cicero's work was not off-limits in principle, and that the boundaries between Cicero and the jurists were more porous than Cicero claimed in his own works.[32]

3. ADVOCATES, JURISTS AND THE MYTH OF CICERO

A juristic text that brings up Cicero several times is the history of Roman jurisprudence written by Pomponius during the reign of Hadrian (D. 1.2.2). Rather than presenting a compilation of views on legal doctrine, the text constitutes a historiographical narrative of legal scholarship from the Regal period onwards. Recent studies have demonstrated extensively that Roman historiographical writings tend to push their rhetorical agendas onto their readership.[33] In line with these observations, this section analyses the agenda of Pomponius' account in its engagement with Cicero.[34] We will see that Pomponius is primarily interested in the figure of Cicero and in constructing him as of marginal importance to the field of jurisprudence. We will also see that Pomponius does so in reaction to polemical attacks by advocates, who take up hostile passages from Cicero's œuvre so as to assert their superiority over jurists.

Regarding the question why the claims of these orators are so important to Pomponius, it should be kept in mind that by his time rhetorical training had been a staple of elite culture for many generations. Authors such as Seneca the Elder, Quintilian and Suetonius give the impression that a tremendous number of people had been through the rhetorical schools that started to

---

[30] Ulpian's discussion of the term *deicere* at D. 43.16.3.8 may be a further case. Although it does not mention Cicero by name, the definition squares with Cicero's definition at *Pro Caecina* 66. Tellegen-Couperus 1991: 46 has argued plausibly that the standard juristic interpretation originates with Cicero.

[31] Nörr 1978: 145–7.

[32] Papinian at D. 48.4.8 cites Iulia's (= Fulvia's) testimony against the Catilinarian Conspirators in support of the claim that women can be heard in cases of *maiestas*. While Papinian mentions that Cicero was consul that year, this is hardly a case of Ciceronian reception as Cicero never mentions Fulvia by name – in contrast to Sallust and Florus. See on this extensively Nörr 1978: 115–21.

[33] See Kraus and Woodman 1997: 1–10 for a discussion.

[34] On the agenda of Pomponius' work more generally, see Nörr 1976 for an extensive discussion.

arise since the Augustan Age. It seems fairly clear that this type of education provided an entry ticket to a political and literary career, as well as to a
career in forensic oratory.[35] It is therefore plausible to assume that men who
made their name as jurists – men such as Pomponius – had spent time in the
rhetorical schools as well,[36] and hence that they were familiar not only with
the schools' literary curricula but also with how the discourse of advocacy
constructed legal history and Cicero's role therein.[37] In order to contextual-
ise Pomponius' engagement with Cicero fully, then, it is necessary to place
it against the predominant narrative that we find in the rhetorical tradition.

A quick glance suffices to note that Cicero is a towering figure in the
rhetorical tradition of the early Empire. From Seneca the Elder's work on
the rise and development of declamatory culture at Rome, we learn that
Cicero's works, especially his orations, were studied intensively, something
we also gather from the work of Quintilian and from Tacitus' *Dialogus*.
While Seneca's preface rhetorically claims that declamatory culture is a mere
footnote to the heights of eloquence reached in Cicero's works, it is perhaps
more telling about the esteem in which Cicero was held that, by the time of
Seneca, the figure of Cicero had grown into a larger-than-life icon of Roman
political oratory. Robert Kaster has pointed out how exceptional it is that
Cicero features in the exercise scenarios of *Suasoria* 6 and 7.[38] The seventh
exercise, for example, asks students to produce a speech advising Cicero
whether or not to burn all his writings in the hypothetical situation that
Antony offers mercy on this condition. Many of the speeches excerpted by
Seneca advise against taking the offer on some variant of the argument that
Cicero's eloquence transcends the mortal condition.

When it comes to Cicero's importance more specifically in forensic
oratory, it is Quintilian who is most explicit about Cicero's all-eclipsing
accomplishments. As part of his discussion that the perfect orator must be
thoroughly educated across the disciplines, Quintilian argues that Cicero
was the one by far closest to reaching this ideal (12.1.15–21). We should note
that in developing these points Quintilian references Antonius' speech on
the ideal orator in Cicero's *De Oratore* and that he himself defends a similar
theory (*De or.* 1.94, 3.189). While the perfect orator of the Ciceronian text
remains nameless, Quintilian's reception of it is premised on a reading that
equates the figure of Cicero with the ideal of *De Oratore*. The same reading
underlies Quintilian's discussion of the relation between rhetoric and juris-

---

[35] Seneca's description of Ovid's days as a student is famous (2.2.8–12). In general, see Bonner
1969, 45 for (still) the best account of this.

[36] Crook 1955 shows that many jurists made a career and achieved top positions under the
emperors.

[37] This is arguably far less the case for the legal–juristic tradition, since specialist juristic education was pursued by only a fraction of the elite young men who went through the rhetorical
schools.

[38] Kaster 1998.

prudence somewhat later on. When Quintilian argues extensively at 12.3 that the perfect orator should have extensive knowledge of the law, we find the following:

> verum et M. Cato cum in dicendo praestantissimus, tum iuris idem fuit peritissimus, et Scaevolae Servioque Sulpicio concessa est etiam facundiae virtus, et M. Tullius non modo inter agendum numquam est destitutus scientia iuris, sed etiam componere aliqua de eo coeperat, ut appareat posse oratorem non discendo tantum iuri vacare sed etiam docendo. (12.3.9–10)

> But indeed Marcus Cato was both the most outstanding in speaking and, likewise, the greatest expert in law; and excellence in speaking has also been granted to Scaevola and Servius Sulpicius, and Marcus Tullius was not only never devoid of knowledge of the law when pleading, but he even began to write something about that, so that it appears that an orator might devote himself not merely to learning the law but also to teaching it.

This passage uses several rhetorical ploys to project Cicero as the pinnacle of legal oratory. First, by placing Cicero at the end of this brief history and by elaborating so much on his qualities, the narrative suggests that Cicero is the culmination of legal history, both of forensic oratory and of legal scholarship. Cicero's capabilities come out even more strongly once we take into account the ancient commonplace that complete intellectual mastery comes with the ability to teach the subject in question.[39] He thus seems to surpass even Cato; for while Cato is praised to a superlative degree, standing out among his peers until at least the generations of Mucius Scaevola and Servius Sulpicius, nothing is said as to whether he ever taught law. Furthermore, we should note that the passage once again evokes the debate on the ideal orator in *De Oratore* by reformulating the speech of Crassus in which he urges passionately that the orator be thoroughly versed in the law (1.166–204).[40] Here we see once more that Quintilian engages closely with Cicero's ideas about the perfect orator, while pushing forth the idea that the figure of Cicero embodies the ideal.[41]

If the text in the block quotation above already suggests that jurisprudence is somehow subordinated to oratory, Quintilian makes this point crystal-clear in the immediately following paragraphs. This time Quintilian takes up a rather polemical passage from *De Oratore* to stress how difficult a task becoming a perfect orator is: many students will not achieve it. We hear that failed students regularly decide to become jurists, designated here by the pejorative term *leguleius* ('pettifogger', 12.3.11 ~ Cic. *De or.* 1.236).

---

[39] See for example Quint. 1 pr.23.
[40] For specific references, see Russell's notes *ad loc.* in the Loeb edition (Russell 2001).
[41] This is admittedly a reading encouraged by the Ciceronian *corpus* itself. The second half of the *Brutus* comes probably closest to saying this flat out.

The problem with these jurists is that they are intellectually less competent or simply lazy individuals (*desidia*, *pigritia*), who despite all this have the nerve to assert the greater usefulness of their type of law (*utiliora*). In all, then, Quintilian not only presents Cicero as the perfect orator according to Quintilian's own – Ciceronian – theory, but his reception of the Ciceronian *corpus* also involves turning Cicero into the icon of advocacy's abusive claim of superiority over jurisprudence.

The letters of Pliny the Younger suggest that the polemical attacks on jurists as found in Cicero's works enjoyed a fairly wide reception among high-profile orators. Three letters, linked by the occurrence of the term *voluntas defuncti*, discuss wills that have been formulated in such a way that the testators' wishes cannot legally be carried out (2.16, 4.10, 5.7). Since the wish of the deceased is perfectly clear in each case, Pliny claims, the solution to the legal tangle should be straightforward. But he also expresses his concern that his view will be rejected by the *iuris consulti* (5.7.2; cf. 4.10.2). By claiming that the jurists are too harsh and suggesting that they are somewhat inferior to himself (for example *convenit inter omnes* [sc. *iuris peritos*] . . . *sed mihi manifestus error videtur*, 4.10.2), his letters invoke a rivalry between orators and jurists similar to the one we saw in the case of Quintilian. Yet since Pliny needs to be careful not to enrage those he needs to persuade, his strategy is to push gently for a seemingly self-evident point, namely that the intention of the deceased take precedence over the debates of lawyers. For the same reason, his engagement with Cicero is rather surreptitious. On the one hand, Pliny's claim that the deceased's wish is *antiquior iure* (5.7.2) may be referring, as Whitton has suggested, to views to this effect associated with Cicero, as found in for example *De Legibus* 1.42.[42] On the other hand, the dilemmas in the three letters seem to evoke the *causa Curiana*, a Republican case that pitted the jurist Scaevola and his literal interpretation of a will against the orator Crassus, who successfully emphasised that the intention of the testator was all that mattered.[43] The case was made famous by Cicero's repeated discussions, which show enduring interest in Crassus' vitriolic disparaging of the jurists.[44] As Quintilian informs us that the case became the exemplar of disputes revolving around letter and intention (7.6.9),[45] Pliny, in constructing his Ciceronian *persona*, evokes a subtext that extols the advocate at the

---

[42] See Whitton 2013 *ad* Plin. *Ep.* 2.16.

[43] Pliny's text does not seem to make any intertextual connections, probably because he needs to be careful not to give too much offence. There is perhaps one exception: '*quid sit iuris* ~ *quod* Scaevola defendebat non *esse iuris*' (*Caecin.* 69).

[44] See for example Cic. *Caecin.* 69; *De or.* 1.180, 2.140–2; *Brut.* 194–8.

[45] La Bua 2006 may be pushing the point too far when he claims that the *causa Curiana* markedly shaped the *controversia* scenarios revolving around the opposition of letter vs spirit of the law. Rather, the *status* was already developed by the rhetor Hermagoras, whose work was used widely by Republican orators (e.g. Bonner 1969: 46–7; Winterbottom 1974: xvii). See below.

expense of the jurist. Thus, even though Pliny is less openly hostile than Quintilian, both authors engage the same polemical trope.[46]

Since rhetorical education was widespread in the early Empire, the discourse about Cicero and the law in the rhetorical tradition provides the intellectual context of Pomponius and his readers.[47] As mentioned above, the long fragment of Pomponius at D. 1.2.2 presents a history of jurisprudence from the Regal period until the reign of the emperor Hadrian.[48] The narrative informs us about generations of jurists with brief notes on their accomplishments, thus resembling other histories of learning such as Cicero's *Brutus* and Suetonius' *On Grammarians and Rhetors*. Pomponius seems to stay closest to the model of the *Brutus*: in addition to engaging explicitly with the *Brutus* at several points, he takes care to list the extant works of most of the jurists featured, and he often inserts a comparative assessment (*synkrisis*) of coeval jurists that brings out the strengths of all involved.[49] A passage from D. 1.2.2.45 about jurists who were active into the Augustan Age illustrates what is at issue here:

> ex his Trebatius peritior Cascellio, Cascellius Trebatio eloquentior fuisse dicitur, Ofilius utroque doctior. Cascellii scripta non exstant nisi unus liber bene dictorum, Trebatii complures, sed minus frequentantur.

> of these Trebatius is said to have been more expert (in the law) than Cascellius, Cascellius more eloquent than Trebatius, Ofilius more learned than either one. Cascellius' writings are not extant except for one book of well-formulated legal maxims, of Trebatius quite some [are extant], but they are less frequently resorted to.

While the passage has raised ample debate about the personal histories of these jurists, for present purposes I will focus on the rhetoric of the *synkrisis*. We should note that the criteria on which Pomponius compares Trebatius and Cascellius, legal scholarship and eloquence, are founded on the same

---

[46] This is not to say that Pliny was hostile to jurists in general, nor that a polemical approach is the only approach found in the rhetorical tradition of the early Empire (cf. e.g. Sen. *Controv.*; Tac. *Dial.* 39).

[47] This is one of my main disagreements with Nörr 1978: he simply assumes that Pomponius is responding to Cicero's attacks on the jurists, whereas I believe that the intervening rhetorical tradition is of great significance.

[48] The following textual note is in order: the Digest credits the passage to a one-book version of Pomponius' *Enchiridion*, whereas at other places it quotes from a two-book version, of which the one-book version may be an abridgement. In any case, I will be assuming that the text can be read as a product of Pomponius' days, and can be meaningfully contextualised in the intellectual culture of the late first and early second centuries.

[49] It is difficult, if not impossible, to decide whether Pomponius' direct model is indeed Cicero's *Brutus*, or whether he works from a tradition of texts of which the *Brutus* is one exponent. References in Quintilian, Tacitus, Gellius and Fronto suggest that Pomponius in all likelihood knew the *Brutus* (see Nörr 1978: 139).

distinction between orators and jurists that we have witnessed in Cicero and the rhetorical tradition of the early Empire. The quotation above is part of a larger passage that activates this rivalry and also stages the figure of Cicero, whom, as we saw, the rhetorical tradition constructed as the alpha male (D. 1.2.2.40–6). In doing so, Pomponius invokes the same *topos* to demonstrate the value of jurists while denying Cicero any importance to legal learning. How does Pomponius do this?

In the first place, while his name is mentioned three times, Cicero is never acknowledged as having contributed anything to the area of law. When Pomponius discusses Quintus Mucius Scaevola the Pontifex, we hear about his seminal contribution to the organisation of the *ius civile* as well as about the many students he educated. Yet while Cicero in his own works emphasises time and again that he studied under Mucius, Pomponius does not even list Cicero among Mucius' pupils. Nor does Cicero's friendship with Servius Sulpicius Rufus receive any attention, even though Cicero himself dwells extensively on it, especially in the *Brutus*. Instead, Pomponius cites Cicero simply as a source of some specific pieces of information in his narrative. At one point, he praises Cicero as an orator by claiming that the *Pro Ligario* is a 'most beautiful speech' (*oratio satis pulcherrima*, 1.2.2.46). But even in this last case, Cicero's presence is marginalised, because Pomponius' elaboration on the case is in all likelihood drawn from the speech of Cicero's adversary Tubero, not from Cicero's own speech.[50] Pomponius thus suppresses the voice of Cicero, the forensic orator, even when bringing up oratory.

Furthermore, Pomponius also resists Cicero's attacks by citing several polemical passages from the *Brutus* while rewriting their narrative to let the jurists emerge as intellectual powerhouses. This strategy can be seen at work at least three times in the passage under discussion here. The first case occurs in Pomponius' mentioning of Lucius Crassus, 'the brother of Publius Mucius, who is called Mucianus: Cicero says that he is the most well-spoken of the jurists' (*frater Publii Mucii, qui Mucianus dictus est: hunc Cicero ait iurisconsultorum disertissimus*, 1.2.2.40).[51] This specific Crassus must be the consul of 131 BC, who was the brother of Publius Mucius Scaevola (father of Quintus) and the father of Licinius Crassus (cos. 92). Several verbal echoes suggest that the praise Pomponius puts in Cicero's mouth is adapted from *Brutus* 145, a discussion of the *causa Curiana* in which the younger Crassus and Quintus Mucius Scaevola served as lawyers. In styling Crassus

---

[50] That is, several facts in Pomponius do not match the account in the *Pro Ligario*. Nörr thinks that Pomponius misremembered the speech, assuming that Cicero's speech was transmitted orally (1978: 137). Yet it is much more plausible to assume that Pomponius is summarising Tubero's (now-lost) speech, which was known to Quintilian. The drama of the story can easily be seen as in line with Tubero's side, rather than that of Ligarius. Pomponius is thus taking the side of Tubero, the jurist in the story.

[51] The transmitted text is Munianus; I follow Mommsen in taking this as a corruption.

as the prototypical orator and Quintus Mucius as the prototypical jurist, Cicero extols Crassus as 'the most learned in law of those who are eloquent' (*eloquentium iuris peritissimus*), while Quintus Mucius is called 'the most eloquent of those who are learned in law' (*iuris peritorum eloquentissimus*, Cic. *Brut.* 145; cf. *De or.* 1.180). As we have already seen, Cicero is primarily interested in setting up this distinction because it serves his larger agenda to claim that orators are the superior class of lawyers. Pomponius, on the other hand, takes up the praise for Quintus Mucius Scaevola and projects it back onto the uncle, thus conflating the famous jurist and the father of the famous orator. By foregrounding juristic accomplishments and emphasising family connections, Pomponius underlines that the Crassi are part of a larger juris- tic clan – perhaps implying that the younger Crassus' success as an orator was made possible by the family's legal expertise.

The biographical section on Servius Sulpicius is the second point at which Pomponius recasts a hostile passage from Cicero's *Brutus*. At *Brutus* 150–7, Cicero argues extensively (1) that his friend Servius Sulpicius Rufus is a superior jurist compared to Quintus Mucius Scaevola, and (2) that Cicero himself outranks Servius by virtue of being an orator rather than a jurist. In making his point, Cicero works with his favoured contrast between orators and jurists. We hear that, in the course of studying rhetoric together, Servius decided to turn to jurisprudence in order to be 'first in the second art' (*in secunda arte primus*, 151), rather than having to stand in Cicero's shadow and be 'second in the first art' (*in prima secundus*). Note that Cicero insists that Servius consciously chose to turn to jurisprudence. Furthermore, Cicero argues passionately that Servius' scholarship is in a different league from Quintus Mucius' because Servius was the first to bring 'dialectic' to jurispru- dence (153).[52] On the other hand, it is immediately obvious that Pomponius' narrative about Servius is rather different. While Pomponius stays close to the *Brutus* when he reports that Servius was the best orator 'certainly after Cicero' (*pro certo post Marcum Tullium*, 1.2.2.43), we then read a rather dra- matic story about Servius' conversion to jurisprudence in which Quintus Mucius Scaevola plays a key part. Servius allegedly consulted Mucius on a point of law, only to realise later that he had misunderstood Mucius' words. The same thing happened a second time. On Servius' third visit Mucius reprimanded him by saying that it was a shame (*turpe*) for a patrician to be ignorant about the law (*ius*) on which the case he was pleading depended. The story ends by saying that Servius, driven by the 'harsh words' (*velut con- tumelia*), decided to devote himself to law. Several differences with Cicero's account stand out. First, Quintus Mucius is portrayed as the godfather of Roman law that most sources make him to be. At the same time, nothing is

---

[52] Cicero is probably inflating Servius' importance – and the explicit surprise of the *Brutus'* interlocutors suggests that the claim was expected to be controversial. The juristic tradition passes over this claim in complete silence (see below).

said about Servius' qualities as a jurist. Second, while Pomponius mentions that Cicero is the best orator, there is no trace of any suggestion that this makes him superior. Rather, it seems that jurisprudence is a separate and challenging world of learning, to which only exceptional individuals turn.

The image that jurisprudence is particularly demanding is further substantiated by a parallel conversion story in Pomponius' treatment of Tubero. We have already seen that Tubero found himself in court against Cicero, who acted as Ligarius' advocate. Before telling us about the trial, however, Pomponius reports that Tubero was 'a patrician and went over from pleading cases to jurisprudence' (*patricius et transiit a causis agendis ad ius civile*, 1.2.2.46), after the trial against Ligarius. The motif of the conversion thus provides an intriguing alternative view on the rivalry between orators and lawyers. In contrast to what we see in Cicero and Quintilian, Pomponius' narrative gives the impression that select individuals turned to jurisprudence after they had started careers as orators; in Servius' case this even took the colossal efforts of an exceptional, erudite mentor. Only the most capable men specialised further in jurisprudence. Note in this connection that nothing negative is said of Servius and Tubero: Servius was one of the best pleaders, and while we hear that Tubero lost his case against Cicero, Pomponius does not disqualify his oratory in any way. We also read that both were extremely successful as jurists: Servius had a tremendous following, and Tubero is called 'most learned' (*doctissimus*). This last statement illustrates once more how Pomponius turns Cicero's hostile narrative in the *Brutus* into a version that is favourable to the jurists. Taking up *Brutus* 117, Pomponius reformulates Cicero's claim that Tubero was 'most learned in detailed argumentation' (*doctissimus in disputando*) into the more scholarly attribute of being 'learned in public and private law' (*doctissimus . . . iuris publici et privati*). Furthermore, while Cicero claims that Tubero's style was 'harsh, rough, uncouth' (*durus horridus incultus*), Pomponius tells us that Tubero wrote 'in an archaic style' (*sermone . . . antiquo*) with the result that his works are not read very often. In Pomponius' hands, the disparaging Ciceronian narratives about jurists are rewritten as more balanced, if not positive, stories.

To sum up, if we juxtapose how the rhetorical tradition of the early Empire and Pomponius' account deal with Cicero in relation to the law, Cicero and his writings emerge as the centrepiece of a fierce polemical debate. On the one hand, the reception of Cicero's theories on the ideal orator by authors such as Quintilian entails casting the figure of Cicero in that role. For Quintilian, a crucial ploy is to assert aggressively the superiority of Cicero-the-perfect-orator over the jurists. On the other hand, while invoking the same Ciceronian intertexts, Pomponius not only constructs Cicero as a mostly irrelevant figure, but he also presents jurisprudence as an exacting and therefore exclusive field of study. In pushing their points, orators and jurists both work with a clearly marked dichotomy between legal oratory and legal scholarship, indicating their reception of Cicero's rhetorical strategy. That orators and jurists felt the need to engage in such polemics, however, suggests that they were talking to each other to some extent, and that the boundaries between the two fields may have been fuzzier than their rhetoric claims them to be.[53] We should take into account here that Cicero was not only the source of the polemical tropes but that he apparently also contributed enough to juristic debates – something we saw in the preceding section – as to be considered a borderline case. While this facilitated his portrayal as an interdisciplinary genius in the hands of the orators, it might also help to explain why, for Pomponius, Cicero warranted explicit exclusion.

4. LEGAL PHILOSOPHERS OF ROME: THE CASES OF CICERO AND LABEO

The question as to Cicero's importance as a philosopher to Roman legal thought is a problematic and highly contested one. The preceding sections of this chapter surveyed all explicit references to Cicero and his writings in the Digest, revealing that Cicero is never mentioned by jurists in relation to any philosophical conceptual elaborations. If this encourages us to study Cicero's reception at the level of ideas, it is crucial that, before turning to the sources, we first address a set of conceptual and methodological questions that have surprisingly often been ignored: what do we mean when we talk about importance, influence, or reception? And how do we establish whether possible connections between texts and ideas found in the output of jurists and in Cicero are meaningful?

As already indicated above, the scholarship so far has usually taken an approach informed by *Quellenforschung*. For example, Dieter Nörr's important work on quotations from Cicero in the jurists studies the manifest and latent influence of Cicero – the latter signifying ideas about which jurists were unaware that they have an origin in Cicero's works.[54] While the search for latent influence may sometimes yield returns,[55] the problem is that such connections are generally hard to trace and to establish beyond reasonable doubt. Illustrative here is the often-held assumption that technical terms found both in the philosophical and in the juristic traditions reached the jurists via Cicero, frequently with the further assumption that the jurists in question must have subscribed to Ciceronian conceptions of the terms, though

---

[53] To the same effect, though from a different perspective, Mantovani 2007 and Bettinazzi 2014 argue that the declamations ascribed to Quintilian at many points reveal in-depth knowledge of technical juristic argumentations.

[54] Nörr 1978 (e.g. 'über latente Einflüsse zu spekulieren', at 142).

[55] For example Tellegen-Couperus 1991 on Cic. *Caecin.* (see above); the case is not mentioned by Nörr.

without crediting him.[56] Prime examples are the notions of natural law and of *aequitas*. Yet several considerations show how problematic this view is.

First and foremost, the concepts are hardly conceptualised explicitly by jurists outside the few excerpts in Digest 1.1, which still seem fairly generic: while the famous passages of Gaius and Ulpian distinguish different types of universal law and hence seem to clash, many scholars have pointed out that it is well nigh impossible to discern philosophical differences between these authors' jurisprudence.[57] Even though Gaius brings up a *naturalis ratio* repeatedly, it never becomes quite clear what this *naturalis ratio* is in conceptual terms. Rather (and perhaps somewhat provocatively), the term functions rhetorically for Gaius to posit an axiom – a starting point that he does not want to elaborate further on in the context of the argument he is making. Because the notion is conceptually unarticulated, the source question also becomes problematic. While Gaius probably found it in earlier juristic works, it is on the present evidence impossible to say whether it entered the juristic tradition through Cicero's works.[58] The spread of the idea of natural law in the philosophical and rhetorical traditions signals that there are many ways, also beyond Cicero, in which it may have reached the jurists.[59]

Much the same case can be made for the concept of *aequitas*. We find the most articulate juristic elaboration in a passage of Marcus Antistius Labeo, a much-admired scholar of the Augustan Age, where he distinguishes between *aequitas naturalis* and *aequitas civilis* – both still vaguely defined (D. 47.4.1.1). Once more, the Ciceronian connection cannot be pressed, because the opposition between written law and equity had already been a commonplace in the rhetorical tradition long before Cicero.[60] Thus the so-called *stasis* theory of the second-century BC rhetorician Hermagoras standardised an argumentative pattern that opposed the letter of the law and more universal considerations of justice.[61] It is essential to note that, rather than embodying a substantive and philosophically developed idea, *aequitas* functions here as a concept that can be fleshed out according to the immediate needs of the forensic orator in the case he is arguing. In short, then, the Ciceronian signature of many of the jurists' theoretical notions cannot be taken for granted,[62] at least not without further evidence.

---

56 For example Ando 2008: 79–92; MacCormack 2014: 254–5.

57 See Atkins 2013: 224–6 for a recent discussion with further literature.

58 Idem: 224–5 suggests that Ulpian's distinction between *ius civile*, *ius gentium*, and *ius naturale* may be taken from Cicero, but that in working with these notions Ulpian is hardly a follower of Cicero.

59 For example in Cic. *Inv. rhet.* 2.67 and *Rhet. Her.* 2.19, which both digest older rhetorical doctrine (cf. Arist. *Rh.* 1.13, 1373b4–9). Stoics and Epicureans (among other philosophers) discuss their conceptions of natural law.

60 For example Cato the Elder (fr. 168.1 = Gell. *NA* 6.3.38).

61 Bonner 1969: 46–7 (see above).

62 Gaius' famous distinction between *res corporales* and *res incorporales* may eventually go

In contrast to a focus on source criticism, which leads us to scholarly *aporia* at best and negative conclusions at worst, a perspective based on reception studies encourages us to ask how jurists appreciate Cicero as a philosopher of law. While we have already seen that the jurists do not connect Cicero with philosophy in the Digest, this does not imply that they do not discuss the role of philosophy in law. Quite to the contrary, several observations indicate that jurists construct the aforementioned Labeo as a foundational figure who appears to displace Cicero by virtue of his expertise in law and philosophy. In the first place, a study of patterns of citation in the Digest yields that Labeo, a relatively early jurist, is cited much more frequently than jurists before him and those for several decades after his death. We should note that Labeo's views are often transmitted through quotations in Ulpian, whose work formed the basis of the Digest by supplying around 40 per cent of the excerpts.[63] Ulpian's interest in Labeo indicates that he must have found Labeo important to the development of legal doctrine.

In line with his profile in the Digest, several texts indicate that the significance of Labeo goes hand in hand with his reputation as a polymath in the early Empire. Thus Pomponius reports that 'Labeo, who had also put work in other fields of learning, set out to make very many innovations on account of the quality of his genius and the faith in his own learning' (*Labeo ingenii qualitate et fiducia doctrinae, qui et ceteris operis sapientiae operam dederat, plurima innovare instituit*, 1.2.2.47). While Pomponius does not single out philosophy as one of Labeo's occupations, his designation of Labeo's learning with the term *sapientia* carries strong philosophical connotations. The picture of Labeo as having philosophical credentials is further substantiated in the work of Aulus Gellius, an author of the second century AD. Gellius' testimony is of particular importance, because, while not a jurist himself, he was a close and interested observer of jurists. His *Noctes Atticae* thus provide a window onto second-century juristic culture independently of the juristic tradition, including its excerptors. While Gellius expresses his admiration for Labeo at many points, his most extravagant eulogy can be found in Book 13:

> Labeo Antistius iuris quidem civilis disciplinam principali studio exercuit et consulentibus de iure publice responsitavit; <set> ceterarum quoque bonarum artium non expers fuit et in grammaticam sese atque dialecticam litterasque antiquiores altioresque penetraverat Latinarumque vocum origines rationesque percalluerat eaque praecipue scientia ad enodandos plerosque iuris laqueos utebatur.[64]

---

back to Cicero's *Topica* 26–7, but the point of both passages is conceptually distinct (see Reinhardt 2003, 259, 263). Yet even if we consider this a case of Ciceronian influence, it remains an open question whether the substance or merely the expository scheme of Roman law have been 'influenced'.

[63] Honoré 2010: 5–6.

[64] Gell. *NA* 13.10.1.

Labeo Antistius devoted himself with the foremost zeal to the study of the *ius civile* and he formulated opinions 'publicly'[65] about the law to those who consulted him; but he was also not destitute of the other good arts and he had immersed himself in the study of grammar and in dialectic and the lofty literature of the olden days and he was steeped in the origins and explanation of Latin words, and he used that knowledge in particular to untie many knots in the law.

The passage underscores Labeo's importance to the *ius civile*. What makes him so erudite and productive is that he was educated across the intellectual board. Even though we hear that antiquarian studies and grammar were the greatest assets to the legal scholar, his mastery of philosophy in the form of dialectic is also highlighted. All this reinforces the account of Pomponius. Yet we should also note that we hear nothing about what we would call legal philosophy: Labeo's valued accomplishments lie in bringing logic to the field of law.[66]

Finally, while so far I have discussed Labeo as someone who is presented as the prime philosopher in the legal sphere, there is some evidence to suggest that, being aware of Cicero's foundational status in legal oratory, some jurists consciously constructed Labeo as the Cicero of Roman jurisprudence. An excerpt of the jurist Paul (early third century AD) brings up a hypothetical case with a fictional subject (D. 34.3.28.4). This subject is called Antistius Cicero. Paul's choice to combine the names of Labeo and Cicero signals that he considered the two historical characters to some extent on a par. It is tempting to take this as a nod at Labeo's and Cicero's status as intellectual patriarchs in jurisprudence and forensic oratory respectively.

5. CONCLUSION

Cicero's reception among the jurists is a complex phenomenon. When it comes to Cicero's writings, especially his speeches, jurists occasionally quote Cicero as a jurist. Above we have encountered several definitions and analogies from Cicero's hand that are credited explicitly to him. In this connection, the watertight separation between orators and jurists that Cicero himself posited collapses to some extent. On the other hand, when it comes to the figure of Cicero and his place in legal history, he turns out to be a controversial character: while Pomponius mentions Cicero but marginalises him, Cicero's role as a philosopher is passed over in complete silence. In his place, Labeo receives full credit. Thus, paradoxically enough, the quotations and the controversy around his person together cement Cicero's place in

---

[65] The meaning of *publice* in this passage is highly contested. To be sure, its possible connection with Pomponius' *publice respondendi ius* (1.2.2.49) is irrelevant to my argument here.

[66] Note that the jurists ignore completely Cicero's similar praise of Servius Sulpicius Rufus at *Brut.* 153 (see above).

Roman law. In the eyes of the jurists discussed above, Cicero was undeniably important to Roman law. This is most evident at points where Cicero is not mentioned but lurks under the surface.

BIBLIOGRAPHY

Ando, C. (2008), *The Matter of the Gods: Religion and the Roman Empire*. Berkeley.

Atkins, J. (2013), *Cicero on Politics and the Limits of Reason: The* Republic *and* Laws. Cambridge.

Bettinazzi, M. (2014). *La legge nelle declamazioni quintilianee*. Saarbrücken.

Bishop, C. (2015), 'Roman Plato or Roman Demosthenes? The bifurcation of Cicero in ancient scholarship', in W. Altman, ed., *Brill's Companion to the Reception of Cicero*. Leiden. 284–306.

Bonner, S. (1969), *Roman Declamation in the Late Republic and Early Empire*. Liverpool.

Crawford, J. (1994²), *M. Tullius Cicero: The fragmentary speeches*. Atlanta.

Crook, J. A. (1955), Consilium Principis: *Imperial councils and counsellors from Augustus to Diocletian*. Cambridge.

Crook, J. A. (1995), *Legal Advocacy in the Roman World*. Ithaca, NY.

Dressler, A. (2015), 'Cicero's quarrels: Reception and modernity from Horace to Tacitus', in W. Altman, ed., *Brill's Companion to the Reception of Cicero*. Leiden. 144–71.

Frier, B. W. (1985), *The Rise of the Roman Jurists: Studies in Cicero's* Pro Caecina. Princeton.

Gowing, A. (2014), 'Tully's boat: responses to Cicero in the imperial period', in C. Steel, ed., *The Cambridge Companion to Cicero*. Cambridge. 233–50.

Harries, J. (2002), 'Cicero and the defining of the *ius civile*', in G. Clark and T. Rajak, eds, *Philosophy and Power in the Graeco-Roman World*. Oxford. 51–68.

Harries, J. (2006), *Cicero and the Jurists: From citizens' law to the lawful state*. London.

Honoré, T. (2010), *Justinian's Digest: Character and compilation*. Oxford.

Howley, J. A. (2013), 'Why read the jurists? Aulus Gellius on reading across disciplines', in P. J. du Plessis, ed., *New Frontiers: Law and society in the Roman world*. Edinburgh. 9–30.

Kaster, R. (1998), 'Becoming "CICERO"', in P. Knox and C. Foss, eds, *Style and Tradition: Studies in honor of Wendell Clausen*. Stuttgart/Leipzig. 248–63.

Kennedy, G. A. (2002), 'Cicero's oratorical and rhetorical legacy', in J. M. May, ed., *Brill's Companion to Cicero. Oratory and Rhetoric*. Leiden. 481–501.

Kraus, C. S. and Woodman, A. J. (1997), *Latin Historians*. Cambridge.

La Bua, G. (2006), 'Diritto e retorica: Cicerone *iure peritus* in Seneca e Quintiliano', *Ciceroniana* 12: 181–203.

Lenel, O. (1927), *Das Edictuum Perpetuum*. Leipzig.

MacCormack, S. (2014), 'Cicero in late antiquity', in C. Steel, ed., *The Cambridge Companion to Cicero*. Cambridge. 251–305.

Mantovani, D. (2007), 'I giuristi, il retore e le api. *Ius controversum* e *natura* della *Declamatio maior* XIII', in D. Mantovani and A. Schiavone, eds, *Testi e problemi del giusnaturalismo romano*. Pavia. 323–85.

Nelson, H. L. W. (1981), *Überlieferung, Aufbau und Stil von Gai* Institutiones. Leiden.

Nörr, D. (1976), 'Pomponius oder "zum Geschichtsverständnis der römischen Juristen"', *Aufstieg und Niedergang der Römischen Welt II* 15: 497–604.

Nörr, D. (1977), 'Cicero als Quelle und Autorität bei den römischen Juristen', in F. Baur, K. Larenz and F. Wieacker, eds, *Beiträge zur europäischen Rechtsgeschichte und zum geltenden Zivilrecht: Festgabe für Johannes Sontis*. Munich. 33–52.

Nörr, D. (1978), 'Cicero-zitate bei den klassischen Juristen', *Ciceroniana: atti del III colloquium tullianum*. pp. 111–50.

Reinhardt, T. (2003), *Cicero's* Topica. *Edited with an introduction, translation, and commentary.* Oxford.

Russell, D. A. (2001). *The Orator's Education: Quintilian.* Loeb Classical Library. Cambridge, MA.

Shackleton Bailey, D. R. (2001), *Cicero's Letters to Friends,* 1–113. Edited and translated. Cambridge, MA.

Tellegen-Couperus, E. O. (1991), 'C. Aquilius Gallus dans le discours *Pro Caecina* de Cicéron', *Tijdschrift voor Rechtsgeschiedenis* 59: 37–46.

Whitton, C. (2013), *Pliny the Younger: 'Epistles', Book II.* Cambridge.

Wibier, M. H. (2014), 'Transmitting legal knowledge: From question-and-answer format to handbook in Gaius' Institutes', in R. Scodel, ed., *Between Orality and Literacy: Communication and adaptation in antiquity.* Leiden. 356–74.

Winterbottom, M. (1974), *Seneca the Elder:* Controversiae *and* Suasoriae. Cambridge, MA.

Winterbottom, M. (1982), 'Cicero and the Silver Age', in W. Ludwig, ed., *Eloquence et Rhétorique chez Cicéron. Entretriens sur l'Antiquité Classique* 28. Vandœuvres-Geneva. 237–74.

Chapter 8

Servius, Cicero and the Res Publica *of Justinian*

Jill Harries

1. INTRODUCTION

In 45 BC, Servius Sulpicius Rufus and Cicero exchanged letters containing reflections on the recent death of Cicero's daughter Tullia. This tragic event was assimilated by both to what they saw as the 'death' of the *res publica*, defined loosely by both as the constitutional order that had underpinned their own success and prestige, and that now, thanks to the victory of Caesar, was no more. However, both also resorted to survival strategies: a continued involvement, somehow, in the affairs of the *res publica*; and the fulfilment of obligations to the interests of clients and friends.[1]

Although the emotions that prompted the exchange were heart-felt (at least on Cicero's side), the pair of letters was also a jointly created literary artefact. Both writers were masters of rhetoric (despite Cicero's allegations to the contrary with regard to Servius in the *Pro Murena*) and their arguments add up to a joint exercise in self-representation as the chief mourners for a defunct *res publica*. As an analysis of what was meant by *res publica*, the letters leave much to be desired in that they may reflect Servius' more limited political and philosophical outlook; Cicero, even when profoundly afflicted by grief, could do better, as is evidenced in the *Tusculan Disputations*, also a response to Tullia's death.[2] In other words, Cicero, as so often, adapted himself to his correspondent.

Cicero's and Servius' concern with helping friends would provide a means to enable the elite under the Empire to survive and prosper as manipulators of networks of power. Among them, Servius' intellectual successors, the Roman jurists, also prospered; his career, and the subsequent perspectives on it, illustrated here through brief analyses of the presence of Servius in Celsus and Pomponius, illustrate how easily the *iuris periti* could adapt to a new constitutional order, by representing it as a continuation of the old. The 'procuratorial' attitude to the role of the *populus* in the *res publica* in

---

[1] For Cicero's overall definition of *res publica*, see Schofield 1995.

[2] *Tusc.* 4.1.1 for laws as directors of *res publica*; for death of Tullia; *Att.* 12.28.2; full discussion and other references at Hammer 2014: 79–87. On the *Tusculan Disputations* as a response to Caesar's victory, with an emphasis on history and education, see Gildenhard 2007.

their exchange is more problematic. The 'fall of the Republic' can be read in many ways; certainly, the ability of the *populus Romanus* to act as an effective element in constitutional governance was an early casualty of Augustus' new system. Cicero and Servius, it will be argued, justify cultural attitudes towards the *populus* that distanced the elite from the *populus* as 'partners' in the *res publica*, thus also subverting Cicero's own philosophical stance on *res publica* as *societas*.[3] This downgrading of the significance of popular participation and consent paved the way for the Augustan regime; parallels between Ciceronian and modern Russian attitudes to 'the people' suggest that these attitudes had (and have) constitutional, as well as social, implications.

2. SERVIUS AND CICERO 45 BC

In their exchange of letters in 45, Cicero and Servius allow the meaning of *res publica* to shift in line with their argument. Servius' letter of condolence mourns the passing of the *res publica* (which Tullia, fortunately for herself, did not live to see), comparing that catastrophe to the obliteration of once great Greek cities.[4] However, Servius then shifts his ground and the *res publica* is resurrected. While the *res publica* as 'constitutional' government was no more, the *res publica*, defined as the Roman civic community, still needed Cicero. Servius thus urged his friend not to seem indifferent to the current situation (*tempora rei publicae*) – or to give the impression of resenting the triumph of the opposing faction. Instead Cicero must continue to supply wise advice to the *patria* (fatherland) and life must go on.

For his part, Cicero, while appreciative of his friend's concern, had more still to say of the *res publica*, now redefined as a source of the activities and status that made life worth living for a leading politician and senator. Famous exemplary men in Roman history who had lost children, Cicero wrote, nonetheless could derive consolation from their possession of the *dignitas*, honourable status, which they could enjoy under a functional *res publica*: the benefits included help for friends, the care (*procuratio*) of the *res publica*, and activities in the law courts and the senate.

Under stress, Cicero reveals a concept of *res publica*, which emphasises the duties of friendship and services to clients over service to 'the people'. While his use of *procuratio* is consistent with his concept of the *res publica* as property owned by the *populus*[5] Cicero, as *procurator*, sees himself as the legal agent for a *populus*, which, by implication, cannot be trusted – and indeed is

---

[3] Atkins 1990; Asmis 2004; Harries 2006: 23–5, 214–15.

[4] *Fam.* 4.4. Cicero's reply is idem:. 4.5.

[5] *Rep.* 1.25.39: 'est igitur ... res publica res populi, populus autem non omnis hominum coetus quoque modo congregatus, sed coetus multitudinis iuris consensu et utilitatis communione sociatus.' Note the lack of independent agency implied by the passive *sociatus*.

not even legally competent – to look after its own affairs.[6] Moreover, his list of activities proper for a man of *dignitas* was headed, not by his obligation to act as *procurator*, but by his duty to supply 'help for friends', which would have included acting as their advocate (*patronus*) in law courts. Cicero's attitude to the *populus* was not shaped by any sense of obligation to constituents or electors. Nor did he see himself as a 'servant' of the *populus*, with any obligation to take account of the superior wisdom of the Roman people. In this discourse of power, *amicitia* and the exchange of favours between equals took precedence over the rights of the *populus* as a political, or even legal, independent agent. The *populus*, therefore (when not the audience to Cicero's comparatively rare speeches *ad populum*) are treated as passive, because incapable of operating as independent agents, and thus in need of the 'care' of his superior wisdom.

Cicero's vision of the *populus* is paradoxical and perhaps self-contradictory, in ways that cannot be explained as deriving from the contexts or genres in which they were expressed. I shall suggest below that modern constitutional theory, when applied to Cicero's analysis of Rome's early constitutional history in *Rep.* 2, accords the *populus* a crucial, albeit limited, role in early Roman state formation, which accords with the functions ascribed to a 'constituent power'. This did indeed die with the Republic, both institutionally and conceptually. But this concession was undermined by the negative attitude implied by the emphasis on *procuratio*. It will also be argued, using a modern parallel, that such cultural attitudes on the part of an elite towards a *populus* were, and are, incompatible with modern, Western ideals of democracy. Despite the well-attested liveliness of the Roman people in public contexts and the importance attached by Cicero and others to the appearance of public support, the late Republican elite, Cicero included, did not view the *populus* as a responsible agent; it was unable to handle freedom (*libertas*) responsibly and required enlightened procuratorship on the part of the elite to perform its functions effectively.

3. LEGUM AUCTORITAS AND THE CONTINUITY OF LAW

Both *res publica* and the rule of law survived the end of Republican government. Emperors would pay lip service to the *res publica* down to the time of Justinian. Justinian's sponsorship of the *Corpus Iuris Civilis* project between 529 and 534 made a direct connection between the *res publica* and the law and was a positive statement on the part of the autocrat that the rule of law was important. Nothing, he claimed, was more deserving of close attention (*studiosum*) than the 'authority of the laws' (*legum auctoritas*), supported by centuries

---

[6] See also Scipio's comment at idem: 1.22.35, that the *procuratio* and *administratio* of the *res publica* are duties inherited by himself (and by implication other eminent public men), and not dependent on popular consent.

of tradition going back to the foundation of the Roman state by Romulus. Nor was this an isolated nod in the direction of ancient history. Elsewhere Justinian justified his reinvention of the praetor in Republican terms; the praetor, he reminded his Byzantine Roman readers, was among the senior magistrates sent out to the provinces, to handle both arms and the laws.[7] Justinian's contemporaries also used the Republic as a reference point for the rise (and fall) of the Roman Empire, and not always favourably. As Marion Kruse put it, *apropos* Justinian's discontinuation of the consulship after 541, 'Jordanes (the historian) heightens the tension inherent in the term *respublica* because the consulship was, for any late antique authors, including Justinian, the defining office of the Republic and its most important survival'.[8]

Jordanes would have agreed with modern late Roman historians, who have assumed that, by the time of the promulgation of Justinian's Digest in 533 AD, the term *res publica* was no more than an empty signifier. The turning point, moderns argue, came in the third century AD, as emperors scrapped the use of Republican magistracies and titles on inscriptions, and the senate was increasingly ignored both as a source of provincial administrators and as a body that had hitherto conveyed both advice, authority and legitimacy.[9] By the early fourth century, this notional Republic had finally given way to a divinely sponsored and unaccountable autocracy. On this view, Justinian's focus on the authority and continuity of law (which echoes the language of a *novella* of Anthemius more than half a century earlier) and the importance of Rome's rise under the Republic is mere antiquarian rhetoric.

The same could also apply to assertions on the part of emperors that they were subject to the rule of law. Claudian, the panegyricist of the emperor Honorius early in the fifth century, provides a representative sample, which could have been guaranteed some impact as it was delivered in public:[10]

> if you ordain or decree any measure to be enacted for the common good, be the first to submit yourself to your own orders; for thus the people are more obser-vant of justice nor do they refuse submission when they see the lawmaker himself obedient to his own law.

Obedience to law, Claudian insisted, was reinforced by respect for the Roman senate, ancient custom and enlightened legal reform. While the rhetoric would have targeted a Roman audience, which could claim more continuity than most with the Republican past, this was a sustained use of loaded terms – 'the people', justice, the obedience of the lawmaker to the laws, respect for the senate and custom, appropriate change – which Cicero himself would have been proud to own.

---

[7] *Novella* 24 pr. For an alternative view, see Kaldellis 2005.
[8] Kruse 2015: 243.
[9] Weisweiler 2015: 19–26.
[10] Claud. *IV cons Hon.* 296–9, 504–7.

Such rhetoric, however conditioned by official conventions, had a prominence in imperial pronouncements and ceremonial that could not be lightly discounted. Sustaining a visible connection between the late antique present and the Republican past was part of a complex strategy of asserting imperial legitimacy by accepting constitutional constraints, which were themselves validated by reference to tradition and history. This process, however, originated not with Constantine but with Augustus, whose adoption of the *tribunicia potestas* in 23 BC gave him permanent curatorship of the interests of the *populus*, relieving them of all constitutional responsibility for their affairs. Under the Principate, all emperors were content to appear 'Republican', through their continued use of Republican magisterial titles and powers, because such symbols provided a convenient mask for an evolving autocracy and a reassuring connection with a remote and idealised past; the rhetoric of continuity was designed both to reassure and to mask change.

The treatment of Servius by later, second-century lawyers demonstrates how continuity between 'Republic' and 'Empire', specifically in the legal tradition, was constructed and maintained through the simple device of failing to acknowledge that there had been a break at all. Successions of jurists through families or descent from teacher to pupil provided the illusion of continuity. So too did patronage. Like many jurists under the Empire, Servius did better with help from his friends; his adherence first to Pompey, who was probably responsible for Servius' consulship in 51, and later Caesar, who appointed Servius to the governorship of Achaea in 46, foreshadowed the elevation of other jurists to high office by emperors. This was not a matter of chance. Servius' lack of clout under the Republican system made him a prime target for the military dynasts in search of useful clients, to provide expert assistance in the creation of what was, already, a set of alternative administrative regimes. By contrast with his belated political success, Servius was a relative failure in his cultivation of eminent people as future jurists (perhaps Cicero's pejorative view of the profession was shared by others); his pupils, as listed by Pomponius, lacked independent distinction or power bases of their own.[11]

4. SERVIUS AND CELSUS

Servius, of course, cannot be held responsible for the absolutism of sixth-century Byzantium, but he would have fitted in well there. As a *iuris peritus*, Servius asked questions of law that required answers, regardless of who was in charge of the government. The adherence of successive emperors in the first and second centuries to what they claimed to be the traditional values

---

[11] D. 1.2.2.44, C. Alfenus Varus (cos. suf. 39), Aulus Ofilius, T. Caesius, Aufidius Tucca, Aufidius Namusa, Pacuvius Labeo, the father of Antistius Labeo.

of government, which included the rule of law, gave to jurisprudence significant protection from the vagaries of autocratic rule; emperors could hardly
jettison traditions of which law was an integral part. But the increased assertion of imperial control over the lawmaking process by both Hadrian, in the
codification of the Praetorian Edict (c. 130 AD), and Justinian, through the
Corpus Iuris Civilis (529–34 AD), were important stages in the consolidation of
power in the person of the emperor. Had Servius lived in the sixth century,
he could have been, perhaps, another Tribonian.

The legal tradition itself drew strength from continuity. Servius' work
could easily be connected to the thinking of those second-century AD
politicians who prospered under Trajan and Hadrian. The Servius of the
senatorial aristocrat and jurist, P. Iuventius Celsus (consul II, 129) was useful
because he was someone who could advise on what was meant by the word,
'furniture' (*supellectilis*), when used by a testator in a will.[12] For a discussion
of his options, he turned to three authorities, all more than a century old,
Antistius Labeo, praetor under Augustus, who had supplied an etymologi-
cal definition of *supellectilis*, Servius and Aelius Tubero. Eminent though he
was, Celsus went out of his way to show his respect for his predecessors:
Tubero's *auctoritas* (authority, prestige, standing) and *ratio* (legal reasoning)
were to be honoured, although Celsus nonetheless declared his preference
for Servius' view.

Cicero's exchange with Servius had mourned the deaths of both Tullia
and the *res publica*; theirs was a rhetoric of discontinuity and the collapse
of the old political and legal order. In the narrative of the imperial jurists,
there is no mention of, still less concern about, the death of Republican
libertas (a 'freedom' that could be read as applying more to the senate than
the population at large). Celsus' deference to Servius, along with Tubero
and other lawyers contemporary with Cicero, such as Aulus Cascellius,[13]
asserts continuity with a legal tradition that was first shaped by the lawyers
who rose to prominence under Cicero's *res publica*. The intellectual pedigree,
constructed by jurists' citations of each other, bridged the gap (as we see it)
between Republic and Empire, by simply – and from their standpoint rightly
– failing to acknowledge it in the first place.

But the world had changed, in some respects. Celsus, like all senators,
owed his status and his high offices to the patronage of the emperor. As a
member of the emperor's *consilium*, Celsus would collude in strengthening
the emperor's control of law, when he supervised the young lawyer from
Africa, Salvius Julianus, in his redacting of the Praetorian Edict into a fixed
form. Moreover, on at least one occasion, Celsus the lawyer strayed into
the world of patronage and *amicitia* that Cicero's exchange with Servius

---

[12] Celsus, Digest XIX at D. 33.10.7 = Lenel vol. 1 Celsus, 168, col. 153.
[13] Celsus, Digest XXV at D. 50.16.158 = Lenel vol 1, Celsus, 215, col. 160; Cascellius is other-
     wise cited only by Labeo and Iavolenus Priscus, with two indirect references in Ulpian.

had placed, for their own purposes, at the heart of what the *res publica* meant to them. With reference to Pompey's Eastern settlement in 63 BC, Celsus described the *lex Pompeia*, the constitution for Bithynia-Pontus, as a *beneficium*.[14] The terms of the discussion suggest that Celsus' copy was incomplete, and that the lawyer, who was also the emperor's man, had no scruples in categorising Pompey's charter as primarily an act of patronage rather than of law.

This provision – which is not typical of the contents of the Digest as a whole – elided the all-important distinction between the making of law as an activity based on rules and legal principles, and the discretionary (and potentially corrupt) culture of doing things for others as acts of (selective) kindness (*beneficium*). As is well known, patronage, *amicitia* and the various forms of assistance afforded by the elite to clients and friends were fundamental to how Roman society worked. Yet the omnipresence of *amicitia*, as an honourable and useful relationship between members of the elite, was also constantly subversive of the rule of law and the 'constitutionality' that both Cicero and Servius claimed to champion, not only because of the discretionary element but also because focus on obligations to individual clients obscured the need to serve the requirements of the *populus* as a whole.

Cicero will be presented below as a champion of the role of the *populus* in the *res publica*, which was essential, but restricted. First however, we should look at Servius' story as Pomponius narrated it, a story in which questions of documentary composition and survival, personal relationships (sometimes dysfunctional) and teacher–pupil succession for the most part trumped those of public service and the *status rei publicae*.

5. SERVIUS AND POMPONIUS

Justinian was far from being the first to ignore the distinction between Republic and Empire. Pomponius' *Enchiridion*, extracts from two versions of which were included in the Digest, is an attempt to preserve and promote a canon of juristic authorities. This is embedded in an account designed to establish the central importance of jurists from the very foundation of Rome (when the *leges regiae* were allegedly codified by C. Papirius) – and to create a narrative without an obvious break. To this end Pomponius, where he could, tried to establish family trees of teachers and auditors, pupils who went on to be famous jurists themselves. But he knew that, with the Republic, he faced problems of transmission and survival, not on constitutional grounds but because his heroes had lived a long time ago. Servius, on his first appearance, provided valuable evidence for predecessors:[15]

[14] D. 50.1.1.2, cited by Ulpian, *Ad Edictum* 2, referring to the *lex Pompeia* of 63 BC.
[15] D. 1.2.2.42.

Mucii auditores, fuerunt complures, sed praecipuae auctoritatis Aquilius Gallus, Balbus Lucilius, Sextus Papirius, Gaius Iuventius: ex quibus Gallum maximae auctoritatis apud populum fuisse Servius dicit.

The auditors of Mucius (Q. Mucius Scaevola Pontifex) were numerous, but of outstanding *auctoritas* were Aquilius Gallus, Balbus Lucilius, Sextus Papirius and Gaius Iuventius; of these Servius declared that Gallus had the greatest *auctoritas* among the people.

Here is Servius, not yet in his own right but as a source of an earlier stage in the evolution of a juristic dynasty constructed through teachers with authority and their pupils. What was awkward for Pomponius was that he was obliged to rely on Servius as the gatekeeper who preserved through his own writings some record of the learning of his predecessors:

Omnes tamen hi a Servio Sulpicio nominantur: alioquin per se eorum scripta non talia exstant, ut ea omnes appetant: denique nec versantur omnino scripta eorum inter manus hominum, sed Servius libros suos complevit, pro cuius scriptura ipsorum quoque memoria habetur.

All these, however, are listed by name by Servius. For their writings do not survive in such a condition on their own account that everyone can have access to them. And so their writings do not circulate at all through people's hands but Servius has incorporated them in his own books and, on account of his writings the memory of these men is also preserved.

This, then, was Servius' first claim to fame, that he had placed on record material from earlier jurists that would otherwise be either completely lost or restricted in circulation to a very few. Underlying this is a concern that is apparent elsewhere in Pomponius with the survival of texts and the accessibility of rare books, which extends also to their readability: Aelius Tubero, for example, affected an archaic style, which made his 'many books' on public and private law unattractive to the reader.[16] This Servius is an author who wrote books for other people who liked books, a type Aulus Gellius would also have appreciated.[17]

In Pomponius' account, Servius the orator, known to and appreciated by Cicero, was subverted and then destroyed by an encounter with Q. Mucius Scaevola Pontifex. Servius begins his public career as a forensic orator second only to Cicero himself (an anachronism, as Cicero's rise to fame postdates Mucius' death in 82 BC). Having enquired about a legal point on behalf of a friend, Servius is twice told the answer and fails to understand it. Q. Mucius loses his temper and declares that 'it was shameful for one who was a patrician and a nobleman and one who pleaded cases to be ignorant

---

[16]   D. 1.2.2.46, 'parum libri eius grati habentur.'
[17]   See Howley 2013.

of the law he was subjecting to discussion'.[18] Pomponius thus obliterates the narrative of Servius' consulship, while personalising his disagreements with the opinions of Q. Mucius. Servius' choice of a legal career is prompted by his feelings of shame – at the contempt shown by Mucius – and affront to his honour, which can only be dealt with by a change of direction.

This refashioning of Servius is anomalous. Resentment about an insult is an unusual launch pad for a legal career. Moreover, having begun with Servius as the guardian of the memory of earlier jurists, Pomponius offers a Servius who, far from being the dutiful successor to a great man, as was usually the case, in fact breaks with him. Brought up in a Rome divided between two principal dynasties (or schools) of lawyers, whose intellectual pedigree he traced back to Ateius Capito and Antistius Labeo, Pomponius venerated the role of *praeceptores* and their auditors as providing continuity through the generations. This should have been the case with Servius as well. One pupil of Mucius, Balbus Lucilius, taught Servius the basics of law, before Servius moved to advanced study with another Mucian auditor, C. Aquilius Gallus, already in the 80s an established *iudex* and *arbiter*. An explanation of this legal–dynastic malfunction was therefore required. Pomponius knew that Servius had disagreed with Q. Mucius on a wide range of matters, including in works provocatively entitled the *Reprehensa Scaevolae Capita*,[19] and the *De Sacris Detestandis* (*The Swearing Away of the Sacra*).[20] However, he did not appear to know why and made no direct reference to the offending texts (although their citation by Gellius shows that they were still available to Romans in the second century). Thus the anecdote did not merely substitute for admitting the intellectual divergence between the two; it also served as a cover-up.

Upon Servius' death 'on embassy' (*in legatione*), Pomponius returns him to the world of Cicero – or nearly. In *Philippic* 9, Cicero had commemorated Servius' service to the *res publica* and his death on embassy to Antonius encamped in northern Italy in February 43, an embassy Cicero had in fact opposed. Pomponius, however, had nothing to say on the involvement of Cicero, the objective of the embassy, or its fraught political context. What mattered was the statue voted on by the *populus* (not the senate, who had voted on Cicero's motion to that effect). It had been placed before the Rostra, 'and today it survives still before the Rostra of Augustus'.[21] The shifts in emphasis may be accidental but they are significant. Servius receives his statue from 'the people', not the senate, Cicero is not mentioned at all, and the location is defined in relation to an imperial monument.

---

[18] D. 1.2.2.43, 'namque eum dixisse turpe esse patricio et nobii et causas oranti ius in quo versaretur ignorare.'

[19] D. 17.2.30; 33.9.3.6; 50.16.25.1; Gaius, *Inst.* 3.149; Gell. *NA* 4.1.17–20.

[20] Gell. *NA* 7.12.1.

[21] D. 1.2.2.43, 'hic cum in legatione perisset, statuam ei populus Romanus pro rostris posuit, et hodieque exstat pro rostris Augusti.'

Pomponius' narrative about Servius concludes with an account of the 180 books ascribed to him. However, he makes one more appearance in a context that illustrates Pomponius' deliberate downgrading of political, in favour of juristic, family identity and status.[22] C. Cassius Longinus, namesake and relative to Caesar's assassin, was *consul suffectus* in 30, and the patron of Masurius Sabinus; for Pliny, he was the mainstay of the Cassian school, which was based in his Roman residence, where, as Tacitus observed, the funeral masks of Brutus and Cassius the tyrannicide were also to be found.[23] None of this family history mattered to the historian of jurisprudence:

> Huic (Sabino) successit Gaius Cassius Longinus natus ex filia Tuberonis, quae fuit neptis Servii Sulpicii: et ideo proavum Servium Sulpicium appellat.

> To him succeeded C. Cassius Longinus, the son of Tubero's daughter, who was also the granddaughter of Servius Sulpicius; and so he called Servius Sulpicius his great-grandfather.

Not only, then, was this Cassius a member of a juristic dynasty, relating him to Servius and Tubero, with no connection to the assassin Cassius – he was also prepared to boast about it.

Pomponius' Servius is a product of the second century AD. Servius' intellectual pedigree, the information he provides on earlier jurists and specifically his contradictions of Q. Mucius, are laid out, and Servius' alleged change of direction, from orator to jurist is accounted for by his *contretemps* with Mucius, the teacher of his teachers. In due course, he becomes the author of numerous books, the teacher of several famous jurists, the diligent state servant, who dies on embassy, and the recipient of a statue. His more obviously 'Republican' aspects are airbrushed from the portrait, including his offices; his relationships with Caesar, Pompey and, crucially, Cicero; and the context of the *legatio*, the senate's abortive negotiation with Antony. Even the location of the statue is defined by its relationship to the Rostra of Augustus, making it in effect an adjunct to the new imperial order. The exclusion of material reminiscent of the old Republic is not fortuitous. For Pomponius, there was no 'old' Republic – only lawyers and their pedigrees, familial or educational, who transcended both the centuries and the vagaries of constitutional change.

6. *RES PUBLICA* AND MODERN CONSTITUTIONALISM

While we cannot know if Pomponius' reworking of history is his own or that of his now lost sources, the effect of his account was to construct a legal continuum that existed independently of political, social or constitutional

[22] D. 1.2.2.51.
[23] Tac. *Ann.* 16.7–9.

context. This allowed the authority of law, as defined by juristic *interpretatio*, to be asserted as an entity that could not be influenced or affected by external factors, such as changes in systems of government from monarchy to collective rule and back again to the imperial autocracy. This fed, in due course, into Justinian's affirmation of law's continuity over the 1,400 years of the Roman *res publica* down to his own day, and into the repeated insistence by panegyrical and other sources on the importance of the rule of law, and the emperor's subjection to it.

Although the *ius civile* as codified by Justinian cannot be described as a constitution in any modern sense, the legitimation both of law and of power rested on related foundations. Rome, of course, had no written constitution, and in that respect differed from the societies usually studied by modern constitutionalists, where 'modern constitutions invariably come into existence as the consequence of some founding act'.[24] However, the issue of how a constitutional order is created and subsequently sustained bears directly on both the Roman *res publica* and later states.

The 'paradox' of constitutionalism has been defined by Loughlin and Walker as a tension between two imperatives: one that governmental power must ultimately be generated by the consent of 'the people', and a second, that 'such power must be divided, constrained and exercised through distinctive institutional forms'. The paradox is that 'people' and 'constitution' can be constructed and shaped by each other, thus rendering the relationship unstable:

> The formal constitution that establishes unconditional authority, therefore, must always remain conditional. The legal norm remains subject to the political exception, which is the expression of the constituent power of the people to make, and therefore also to break, the constituent power of a state.

For moderns, the 'constituent power' must be 'the people' for a constitution to be legitimate, although some flexibility is accorded to what 'the people' might consist of in any given situation. Moreover, although (on the American model) it is possible to identify the moment when a constitution comes into being, the creation of a constitutional order can also be a process of unspecified duration. When these theories are applied to Cicero's thinking on the *res publica*, for which he claimed the status of *procurator*, it appears that he did indeed construct 'the people' as the constituent power, albeit with limits as to its role, and that he had a clear idea of who, in philosophical terms, 'the people' were. Moreover, he saw the formation of the Roman constitution as a process, extending over centuries.

The *res publica*, Cicero's Scipio Africanus argued, was owned by the *populus*, and the *populus* was defined, not as a haphazard collection of

---

[24] Loughlin and Walker 2007: 3.

individuals but as an assemblage of a large population (*coetus multitudinis*) 'brought together in a partnership' (*sociatus*) by legal consent and mutual self-interest (*iuris consensu et utilitatis communione*). Although Cicero appears to ascribe agency to 'the people', for whom it is part of the law of nature that they wish to live in communities, the use of the passive *sociatus* is ambiguous; there is no space to acknowledge that those who constitute the *coetus* must choose to make the partnership contract with each other as individuals. Instead a partnership is created for the *coetus* as a collective 'brought together' by two further abstracts, legal consent and common interest. This use of language may not be fortuitous; reducing 'the people' to a philosophical abstract endowed with a collective identity, constructed by a legal concept, *societas*, downgrades the importance of individual agency in state formation.

Next, Scipio's *coetus* constructs its dwellings on a fortified site, calls it a town or city and builds shrines and meeting places. Only then does a 'constitution' take shape:[25]

> Omnis ergo populus, qui est talis coetus multitudinis, qualem exposui, omnis civitas, quae est constitutio populi, omnis res publica, quae, ut dixi, populi res est, consilio quodam regenda est, ut diuturna sit. Id autem consilium primum semper ad eam causam referendum est quae causa genuit civitatem.

> Every people, therefore, which is the assemblage of a large population, as I have described, every citizen community, which is the constituted state of the people, and every *res publica*, which, as I said, is the entity owned by the people must be governed by some kind of guiding power, so that it may endure. And this guiding power must always first be attributed to the same root cause that generated the citizen community.

Although Cicero uses no single word for 'constitution', the formation of the *consilium*, involving the *coetus*, the *civitas* and the *populus* marks the moment at which a constitution, notionally, comes into being. At this point, the choice is made (we are not told how) between the three primary types of government: monarchy, aristocracy or democracy. Any of these, Scipio says, is viable, provided that the ties (*vinculum*), which first bound men together in the partnership of the *res publica*, hold firm.[26] All three forms of government, therefore, still depend on the continuation of the partnership formed for (but not so clearly by) 'the people'; this, in its turn, is based on legal consent and the common good.

As 'owners', on the strength of the partnership established among themselves, Cicero's *populus* was the prime source of legitimacy for all forms of government and constitutions. However, the power to act, in practice

---

[25] *Rep.* 1.26.41.

[26] Idem: 1.26.42, 'si teneat illud vinculum, quod primum homines inter se rei publicae societate devinxit.'

ascribed to the *populus*, is left undefined. The result is a paradox. In line with modern constitutional theory, Cicero concedes to the *populus* its status as the constituent power with an ongoing watching brief on its governance (including, in theory, the option of majoritarian democracy). At the same time, Cicero is either vague or restrictive on how in practice that power was or should be exercised.

His narrative of the founding of a real constitution, that of the Roman *res publica*, also ascribed to Scipio, further clarifies the rights of the *populus* as beneficial 'owner' of the *res publica*. It also suggests that what we now see as 'constituent power' may be ascribed to more than one authority, requiring a differentiation between the role of 'constituent power' or 'powers' in the creation and legitimisation of the constitution, and the ability of the 'constituent power' to break the power of the state as 'constituted', by withdrawing consent or by disrupting or changing the institutions it has initially authorised.

In his preliminary remarks, Scipio invokes the authority of Cato the Elder in explicitly rejecting the creation of the Roman constitution as the work of a moment or of one individual.[27] Unlike Greek lawgivers, he said, such as Minos in Crete, Lykourgos in Sparta and, in Athens, Theseus, Draco, Solon and Cleisthenes, the Roman *res publica* was not the creation of one mind but of many. The *res publica* had a founder, Romulus, responsible for the choice of site (much space is devoted to the advisability of not being by the sea), the union with the Sabines, and the creation of the advisory senate. He also instituted the taking of the auspices, a practice conducive to the security (*salus*) of the *res publica*, and the founding of the College of the Augurs, 'which was the foundation (*principium*) of our *res publica*'.[28]

Because so much of Rome's early history was the stuff of legend, Cicero had some leeway in handling the tradition. The choice, therefore, to foreground, as he did, the importance of popular consent and ratification, is significant. From the death of Romulus onwards, the *populus* asked and were granted by the senate a decisive voice, both in the continuation of the monarchy and the appointment of successive kings.[29] In response to the people's insistence on a new king, the senate appointed an *interrex*, and, after a search, 'the people', on the advice of the senate, chose Numa Pompilius, credited with the establishment of Rome's religious institutions.[30] On Numa's death, the *Comitia Curiata*, presided over by the *interrex*, chose Tullus Hostilius, whose prompt response was a request to the *Comitia* directly for ratification of his position:[31]

[27] Idem: 2.1.2 although later (2.11.21) he credits Romulus with the formation of a fully-grown *populus*.
[28] Idem: 2.9.16.
[29] Idem: 2.12.23–13.25.
[30] Idem: 2.13.25, 'patribus auctoribus sibi ipse populus adscivit.'
[31] Idem: 2.17.32.

> Et ut advertatis animum, quam sapienter iam reges hoc nostri viderint, tribuenda
> quaedam esse populo . . . ne insignibus quidem regiis Tullus nisi iussu populi est
> ausus uti.

His successor, Ancus Martius, maternal grandson of Numa, was chosen by 'the people', and the choice was confirmed by a curiate law.[32] When he too died, the fifth king, Lucius Tarquinius Priscus, was elected unanimously and he too passed a law *de suo imperio*.[33] Thus the pattern was established of a double popular vote, first making the choice and then, once the nominee had consented, confirming it with a *lex de imperio*.

Despite Cicero's insistence on popular consent, however, his treatment of the *populus* falls short of crediting them with creating the institutions of the *res publica*. The *populus* therefore were the 'constituent power', in the sense that they chose, and by their choice gave delegated authority to, those who would proceed to create over time the institutions of the *res publica* using their own judgement. The architects of the reforms that 'constituted' the *res publica* were the kings, and the *populus*, having chosen the king, had no further direct say. Instead, Romulus was responsible for the city, the senate and the auspices; Numa, the various priesthoods, including the Salii and Vestal Virgins and the necessary rituals, making them onerous but not expensive; and Tullus Hostilius the meeting places for senate and people, and the *ius fetiale*, the binding rules, governing the declaration of war. Ancus Martius made no reforms but expanded the city and Tarquinius Priscus expanded the senate, and reformed the cavalry.

Could the *populus* be credited with the ability to act as the constituent power, given their largely passive role? With the accession of the sixth king, Servius Tullius, the tension between the *populus* as the 'owner' of the *res publica* and thus of the ruler, and the role of the ruler himself as the author of constitutional reform, became more apparent. 'Laelius' observed that Servius Tullius 'had the best insight of all into what the public interest required'.[34] Yet his legitimacy was open to challenge. As Scipio confirmed, Tullius was traditionally believed to be the first to have reigned 'without the order from the people' (*iniussu populi*). Indeed, as the monarchy entered its phase of degeneration Tullius engaged in a cover-up, by taking over following Tarquinius' murder and ruling in his name, concealing his predecessor's death until his own position was secure. He did not consult the senate either, but, after Tarquinius' funeral, took his request for power to the people and, after receiving their endorsement, authorised the usual curiate law. His main reform, so admired by 'Laelius', would have gone down less well with the majority of the *populus*; the creation ascribed to him of the *Comitia*

---

[32] Idem: 2.18.33, 'a populo est Ancus Martius constitutus.'
[33] Idem: 2.20.35, 'cunctis populi suffragiis rex est creatus L. Tarquinius.'
[34] Idem: 2.21.37, 'qui mihi videtur in re publica vidisse plurimum.'

Centuriata concentrated voting power in the hands of the elite. The pretext of universal suffrage was maintained, while 'the greatest voting power lay with those in whose interest it most was that the welfare of the *civitas* was maintained'.[35]

Cicero's view of the role of the *populus* was conditioned by the Roman understanding of the nature of different kinds of power. *Potestas*, also used of the power of fathers over households, lay with the magistrates; *auctoritas* lay with the senate; and *libertas* with the *populus*;[36] and unless they were properly distributed, the *status rei publicae* would be destabilised. But although they had the 'freedom' to own, their role in the state in Cicero's day was limited to that of responding to prompts from the elite concerning legislation, voting in elections; in those held by the *Comitia Centuriata*, the upper classes were privileged, a state of affairs justified by 'Scipio', on the grounds that a principle in constitutional governance (*in re publica*), which should always be upheld was that 'the greatest number should never hold the greatest power'.[37] This passive or reactive role is echoed in Cicero's terminology with reference to the behaviour of the *populus* in the early centuries of the Republic, when, although the people were 'free', the government lay with the *auctoritas* of the senate;[38] reforms were brought about by the senate, while the people acquiesced, *populo cedente* or *populo patiente atque parente*.[39]

Thus far, this line of thought, which favoured aristocratic governance but gave a protected, albeit passive constitutional role to the *populus*, along with such legal rights as that of *provocatio* (appeal), is what we would expect of Cicero, even as mediated through the figure of Scipio Aemilianus. But in consigning the *populus* to a passive constitutional role, both in the evolution and the preservation of the *res publica*, while also, in the letter to Servius, assigning to himself and to fellow members of the elite the powers of acting as *procurator*, on behalf of the *populus* as owner of the *res publica*, Cicero effectively nullified the ability of the *populus* to take action on its own initiative to protect its interests.

7. CULTURES OF POWER: MODERN RUSSIA

Cicero's representation of 'the people' as being occasionally active and assertive, not always in their own best interests, but otherwise passive recipients

---

[35] Idem: 2. 22.40, 'et is valebat in suffragio plurimum, cuius plurimum intererat esse in optimo statu civitatem.'

[36] Idem: 2.33.58, 'ut et potestatis satis in magistratibus, et auctoritatis in principum consilio, et libertatis in populo sit'; on *libertas*, as, among other things the freedom to 'own' in Cicero's public sense of 'owning' the *res publica*, see Hammer 2014: 52–8.

[37] *Rep.* 2.22.39, 'ne plurimum valeant plurimi.'

[38] Idem: 2.32.56; cf. 2.31.55, 'modica libertate populo data', so that the *auctoritas* of the *principes* could be strengthened.

[39] See Idem: 2.32.56; 35.60; 36.61.

of enlightened leadership by the elite was a cultural, as much as a constitutional, phenomenon. As Michael Urban's study of elite political discourse in post-communist Russia maintains, 'Cultures of power express themselves as discursive strategies, rooted in group habitus, by means of which actors on the field of politics stake out positions yielding access to desired things'.[40] Cicero (and Servius) would doubtless have been appalled to be accused of framing arguments about *clientelae*, public service or constitutional theory with a view to enhancing their own status. Nonetheless, Cicero's (and Scipio's) philosophical position both explains and validates Cicero's political preference for the exercise of *auctoritas* by an enlightened elite. Nor was this a deliberate or conscious tailoring of theory to practice. As Urban puts it, 'Rather than a collection of beliefs and values held by individuals, that are thought to cause some effect in behaviour, culture appears here as meaning integral to, or coextensive with, that behaviour itself'.[41]

While the parallels with modern Russia should not be pushed too far, the overlaps with Ciceronian attitudes towards 'the people' are striking. The power of the Russian elite, though different in composition from that of Rome, was based, as it was in Rome, on networks of power and personal relationships, designated favourably as 'teams' or, unfavourably, as 'clans', a linguistic distinction reminiscent of the Romans' designation of opposing groups as 'factions'. Urban's interviews with a selection of men and women involved in government from the late 1980s to the present identified four distinctive perceptions of the Russian people; 'as inert; as in need; as degraded; and as easily manipulated'.[42] The first perception, partly grounded in tradition, was of the people as either 'vegetables' or 'god-bearers' or both, who were liable to act on the basis of irrational impulses. The second was expressed, as a minority view, positively in terms of ability to provide practical help to constituents; more often respondents expressed an abstract dedication to popular welfare, which did not, at least in the speakers' view, entail helping individuals, reminiscent of Cicero's often generalised rhetoric on public service, as contrasted with his active efforts on behalf of clients. The third element, degradation, blamed the 'vegetable' state of the people on wider corrupt practices on the part of the elite, not least the introduction of mass capitalism; Roman moralists, such as Sallust, might have spotted parallels with the corrosive effect of the riches of empire on social mores. The fourth, which criticised the people as too easily fooled by populist rhetoric, resulting in their preferring the 'bad' leader Yeltsin to the 'good' leader Gorbachev, has a long classical pedigree in the denigration of orators as deceivers (and Cicero's own boasts, as over his defence of Cluentius in 66, of how he pulled the wool over the eyes of credulous judges).

[40] Urban 2001: 4–5.
[41] At 5.
[42] Idem: 78–87.

Of these, the first two are the most significant to Cicero's cultural perspective. As we have seen, Cicero's 'people', having asserted itself positively with its choice of the first five kings, gradually slipped into more passive mode. While retaining the constitutional power to 'concede' or 'allow', the People of the early Republic wisely submitted itself for the most part to the *auctoritas* of the senate. However, as Hammer pointed out, the partnership (*societas*) that constituted the *res publica* was also a matter for negotiation, and if the balance of powers was uneven, or the people acquired a taste for too much 'freedom', such negotiations could undermine the stability of the entire *res publica*:

> grant a measure of freedom to the People, as did Lycurgus and Romulus, you will not grant them a sufficiency of liberty but will whet their appetites for more, when you give them no more than a mere taste of it.[43]

Indeed, 'Scipio' argued, as history had shown, a people with too much freedom had no idea how to use it, indulged in all kinds of excesses and ended up under the rule of a tyrant.

Cicero's 'people', therefore, although entitled to be 'granted' legal rights and freedom, was best off, when it acquiesced in the *auctoritas* of the enlightened elite. But obligations were reciprocal. On Urban's second category, the people as in need, Cicero agreed that, as individuals, they were entitled to protection and the elite were expected to provide it: under the early Republic, before inequalities of wealth had taken hold, 'the virtuous conduct of each in public life was the more welcome, because in their private dealings, they made every effort to assist individual citizens with practical assistance, advice and material support'.[44] However, as a constitutional entity, a member of the *populus* as a voter in elections or on legislation was not susceptible to 'assistance'. However, he could be, and was, manipulated (Urban category 4) by (alleged) bribery, rhetoric in the *contio*,[45] and as a member of a jury in public trials. Cicero praised 'the people' to their faces, as in his speech for Pompey's command in 66, or his rejection of the agrarian bill in 63, by posing as a true *popularis*; it was a tribute to his skill as a speaker that he could also, as he did Rullus in 63, persuade them to vote against their own interests. Here, unlike in the Russian example, which ascribed the deceit to others, it was the manipulator himself who boasted of his power to hoodwink the unwary.

---

[43] *Rep.* 2.28, 50.
[44] Idem: 2.34.59.
[45] Mouritsen 2001: 38–62.

8. CONCLUSION

The formulation, study and interpretation of Roman law was an elite pre-
rogative; its practitioners required the leisure that came with wealth, and
access to power networks, which could both use and disseminate their
work. Lawyers, therefore, had employment and status, whatever Rome's
system of government, provided the preserves and privileges of their sector
of the elite were safeguarded. It followed that, along with the jurists, the
continued survival of a *res publica*, which originated with *iuris consensus*, was
also guaranteed, not as a specific constitutional entity, but as a civic community governed by law. Pomponius' and Celsus' assertion of continuity,
therefore, may not have been as tendentious as appears at first sight. They
asserted the continuity of law (and Servius' place within that continuum),
because that was genuinely the case. Justinian, several centuries later, would
do the same.

Nor was jurisprudence the only elite occupation to be relatively unaf-
fected by constitutional change. Cicero's focus in his letter to Servius on
helping his friends as a bereavement strategy would also be continued by
the elites under the Empire; patronage, friendship, the cultivation of clients
were the bedrock of aristocratic power down to the Fall of Rome in the
fifth century. All this rendered the *populus* dispensable. Cicero's notion (as
expressed by 'Scipio') of the enlightened aristocrat, empowered to act as a
procurator for a *populus* bound into the contractual partnership of the *res
publica*, denied to the *populus* the right or indeed the legal capacity to act
for itself. Whatever may be thought of Roman 'democracy', the cultural
assumptions of Cicero, the self-proclaimed *procurator* of the people, show
that he was no democrat; for him the *populus* must always be legally dependent on those who knew better.

Cicero's historical construction of the role of the *populus* in the evolution
of the Roman constitution therefore contained a paradox. On the one hand,
the people had ultimate authority, especially under the early kings, as the
'constituent power' that chose the kings, who then, under power effectively
delegated by the people, established the institutions of the *res publica*. On the
other, as their role became more passive, the *populus* was 'granted' freedom
and rights, or ceded reforms, through a process of largely passive consent.
This version of history was not intended as the tendentious self-justification
of elite values, but reflected the interaction, or confluence, of Cicero's elite
culture with the actions and behaviour that had characterised his entire
political career.

Such attitudes had constitutional consequences in that it rendered more
acceptable a *res publica* without the *populus*. Perceptions on the part of
members of the modern Russian political elite of their *populus* as inert and
irresponsible, requiring assistance but vulnerable to manipulation, provide
an instructive echo of Cicero's perspectives. Without seeking to make judge-

ments on the present state of Russian 'democracy', an elite, be it Roman or any other, which, as a collective, has access to power and wealth, without the requirement to seek endorsement from the wider population,[46] and which also expresses cultural attitudes that are dismissive or contemptuous of the ability of the *populus* to make rational decisions for itself, is unlikely to go out of its way to safeguard the people's constitutional prerogatives. In 45 Cicero and Servius condemned Caesar's autocracy, yet both, in their different ways, would contribute to its perpetuation.

BIBLIOGRAPHY

Asmis, E. (2004), 'The state as partnership: Cicero's definition of *Res Publica* in his work On the State', *History of Political Thought* 25: 569–99.

Atkins, E. M. (1990), '*Domina et regina virtutum*: justice and *societas* in *De Officiis*', *Phronesis* 35: 258–89.

Gildenhard, I. (2007), Paideia Romana: *Cicero's Tusculan disputations*. Cambridge.

Hammer, D. (2014), *Roman Political Thought from Cicero to Augustine*. Cambridge.

Harries, J. (2006), *Cicero and the Jurists: From citizens' law to the lawful state*. London.

Howley, J. A. (2013), 'Why read the jurists? Aulus Gellius on reading across disciplines', in P. J. du Plessis, ed., *New Frontiers: Law and society in the Roman world*. Edinburgh. 9–30.

Kaldellis, A. (2015), *The Byzantine Republic: People and power in New Rome*. Cambridge, MA.

Kruse, M. (2015), 'A Justinianic debate across genres on the state of the Roman republic', in G. Greatrex and H. Elton, eds, *Shifting Genres in Late Antiquity*. Ashgate. 233–45.

Lenel, O. (1889), *Palingenesia iuris civilis*, 2 volumes. Berlin.

Loughlin, M. and Walker, N., eds (2007), *The Paradox of Constitutionalism*. Oxford.

Mouritsen H. (2001), *Plebs and Politics in the Late Roman Republic*. Cambridge.

Schofield, M. (1995), 'Cicero's definition of *res publica*', in J. G. F. Powell, ed., *Cicero the Philosopher: Twelve papers*. Oxford. 63–83.

Urban, M. (2001), *Cultures of Power in Post-communist Russia: An analysis of elite political discourse*. Cambridge.

Weisweiler, J. (2015), 'Domesticating the senatorial elite', in J. Wienand, ed., *Contested Monarchy: Investigating the Roman Empire in the fourth century AD*. Oxford. 17–41.

---

[46] Presidents of Russia require to be elected every six years; their *consilia principis*, selected, as were those of Roman emperors, on the basis of *amicitia*, do not.

Part III

On Legal Practice

Chapter 9

Cicero and the Italians:
Expansion of Empire, Creation of Law

Saskia T. Roselaar

1. INTRODUCTION

As the Roman state expanded its territory, the peoples of Italy were gradually incorporated into the Roman framework, either as full or partial citizens or as nominally independent allies. In the third century BC a bewildering variety of legal statuses existed in close proximity within the Italian peninsula, which meant that people of different statuses were obliged to interact regularly. The Roman state endeavoured to accommodate these needs by creating new legal instruments, for example *commercium* and *conubium* – which, however, were only available to Latins, not to all Italians. The office of *praetor peregrinus* was created in 241 BC to deal with legal conflicts between Romans and Italians. Nevertheless, not all conflicts that involved people who held a different legal status could easily be resolved; new legal instruments were created throughout the Republic.

Most Italians still suffered from legal disadvantages in their dealings with Romans, for example because they did not hold *commercium*, which made it difficult to do business with Romans and to join in commercial partnership with them, or because they could not inherit from or bequeath to Romans because of their lack of *conubium*. Moreover, their possessions, especially land, were constantly under threat of confiscation by the Romans, as became clear during the Gracchan land reforms. Recourse to the *praetor peregrinus* availed the Italians very little in these situations. These legal handicaps may have been among the main reasons for the outbreak of the Social War in 91 BC: the Italians demanded, among other things, legal equality with their Roman business partners.

In the early first century BC, after the Social War, all Italians were granted Roman citizenship. However, it took a while before the Roman state was willing to grant them the full benefits of this status; it attempted to limit the voting rights of Italians by entering them in a small number of voting *tribus*, and are most unlikely to have assigned all Italians a *tribus* until the census of 70 BC.

This chapter will investigate the legal status of Italians in the second and first century BC. In theory, at least after 70 BC, Italians were equal to the old Roman citizens, in that they could avail themselves of the same legal

instruments provided by the Roman state. Nevertheless, there are indications in Cicero's work that not all Italians were considered equal by the
Romans who sat in judgement on their cases. Sometimes Cicero seems to
fight against prejudice held about Italians, making it necessary for him to
point out that Italians are perfectly capable of acting as witnesses, or arguing
that they possess the same moral qualities as Romans and should therefore
be treated equally under the law.

Furthermore, Cicero and other sources also indicate that not all Italian
communities shared exactly the same laws; communities could 'ratify'
Rome's laws to make them valid locally (the so-called *fundus fieri*), which
suggests that in administrative matters Italian communities retained their
own laws and customs. This chapter will investigate the integration of
Italy in Roman legal procedure, as well as the practical and legal prejudice
that Italians seem to have suffered in their legal affairs through the eyes of
Cicero – not only the most famous Roman lawyer in history, but also an
Italian.

2. THE LEGAL STATUS OF ITALIANS BEFORE THE SOCIAL WAR

During their conquest of Italy the Romans devised various legal instruments to regulate their relations with people who did not possess Roman
citizenship. One of the issues that needed regulation was trade: laws had to
be formulated to enable trade between people from different political entities. It is often assumed that the main instrument devised by the Romans to
regulate trade with *peregrini* – a term that included all non-citizens, including
Latin and Italian allies – was the *ius commercii*. It is usually assumed that *commercium* was a right that could be granted to non-citizens, permitting them
the use of certain legal instruments related to trade that were otherwise only
available to citizens.

I have explored elsewhere the legal status of Italians in the third and
second century BC, and especially the importance of *ius commercii* and *ius
conubii*.[1] In short, in contrast to what is believed by many scholars, I believe
that only the inhabitants of Latin colonies enjoyed these two privileges,
while other allies did not. These were aimed at maintaining the strength of
the Latin colonies, thus serving a military purpose – the most important role
that any ally served in the eyes of Rome. *Conubium*, *commercium* and the *ius
migrationis* formed clearly defined instruments of Roman hegemony, with
which it kept a close watch on the strength of its Latin colonies. The Roman
state was not eager to grant these rights to anyone else, including Italian
allies; the three rights – separately or together – could be granted as rewards

---

[1]   Roselaar 2013a; 2013b.

for loyalty to the Romans, either to individuals or to towns or peoples, but the recorded number of such grants is rather limited.[2]

Many scholars argue that trade between Romans and non-citizens was severely limited or even completely impossible when *peregrini* did not enjoy *commercium* with Romans. However, the only possible limitation on trade between Romans and *peregrini* concerned *res mancipi*, to which people without *ius commercii* were not admitted. Trade in *res nec mancipi* could always take place, and could be protected by the praetor; and even trade in *res mancipi* could be protected by the praetor if he so chose. Allies were not allowed to use the Roman *legis actiones*, but this does not mean that they could not pursue a lawsuit. If there was no available *legis actio*, the matter could be resolved by an informal oral statement of the plaintiff and defendant, to be judged by the praetor. The praetor could use an *actio in factum* ('action considering the facts') or *actio utilis* ('useful action', which could be added if the law did not quite match the facts). Where Roman law could not be applied, the praetor could protect the interests of a *peregrinus* by means of an *actio ficticia*; this ordered the judge to proceed as if something was the case, which in fact was not true.[3] Thus the praetor could treat the plaintiff as a Roman citizen when in fact he was not, through the fiction *si civis romanus esset*.[4]

Peregrini were also protected against disruption of their possessions by the possessory interdicts. The *interdictum uti possidetis* protected the person who was in actual possession, provided he had not obtained the item 'by violence, stealth, or on sufferance' (*vi, clam,* or *precario*) from the other party. Through an *interdictum utrubi*, the possession of a movable thing was declared to belong to the party who had held it the greatest part of the past year. The *interdictum unde vi* protected someone who had been driven by force from his possession. These interdicts had probably existed since the late third or early second century BC and could be granted to *peregrini* by the praetor.[5]

Legal transactions were based on *bona fides*: this was the basis of social life. If someone did not perform a task entrusted to him, he damaged the community as a whole, because he undermined the social values on which it was based.[6] Transactions depended on adherence to moral standards, 'as ought to be good conduct between good men' (*societas omnium bonorum*).[7]

---

[2] Coşkun 2009.

[3] Sotty 1977.

[4] Gai. *Inst.* 4.37. See Coşkun 2009: 49–50.

[5] Festus 260–2 L mentions Aelius Gallus (*fl.* 170–150 BC) as the oldest authority. In Ter. *Eun.* 319–20, written c. 161, refers to the *interdictum uti possidetis*; while Plaut. *Stich.* 696: *Age dice uter utrubi accumbamus* and 750: *Utrubi accumbo? – Utrubi tu vis*, seems to refer to the *interdictum utrubi*. The *interdictum unde vi* is mentioned in the *lex agraria* of 111 BC, l. 18–9. See Crawford 1996: 164; Roselaar 2010:114–6.

[6] Cic. *Rosc. Am.* 111–13; *Nat. D.* 3.74. See Harries 2013: 118.

[7] D. 17.2.1.1.

The so-called *bonae fidei iudicia* protected the consensual contracts of *emptio-venditio* (buying and selling), *locatio-conductio* (leasing and hiring), *societas* (partnership), and *mandatum* (performance of services for free). These developed gradually: the contract of *emptio-venditio* was probably the earliest and had been fully formed by c. 200 BC, *locatio-conductio* in the mid-second century, and *mandatum* by 123 BC.[8] These contracts were accessible to *peregrini*; they were simple agreements between two people and required no special status.

The praetors were the most important magistrates in the development of law: they could introduce new regulations to deal with issues that were not covered by the *ius civile*, or new instruments of law for those who could not use the *ius civile*. These new regulations were collectively called the *ius honorarium*, the body of law created by the magistrates of the Roman Republic. We may conclude that the number of people enjoying *commercium* was much smaller than is assumed by many scholars, but also that it was much less important in trade than is often thought. However, in certain situations the lack of Roman citizenship caused limitations in the possibilities for economic gain that Italians enjoyed. When trading in *res mancipi*, the legal position of an Italian partner in trade was worse than that of the Roman party, despite the possibility that the praetor would protect an Italian party. Furthermore, it was impossible for Italians to inherit from or make bequests to Romans if they did not enjoy *conubium*. This meant that they were not fully free to decide on the best possible strategy for managing their property, which could have negative effects on their financial position. Furthermore, Italians suffered from various legal and economic disadvantages, which gradually led to more and more dissatisfaction with their position *via-à-vis* the Roman state, and eventually to the outbreak of the Social War in 91 BC.

3. THE SOCIAL WAR

Many explanations have been given for the outbreak of the Social War: a universal desire for Roman citizenship; the cultural Romanisation of Italy; Italian grievances over Roman abuse, and dissatisfaction with their political, military and/or social position. Not all these explanations are equally likely; the cultural Romanisation of the Italians especially is now generally rejected.[9] In my view, it is likely that economic grievances were the most important reason for the outbreak of the Social War.[10] First, problems surrounding the distribution of *ager publicus* were among the economic

---

[8] *Mandatum* appears in *Rhet. Her.* 2.13.19. See Watson 1961; 12–13, who argues that *mandatum* became legally recognised between the time of Plautus and that of Cicero. See Fiori 1998–9.

[9] Most forcefully argued by Mouritsen 1998.

[10] I argue this in more detail in Roselaar forthcoming.

concerns of Italians in the late second century.[11] This land was in theory accessible only to Roman citizens, so that Italians had no legal right to use it. I have dealt extensively with *ager publicus* elsewhere,[12] but for now it suffices to say that many Italians had continued to work this land after it had been confiscated. When the Gracchan land commission started its work in 133, the distribution of the land worked by Italians, although legal from a Roman point of view, caused much opposition among its Italian holders. It is in the context of the debate about *ager publicus* in the 120s BC that we hear for the first time about the idea of granting citizenship to Italians; clearly the two issues were closely connected. It was suggested that the Italians would be more willing to give up their land if they received citizenship in exchange.[13] This at first sight looks rather odd: why would Italians prefer Roman citizenship, which did not have any direct economic benefits, to the possession of land, which clearly brought in large profits? However, in fact there were tangible material benefits to having citizenship.

Italians had used Roman *ager publicus* for a long time, never considering that it could be taken away from them. Suddenly these possessions became insecure; very importantly, the Italians suffered from the fact that measurements made by the land commission were done very quickly, and not always very accurately.[14] It seems that Italians suffered more than Roman citizens from incorrect measurements and that in some cases their private land was taken by the Roman state for distribution. Gaining citizenship would give the Italians some measure of protection against all this. Citizens were protected against random confiscations of their private land during land distribution schemes; rather than having to approach a Roman senator to gain redress, which in this case proved ineffective, they would have access to the Roman courts to protect their rights of ownership of privately owned land.

There were other direct economic advantages of having citizenship: for example, the Italians were still paying taxes for the upkeep and payment of the contingents they sent to the Roman army. The Romans had not paid any direct taxes since 167.[15] Furthermore, a very profitable business only open to Romans was tax-farming in the provinces and bidding for public contracts let out by the state, for example for building projects. Italians could only become involved in tax-farming and other public contacts indirectly, by entering into a partnership with a Roman, but this was not as profitable as being a *publicanus* in their own right.[16] Badian argues that very quickly after

---

[11] Nagle 1973; Kendall 2013: 142–66.

[12] Roselaar 2010.

[13] App. *B Civ.* 1.21: 'The Italians were ready to accept this, because they preferred Roman citizenship to possession of the land.' See Nagle 1973: 368; but he agrees that the supposed Italian willingness to accept citizenship in exchange for land was indeed strange.

[14] App. *B Civ.* 1.18–9.

[15] Brunt 1988: 120–1.

[16] Badian 1972: 57–8, 97; Kendall 2013: 121–2.

gaining citizenship Italians started to bid for public contracts.[17] This is difficult to corroborate, since the sources – mostly Cicero – do not record the backgrounds of the *publicani*.[18] Cicero does, however, emphasise the close bond between the *equites*, the *publicani* and the upper classes of Italian towns. When defending Plancius from Atina, he emphasised his Italian origins on the one hand, and on the other his position as a *publicanus*: 'The flower of the Roman knighthood, the ornament of our society and the backbone of our political life, is to be found among the body of tax-farmers'.[19]

Finally, cultural developments in second-century Italy were important. Many areas of Italy show great cultural sophistication, influenced by the Greek world, for example in building stone theatres and monumental temple complexes. Italy was often ahead of Rome in these developments, erecting sophisticated buildings and artworks that had not yet been introduced in Rome. Italian elites were rightly proud of these achievements, but the Romans could easily depict the Italians as backward, boorish, and uncivilised (see below). This depiction clearly did not match the image that Italians held about themselves, of sophisticated and civilised people engaged in a Mediterranean-wide cultural exchange. As Roman citizens the Italians would have greater social prestige in the eyes of existing Roman citizens. They would also be protected against random abuse from Roman magistrates, as occurred regularly in the late second century BC.[20] Velleius indicates that the Italians indeed felt that they were seen as 'foreigners and aliens' by the Romans, although they felt closely related.[21] However, even if prestige was an important consideration, the tangible benefits of having citizenship were likely to be more important.

Of course the Romans could see that their allies were unhappy; they in fact recognised the validity of the Italians' grievances. One way of showing this was to take action against magistrates who abused their powers. In 123 the *lex Acilia repetundarum* was passed on the instigation of Gaius Gracchus, which allowed for a set procedure for the prosecution of extortionate officials. This was probably available to both Italians and provincial allies. An ally who successfully prosecuted a Roman magistrate was to be granted (Roman) citizenship, or, if he preferred to keep his own citizenship, to receive *provocatio* and freedom from military service and public services (*munera*) in his hometown. Thus, the law recognised that not all allies might want to become citizens and offered *provocatio* as an alternative reward.

The *lex Acilia* was unfortunately not very effective. Most governors

---

[17] Badian 1972: 96–7. Mouritsen 1998: 92–3 does not believe many Italians wanted to become *publicani*.

[18] Brunt 1988: 126–7.

[19] Cic. *Planc.* 24.

[20] E.g. Gell. *NA* 10.3. See Dart 2014: 56–9; Roselaar forthcoming.

[21] Vell. Pat. 2.15.2, see App. *B Civ.* 1.35.

who were prosecuted were acquitted; only a few successful prosecutions are known. The only recorded cases of people receiving citizenship after a prosecution are those of L. Cossinius from Tibur, who prosecuted a Roman between 106 and 90, and another Tiburtine, T. Coponius.[22] This indicates that the law was passed, at least in part, because of the Italians' dissatisfaction with the way they were treated. However, the fact that so few people gained citizenship through a prosecution shows that the possibility of becoming a citizen by prosecuting a magistrate was quite limited – or that Italians who were successful chose *provocatio* rather than citizenship.

Around the same time, Latin allies were given the opportunity to receive citizenship through the *ius adipiscendi civitatem Romanum per magistratum*, that is, the 'right to receive Roman citizenship through holding a magistracy'.[23] Unfortunately much uncertainty exists about the contents of this right. It is assumed that this regulation allowed magistrates of Latin towns to become Roman citizens after the term of their magistracy. The *lex Acilia repetundarum* awards successful prosecutors either Roman citizenship, or, if they do not wish to become citizens, *provocatio* and *vacatio* are awarded. This option is given to '[whoever of them . . .] shall not have been [?duumvir, consul, dicta]tor, praetor or aedile'. Apparently those who exercised these offices in their hometowns had been granted *provocatio* and *vacatio* because of their service – another important indication that allies did not necessarily want to become citizens, but that their grievances were recognised by the Roman state. Most scholars argue that the *lex repetundarum* introduced the *civitas per magistratum*, or at least that it was introduced around 125,[24] although this date has been disputed.[25]

Further evidence for the existence of the *civitas per magistratum*, at least in the early first century BC, comes from Asconius: he states that Pompeius Strabo gave some towns in the Po Valley 'Latin rights, so that they would have the same rights as the other Latin colonies, namely to receive citizenship through exercising a local magistracy'.[26] If Asconius means by 'other Latin colonies, those that existed at the time, that is, before the Social War when the Latins were given citizenship, then this means that the people of these colonies had this right since before the Social War. It seems reasonable therefore that *civitas per magistratum* was introduced either by the *lex Acilia* or at some point between 122 and 87.[27] This was another way in which the Roman state tried to assuage the grievances of its allies, at least of the Latin colonists among them.

---

[22] Cic. *Balb.* 53–4.
[23] Crawford 1996: 111; Mouritsen 1998: 99–108.
[24] E.g. Brunt 1988: 97; Dart 2014: 60–1.
[25] E.g. Sherwin-White 1973: 112; Galsterer 1976: 96.
[26] Asc. 2–3C.
[27] See in more detail Roselaar forthcoming.

However, this does not necessarily mean that all Latins and allies wanted to become Roman citizens: all these problems could have been solved by other means, such as a more equal distribution of booty acquired in wars, opportunities to share in the exploitation of the provinces, and protection against random abuse and the expropriation of land by Romans. This had indeed been attempted by the *lex Acilia*, but had proven ineffective. Thus, for most Italians Roman citizenship was not a goal in itself, but a means to an end, namely the improvement of their economic situation. The Italians did not necessarily want citizenship for cultural reasons: in the late second century, many Italian towns were still proud, wealthy and important. There was no reason to assume that the Italians wanted to abandon their local citizenship and become Romans. However, eventually they saw no other choice, since they realised that other measures to protect their interest were ineffective. Legally, economically and socially their interests would best be served by becoming Roman citizens.

After the Social War the Romans still refused to share the advantages of citizenship with the Italians. Although the allies had now been given citizenship, the Romans were still not happy with the idea. In fact, various tricks were devised to prevent them from exerting any actual influence.[28] There is some debate about when and how the new citizens were finally included on the Roman census lists and assigned to a voting tribe. At first it was proposed that new citizens would be placed in a small number of newly created voting tribes,[29] but these were most probably never created. The census of 89 failed, meaning that new citizens were not enrolled into the *tribus* or the census classes, which would have allowed them to vote in the *comitia centuriata*. This was especially important for wealthier Italians, who would have joined the higher classes of the *comitia centuriata* and thus been able to make a real difference. A new census was held in 86, but the census figure for this year as reported is only 463,000, suggesting that the Italians were not registered in the tribes.[30]

This Roman reluctance to give the Italians what was theirs by right was clearly perceived as a new insult by the Italians. They showed their interest in the matter by supporting the various Roman politicians who claimed to be able to give them full citizenship rights: Marius, Sulpicius, Cinna and Sulla all tried to recruit the Italians.[31] The next recorded census was not held until 70 BC; this meant that the new citizens would not enjoy full voting rights until 70, or at least not in the *comitia centuriata*. They might have been able

---

[28] App. *B Civ.* 1.49, 53–5; Livy *Per.* 76–7; Plut. *Sull.* 8; Vell. 2.19.1, 2.20.2. See Sherwin-White 1973, 156–7.

[29] App. *B Civ.* 1.49; Vell. Pat. 2.20.2; Sisenna fr. 17 Peter (3.50 B).

[30] Cic. *Arch.* 11; Cass. Dio 37.9.3; Livy *Per.* 63, 98.3; Jer. *Chron.* 85. See Dart 2014: 103–4; Roselaar forthcoming.

[31] App. *B Civ.* 1.77–82, 93; Plut. *Sull.* 25; Strab. 5.4.11.

to vote in the *comitia tributa*, if they had indeed been assigned to a *tribus*, but for voting rights in the *comitia centuriata* their property had to be recorded in the census. At this time indeed a much larger number of citizens – 910,000 – was recorded than in 86; finally all new citizens and their property were registered. Thus, after the census of 70 BC, all Italians were full Roman citizens and thus held the same legal status as the Romans.

As we can see, the Roman state in the late second century BC was very aware of the grievances of the Italians and the importance of keeping them happy. However, the measures introduced to solve these grievances were ineffective. This was often the result of conflicts within the Roman ruling class, especially in the debate about whether the Italians should be given citizenship. Nevertheless, legal instruments were gradually created that were available to Italian allies, such as the *bonae fidei iudicia* and the interdicts. Gradually, therefore, the Italians were integrated into Roman political and legal life. However, this process was not fully complete after the Social War, and in fact continued throughout the first century BC.

4. PREJUDICE AGAINST ITALIAN ALLIES AND THE *IUS CIVILE*

The Italians in the first century BC shared the same legal status as the old Roman citizens, even if they sometimes suffered from prejudice. The ambiguous reputation of Italian towns is clear from Cicero's works: he does not hesitate to present them as the sources of all virtue, although he could also present them as backward if it suited his purposes. The most explicit example of Cicero extolling the virtues of an Italian town (his home town, Arpinum) occurs in the speech for Publius Sulla of 62 BC. He says to the defence lawyer:

'This is what I mean', says he, 'that you come from a municipal town', I confess that I do, and I add, that I come from that municipal town from which salvation to this city and empire has more than once proceeded. But I should like exceedingly to know from you, how it is that those men who come from the municipal towns appear to you to be foreigners. For no one ever made that objection to that great man, Marcus Cato the Elder, though he had many enemies, or to Tiberius Coruncanius, or to Marcus Curius, or even to that great hero of our own times, Gaius Marius, though many men envied him. In truth, I am exceedingly delighted that I am a man of such a character that, when you were anxious to find fault with me, you could still find nothing to reproach me with which did not apply also to the greater part of the citizens. And if we seem to you to be foreigners, whose name and honours have now become familiar topics of conversation and panegyric throughout the city and among all men, how greatly must those competitors of yours seem to be foreigners, who now, having been picked out of all Italy, are contending with you for honour and for every dignity! And yet take care that you do not call one of these a foreigner, lest you should be overwhelmed by the votes of the foreigners.[32]

A number of interesting observations can be made from this passage: firstly, Cicero himself was accused by the prosecution lawyer, Torquatus, of being a foreigner (*peregrinus*). In legal texts a *peregrinus* was someone who did not possess Roman citizenship, and could therefore not partake in *ius civile*. Furthermore, such a person suffered from prejudice: he was not considered a true member of Roman society, even if he lived in Rome. Cicero, on the other hand, turns the argument on its head by saying that many of the most famous men in Roman history, including some of the kings, had arrived in Rome from elsewhere; this did not mean that they were excluded from performing great deeds for the Roman state. In the eyes of city-born Romans, their Italian origins could be used to insult their character and, more importantly, as an indication of their unfitness for public office. In fact, Cicero counters, men from Arpinum have twice saved the Roman Republic: first Gaius Marius, who repelled the Cimbric invaders in 101 BC, then Cicero himself when he dealt with Catiline's conspiracy.

Furthermore, Cicero refers to more new men entering the Roman state in recent times. Cicero thinks that, if a longstanding citizen town like Arpinum already seems foreign to Torquatus, then all these new citizens must seem even more exotic. Cicero suggests that there is a kind of hierarchy among the Italian towns, with those that had citizenship for longer being seen as less foreign than those just admitted. These new citizens also formed a tangible danger for the old city-born Romans, since all these people had the right to vote and to be elected as magistrates in Rome. Thus competition for public office had increased enormously, and the power of new Italian citizens to vote threatened to swamp the power of the old Roman citizens. Therefore, Cicero warns Torquatus, he must be careful about whom he calls a foreigner – before he knows it he may lose out on public office because the 'foreigners' vote against him.

On the other hand, Cicero does not hesitate to use prejudice against Italian towns if it suits his case. In *De lege agraria* he takes a stab at Capua, where a new colony was planned. He points out the arrogance that is traditional to Capuans, as well as the danger they present to Rome:

> Though similar officers in the other colonies are called duumvirs, these men chose to call themselves praetors. But if their first year of office inspired them with such desires as that, do not you suppose that in a few years they would be likely to take

[32] Cic. *Sull.* 22–5. Although the speech was in defence of Publius Sulla, it was also Cicero himself who was under attack; some accomplices of Catiline had been arrested and put to death without a trial on the senate's order, which was executed by Cicero; this had caused much resentment against him. For other instances of prejudice against Italians, see *Clu.* 197; *Cael.* 5; *Mur.* 15–7; *Phil.* 3.15–17. See Roselaar forthcoming.

a fancy to the name of consuls? In the next place, they were preceded by lictors, not with staves, but with two fasces, just as lictors go before the praetors here . . . But after this, it was almost more than one could endure, to see the countenance of Considius. The man whom we had seen at Rome shrivelled and wasted away, in a contemptible and abject condition, when we saw him at Capua with Campanian haughtiness and royal pride, we seemed to be looking at the Magii, Blossii, and Vibellii.[33]

Cicero is talking here, in 63 BC, about the colony in Capua founded in 83 BC, led by Considius and Saltius; this colony contained many Roman settlers, so that the inhabitants of Capua were not in fact all native Capuans. However, Considius, as Cicero represents him, saw Capua as his own little kingdom and behaved with the arrogance of the previous Capuan leaders, the Blossii, Magii and Vibellii. If Capuan institutions reflected Rome's, then the Capuans were not only arrogant in using the same terms for magistrates as Rome did, but could also form a real threat if at some point – under Considius' leadership – they desired to form an alternative state rivalling Rome, as had been done by the Italian rebels in the Social War.

What lies behind this kind of prejudice is the debate about who deserves to be a citizen. All citizens of the Roman state were subject to the *ius civile*. The *ius civile* is defined by Cicero as 'a system of proportional fairness [*aequitas*] set up for those with a shared citizenship to claim what is rightfully theirs'.[34] Throughout his works Cicero says much about what it means to be Roman citizen: it is determined by 'ethical continuity' (*mos maiorum*), which includes culture, descent and political identification with the *res publica*.[35] The *res publica* is defined as the *res populi*, but 'a people is not a collection of all human beings joined in whatever way, but a coming together of a multitude of people in agreement with respect to law and a partnership with respect to the common good'.[36] Cicero on many occasions emphasises the importance of the *ius civile* and the rule of law. The rule of law is the basis of any state; violence is fundamentally incompatible with it.[37] The loss of law would cause 'great detriment to the citizen community [*civitas*]'.[38]

---

[33] Cic. *Agr.* 2.93. See also Cic. *Fam.* 7.1.3; Cic. *Leg.* 3.36, where he makes fun of unimportant small town events.

[34] Cic. *Top.* 9: 'Ius civile est aequitas constituta eis qui eiusdem civitatis sunt ad res suas obtinendas.' He is aware that the ideal is not always achieved, however: *Inv. rhet.* 2.65; see Harries 2013: 111, 115.

[35] Dench 2013: 122.

[36] Cic. *Rep.* 1.39: 'res publica res populi, populus autem non omnis hominum coetus quoquo modo congregatus, sed coetus multitudinis iuris consensu et utilitatis communione sociatus.'

[37] Cic. *Caecin.* 5: 'those rights which concern all men, which were established by our ancestors, and have been preserved to this time; while, if they were taken away, not only would some part of our rights be diminished, but also that violence, which is the greatest enemy to law, would seem to be strengthened by that decision.' See Frier 1985: 171–83.

[38] Cic. *Caecin.* 75. See Harries 2006: 186.

This means that by definition those who are not citizens do not fully participate in the *ius civile*. However, Cicero, as the defender of new citizens of Italian background and those who did not hold citizenship at all, has to look for a different community that included everyone whom he defended. Cicero therefore emphasises a community of humanity, of which in theory everyone could become a member. Membership of this community is not determined by legal status, but by political and moral values, so that Cicero must offer a clear definition of who is or can become a member of it.[39] For this he turns to the *ius gentium*, the 'natural' laws that are common to all humanity. He sees Roman law as sharing elements of natural law, as long as it is created and maintained by men who possess 'Roman' virtues. Cicero argues that these virtues can be taught to both Roman citizens and aliens.[40] Therefore, citizenship, in his view, should not solely based on parentage or birthplace, but be opened to all those who share 'Roman' values or contribute positively to the Roman state.

What is most important, according to Cicero, is the shared history of a community; this is more important than shared emotional bonds between the inhabitants. Because the community is formed through historical events, fluidity is possible in its citizenship. Especially in early Rome, as Cicero (a Roman citizen) emphasises, citizenship was constantly renegotiated, often violently.[41] He constructs a nostalgic version of Rome's early history, in which the Romans were always respectful, never more violent than necessary, and brought Roman law to those they conquered. Early Roman leaders aimed to protect their clients and the peoples who enjoyed friendship with the Roman people, and to bring them prosperity.[42] The value of the *mos maiorum*, so important for Roman society, was fully exploited by Cicero: he constantly refers to examples from ancient history, as in the passage of the *Pro Sulla* cited above. In the *Pro Balbo*, Cicero also emphasises the importance of new citizens to Rome: the Sabines, Volsci, Hernici and Latins, and the people from Tusculum and Lanuvium. The fact that the Italians had been so important in the early Republic gives his argument extra weight.[43]

Cicero does not usually make distinctions between different Italian towns. He usually ascribes certain moral values to specific peoples, rather than to individual towns.[44] This allows him to present the Italians as occupying the moral high ground, shocked at the behaviour of Roman politicians and

---

[39] Subacus 2015: 84.
[40] Cic. *Off.* 3.27: 'Those who say that regard must be had for citizens, but deny it to foreigners, these tear apart the common partnership of the human race.' See Subacus 2015: 91.
[41] Subacus 2015: 125–6.
[42] Cic. *Div. Caec.* 66.
[43] Cic. *Balb.* 31.
[44] E.g. *Leg. Agr.* 2.95: 'The Ligurians, being mountaineers, are a hardy and rustic tribe . . . The Campanians were always proud from the excellence of their soil, and the magnitude of their crops, and the healthiness, and position, and beauty of their city'. See Dench 1995: 85–94.

magistrates, and as opponents of tyranny. Regularly he states that *tota Italia* is shocked at abuse from Roman magistrates; in the triumviral period, *tota Italia* wants *libertas*.[45] Thus because the Italians represent traditional 'Roman' virtues, they are worthy of citizenship. A good example of a deserving citizen is Cluentius, from Larinum in southern Italy. He 'guards that well-known nobility among his own people and status handed down by the ancestors in such a way that he achieves the weightiness, firmness, good name and generosity of the ancestors'.[46] Cicero is deliberately vague on which ancestors he means: only Cluentius' direct, local ancestors, or the Roman nobility of old, who were the quintessential examples of weightiness, firmness, good name and generosity. By implication, he suggests that Cluentius is one of the Italians who represents traditional Roman virtues.

Therefore, political loyalty was an important criterion for inclusion in the Roman state. Cicero famously stated that he, like all Romans who were born in an Italian town, had two *patriae*: 'I think, that there are two fatherlands for him and all those from municipalities, one from nature, the other from citizenship'.[47] There was a clear hierarchy between the 'natural' and the 'legal' *patria*:

> The one which takes its name from the state as a whole should have first place in our affections. That is the country for which we should be willing to die, to which we should devote ourselves heart and soul, and on whose altar we should dedicate and consecrate all that is ours. Yet the one which gave us birth is dear to us in a way not very different from that which took us in. And so I shall always insist that this is my country, even though the other is greater and includes this within it.[48]

In *Pro Balbo*, Cicero uses political loyalty to Rome to argue for citizenship based on emotional and political affiliation. One's feelings and actions towards the Republic are what determine whether someone is worthy to be a citizen. The state is united by a shared sense of identity that comes from loyalty to the Republic: 'I wish that those who everywhere are the defenders of this empire, could come into this state, and that all those fighting against the republic be put out of the state'.[49] Thus, everyone who has something to contribute to the Roman state should be welcomed as a citizen.

Not only political values, but also culture created a community of

---

[45] Abuse: Cic. *Verr.* 1.54; *Phil.* 2.105–6; Cic. *Cat.* 2.25: 'all Italy' opposes Catilina; *Red. Quir.* 16: 'all Italy' asks Pompey to speak for Cicero; *libertas*: *Phil.* 3.32, 10.19, 13.39. See Dench 2013: 128.

[46] Cic. *Clu.* 196: 'Praeterea nobilitatem illam inter suos locumque a maioribus traditum sic tuetur ut maiorum gravitatem, constantiam, gratiam, liberalitatem adsequatur.'

[47] Cic. *Leg.* 2.5: 'Ego mehercule et illi et omnibus municipibus duas esse censeo patrias, unam naturae, alteram civitatis.'

[48] Cic. *Leg.* 2.5.

[49] Cic. *Balb.* 51. See Subacus 2015: 148–9.

humanity. Cicero emphasises this especially in the *Pro Archia*, since Archias was a poet whose works glorified the Roman state.[50] He starts out by creating a bond between himself, the jury and Archias, who are all part of the same community.[51] Cicero argues that learning and literature are typical values of the Roman elite, and that Archias shares this cultural kinship. Thus both his kinship with Roman culture and his tangible contribution to Rome's power make him worthy of citizenship.

In the *Verrines*, Cicero combines the arguments of cultural similarity to Rome and political loyalty to the Roman state. He argues that the Sicilians possess typically Roman characteristics, while on the other hand Verres is not a true Roman at all because of his corruption. He establishes clear characteristics for what makes someone a virtuous Roman, and argues that anyone can claim these qualities. On the other hand, he also praises Sicily's importance and past loyalty to Rome: 'Sicily first of all foreign nations devoted herself to the friendship and loyalty of the Roman people. First of all to be called a province, that which is an ornament of empire'.[52] Although the Sicilians were not in fact Roman citizens, they certainly deserved to be treated as if they were, Cicero argues.

All this prejudice against Italians could obviously be a problem if they became engaged in a lawsuit. Much of Cicero's pleading is aimed at establishing the Italian or provincial defendants as worthy characters who deserved to be protected by Roman law. In many cases he was successful, as his clients won their case. Most Italians of course never got into legal trouble, but this does not mean that they never suffered from prejudice legal and economic affairs. For example, in the *Pro Fonteio* Cicero argues that Naevius was 'a worthy man, but one who had not been brought up in such a manner as to give him the opportunity of becoming acquainted with the rights of a partnership and the duties of a trustworthy manager'.[53] As we saw above, the rules of *bona fides* underwrote all business and legal transactions. It was necessary to be acquainted with Roman law and the unwritten social rules of trade; an Italian who traded little with Romans would not be able to acquire this knowledge and therefore be at a disadvantage. Having citizenship would

---

[50] Cic. *Arch.* 14. Archias wrote in Greek, which ensured that Roman glory was spread through as large a part of the world as possible: 'Moreover because Greek is read in nearly all races, Latin is contained in its own, narrow, limits. By which, if those things which we do are defined by the regions of the whole world, we ought to desire that where the weapons of our armies have come, our glory and fame reach to the same place' (*Arch.* 23). Archias thus has *duae patriae* as well: 'his Greekness is just as important as his constructed Romanness and in fact plays an active role in the continual affirmation of what it means to be Roman' (Subacus 2015: 144–5).

[51] Cic. *Arch.* 3: 'before this order of most literate men, your humanity . . . that you allow me to speak a little more freely concerning a zeal for humanity and letters.'

[52] Cic. *Verr.* 2.1.2–3; see 2.2.2–11. See Lintott 2008: 95.

[53] Cic. *Font.* 11–2.

open up more opportunities to use the *ius civile*, leading to a closer knowledge of Roman law among Italians.

5. *FUNDUS FIERI*: ROMAN LAW AND THE ITALIANS

It stands to reason that all Italians, after being made Roman citizens, had to adhere to Roman law. However, some debate has been caused by what Cicero says about the concept of *fundus fieri* in *Pro Balbo*:

> What can possibly be said more ignorant than that it is requisite for the federate cities to ratify such a transaction? (*quid enim potuit dici imperitius quam foederatos populos fieri fundos oportere?*). For that is not a right peculiar to federate cities, but to all free nations . . . When the Roman people had ordered anything, if the allied peoples and the Latins had adopted and ratified it, and if the law which we had among ourselves was in this manner established among some people on a firm footing, then that people should be bound by the obligations of that law; not in such a manner as to detract in the least from our privileges, but that those nations might enjoy either that law which was established among us, or some other advantage and benefit . . . The Latins have adopted whatever of them they have chosen; even the *lex Iulia* itself, by which the rights of citizenship were given to the allies and to the Latins, it was decreed that those people who did not ratify the law should not have the freedom of the city, which circumstance gave rise to a great contention among the people of Heraclea and of Neapolis, since a great part of the population in those states preferred the liberty which they enjoyed by virtue of their treaty with us to the rights of citizenship. Lastly, this is the meaning both of that law and of that expression, that the peoples who do ratify it enjoy its advantages owing to our kindness, and not owing to any right of their own [*ut fundi populi beneficio nostro, non suo iure fiant*].[54] When the Roman people has enacted anything, if it be a matter of that sort, that it appears it may be granted also to some other nations, whether joined to us by a treaty, or free to decide themselves which law they prefer using, not about our affairs, but about their own; then it seems necessary to inquire whether they have adopted and ratified our law, or not; but the Senate never intended that those peoples should have the power of ratifying or declining to ratify measures which concern our republic, our empire, our wars, our victory, and our safety [*de nostra vero re publica, de nostro imperio, de nostris bellis, de victoria, de salute fundos populos fieri noluerunt*].[55]

Cicero has to explain the concept of *fundus fieri* in order to support Balbus' claim to citizenship. He argues that Balbus, from Gades in Hispania,

---

[54] Elmore 1916, 35–6 argues that *beneficio nostro, non suo iure fiant* means that *fundus fieri* was a privilege granted to foreign states by Rome, perhaps as a result of a petition by the community. But this cannot be deduced from Cicero's words; he refers to the individual benefits that the allies received.

[55] Cic. *Balb.* 20–2.

had accepted citizenship from Pompey under the *lex Gellia Cornelia* of 72 BC. The prosecutor argued that Balbus was not a citizen because his hometown had not adopted this particular Roman law, that is, had not become *fundus* to it. Against this, Cicero argues that the formal adoption of a Roman law was necessary only where the internal affairs of a community were concerned. Furthermore, Rome was free to grant its citizenship to individual foreigners as a reward for service. Thus, it is a fundamental Roman right to retain or renounce the citizenship: 'for these are the firmest foundations of our freedom, that each man is his own master in retaining or giving up his citizenship'.[56]

Scholars have proposed different theories about whether Roman law applied to the Italians. Salmon mentions a number of other second-century BC laws that he thinks applied to the allies: the *lex Voconia* about female inheritances, as Cicero mentions in *Pro Balbo*, the *lex Appuleia* and *lex Furia* (both *de sponsu*), and the *lex Fannia* of 161 and *lex Didia* of 143, both sumptuary laws.[57] Harris, on the other hand, convincingly argues that the *leges Appuleia* and *Furia* probably only applied to Roman citizens in Italy and the provinces. The most important argument for this is that both laws were still valid in Gaius' time, so that Gaius' text cannot be used as evidence to argue that it applied to Italian allies before the Social War. Moreover, the use of *sponsio* was restricted to citizens in any case, so that it was not relevant to Italian allies before they received citizenship.[58] In 161 a sumptuary *lex Fannia* was passed; eighteen years later a *lex Didia* specified that this also applied to *Italici*.[59] If this is true, it would be a very unusual innovation for this period, leading us to doubt that Macrobius really meant Italian allies when using the term *Italici*. It is possible that he meant 'Roman citizens living outside of Rome', since the *lex Fannia* was concerned with spending during the *Ludi Romani* and other festivals in Rome, so that Romans living outside the city could easily use the argument that it did not apply to them.[60] Macrobius emphasises the difference between town and country, and it is very likely that he did not realise that Italians had not held Roman citizenship in the second century BC.[61]

Aulus Gellius states that even though the inhabitants of a community were Roman citizens, it was only bound by Roman laws if it became *fundus*

---

[56] Cic. *Balb.* 31: 'Haec sunt enim fundamenta firmissima nostrae libertatis, sui quemque iuris et retinendi et dimittendi esse dominum.'

[57] Gai. *Inst.* 3.121–2: 'But, as the *Lex Furia* only applies to Italy, the result is that in the other provinces both sponsors and guarantors, like sureties, are perpetually liable; and each one of them is bound for the entire amount of the debt, unless they are, to a certain extent, relieved by the letter of the Divine Hadrian', Salmon 1967: 324.

[58] Harris 1972: 642.

[59] Macr. *Sat.* 3.17.6.

[60] Harris 1972: 644.

[61] Idem: 644; Roselaar 2013a.

of them.[62] As Elmore argues, Gellius is wrong: those who had Roman citizenship should follow Roman law.[63] This means that a community could not make itself *fundus* to the *lex Iulia* while retaining its own municipal laws. Only towns that are *foederati* or *liberi* could make themselves *fundi*, as Cicero in fact states.[64] Elmore argues that all Latin colonies were *fundus* of all Roman laws, but that they could choose not to follow them in each case.[65] However, Harris argues that those communities that did adopt Roman law were mostly Latins, and that Italians did so only rarely.[66] There in fact is very little evidence about how many Roman laws the Italians, or in fact the Latins, adopted. Sherwin-White assumes that the *Tabula Bantina* is an example of *fundus fieri* and that the community of Bantia had adopted a Roman law, in this case the *lex Appuleia de maiestate*.[67] However, if indeed this was a *lex de maiestate*, it could easily be argued that it was part of the laws *de nostra vero re publica* et cetera, which Cicero mentions. Indeed treaties between Rome and other communities, whether *aequus* or *iniquus*, included a clause to maintain the *maiestas* of the Roman people – this was the 'international' version of *fides*.[68] This law unfortunately therefore cannot be used as an example of *fundus fieri*. Criminal laws were not open to *fundus fieri* either: 'crimes committed in Italy which require a public investigation, such as treason, conspiracy, poisoning, and assassination, are under the jurisdiction of the senate'.[69]

Quite strikingly, Cicero mentions that the Latins and Italians even had the right to adopt or reject the terms offered in the *lex Iulia*. Indeed, as Cicero states, if the Roman state wanted to make an allied state benefit from some Roman measure, it had to be checked whether it was *fundus*, because the allied state must always retain the possibility to use its own law.[70] It is understandable that great debate surrounded the *lex Iulia* in some Italian communities: although we have seen that Roman citizenship could offer many advantages, many people would not have been convinced that it was worth giving up their independence.

It must be emphasised that there is a difference between being citizens with access to the *ius civile*, and following the Roman system of administration. All Roman citizens were indeed subject to the *ius civile*, but not all

---

[62] Gell. NA 16.13.6: 'Municipes ergo sunt cives Romani ex municipiis legibus suis et suo iure utentes, muneris tantum cum populo Romano honorari participes, a quo munere capessendo appellati videntur, nullis aliis necessitatibus neque ulla populi Romani lege adstricti, nisi in quam populus eorum fundus factus est.'

[63] Elmore 1916: 37.

[64] Hardy 1917: 134.

[65] Elmore 1916: 37.

[66] Harris 1972: 645, *contra* Brunt 1965: 101.

[67] Sherwin-White 1973: 130.

[68] Polyb. 21.32.2; Liv. 38.11.2.

[69] Polyb. 6.13.4. See Hardy 1917: 134; Harris 1972: 644–5.

[70] Elmore 1916: 38–40.

Italian communities had the same constitution. The *Tabula Heracleensis*, a municipal charter dated to c. 44 BC, states that:

> whoever is or has been commissioned by a law or a plebiscite to give a charter for a *municipium fundanum*, or the citizens of that *municipium*, whatever supplements, amendments, or corrections are made to this charter in the year immediately after the people authorise this law shall be binding on the *municipium fundanum*, as they would have been if these had been incorporated by him when first he gave a charter on the authority of the law or the plebiscite.[71]

Some debate has focused on the term *municipium fundanum*. *Municipia* were usually communities of Roman citizens, which would mean that their inhabitants were subject to Roman law in any case.

However, the *Tabula Heracleensis* suggests that local constitutions differed from place to place, which is indeed shown by other sources as well. For example, the number and character of local magistracies varied in the first century: Arpinum had three aediles, for example.[72] Bispham reasonably argues that the *municipia fundana* were those communities that had made themselves *fundi* to the *lex Iulia*, and thus become *municipia*; but, as he rightly points out, there was no immediate need for them to change their constitution, as long as they fulfilled their military and other duties towards the Roman state.[73] It is therefore likely that much variation still existed in the laws of the Italian communities after the passage of the *lex Iulia*, despite the fact that all Italians now were Roman citizens, and that only in 44 BC was an attempt made to bring them into line. The *Tabula Heracleensis* also shows the autonomy that these communities still held over their own constitution – when more than a year had passed after their foundation, they would have to agree to any changes to their municipal laws.

---

[71] *Tab. Her.* l. 159–63 (text Crawford 1996): 'sei qui<d> is post h(anc) l(egem) r(ogatam) in eo anno proxumo, quo h(anc) l(egem) populus iuserit, ad eas leges <addiderit commutauerit conrexerit>, municipi{ei}s fundanos/ item teneto, utei oporteret, sei ea<e> res ab eo tum, quom primum leges eis municipibus lege pl(ebei)ue sc(ito) dedit,/ ad eas leges additae commutatae conrectae essent, neue quis interced<i>to neue quid facito, quo minus/ ea rata sint quoue minus municipis fundanos tenea<n>t eisque optemperetur.'

[72] Cic. *Fam.* 15.15.1.

[73] Bispham 2007: 166. See Knapp 1980: 30; he argues that the list headed by *Fundi*, in Festus' list of *praefecturae*, had led to the creation of the general name *municipia fundana* to indicate all towns that needed a new charter. This is very unlikely: first, there were more towns in need of changes in their charters than just the *praefecturae* listed by Festus; and secondly, since the term *fundus fieri* already existed, it would create confusion if it was now applied to a different type of town. Sherwin-White 1973: 167–8 argues that this regulation refers only to the *municipium* of Fundi, but this seems unlikely in a law of general relevance. See Galsterer 1976: 98.

6. CONCLUSION

It is clear that law and the expansion of the Roman state went hand in hand. As the Roman Republic expanded, it conquered first the whole of Italy and then large parts of the Mediterranean. The Romans could not simply order their Italian and provincial allies to obey them, but had to give them a share in the profits of empire. At first only the Latin colonies were given any legal advantages with regard to their political and economic position. During the second century BC, however, the Italians became dissatisfied with their position, especially because of economic disadvantages. The Roman state introduced various new laws in order to satisfy them, but without much success. In the end only a grant of Roman citizenship could placate their wishes.

Thus, at least after 70 BC, Italians were equal to old Roman citizens, in that they could avail themselves of the *ius civile*. Nevertheless, there are indications in Cicero's work that not all Italians were considered equal by the Romans who sat in judgement on their cases. Cicero often had to fight against prejudice held about Italians and other allies, arguing that they possessed the same moral qualities as Romans and should therefore be treated equally under the law.

Even if all Italians shared access to the *ius civile*, this does not mean that all Italian communities had the same constitution. They could 'ratify' Rome's laws to make them valid locally through the process of *fundus fieri*. Even after the municipal laws of Caesar in 44 BC created more unity in Italian local administration, Italian communities retained control over their own laws and customs.

As the Roman state continued to expand, the inhabitants of the provinces adopted the place that the Italian allies had taken in the hierarchy of peoples. As with the Italians earlier, the Roman state acknowledged that these people needed a means of protection against Roman abuse. Moreover, if Rome wanted to maintain its status as most powerful state in the Mediterranean, it had to act against abuse carried out by Roman magistrates – otherwise, the status of the *res publica* would be damaged.[74] Still, the Romans were not ready to give the provincials citizenship. Instead, two important mechanisms for existed: treaties and the *lex repetundarum*; Cicero used both of these many times in his speeches for provincial clients. Eventually, these proved insufficient to really protect the allies, but citizenship for all provincials was long in coming.

---

[74] Subacus 2015: 192–3.

BIBLIOGRAPHY

Badian, E. (1972), *Publicans and Sinners: Private enterprise in the service of the Roman Republic*. Oxford.

Bispham, E. (2007), *From Asculum to Actium: The municipalization of Italy from the Social War to Augustus*. Oxford.

Brunt, P. A. (1965), 'Italian aims at the time of the Social War', *Journal of Roman Studies* 55: 90–109.

Brunt, P. A. (1988), *The Fall of the Roman Republic*. Oxford.

Coşkun, A. (2009), *Bürgerrechtsentzug oder Fremdenausweisung? Studien zu den Rechten von Latinern und weiteren Fremden sowie zum Bürgerrechtswechsel in der Römischen Republik (5. bis frühes 1. Jh. v. Chr.)*. Stuttgart.

Crawford, M. H. (1996), '*Tabula Heracleensis*', in M. H. Crawford, ed., *Roman statutes* I. London. 355–91.

Dart, C. J. (2014), *The Social War, 91 to 88 BCE: A history of the Italian insurgency against the Roman Republic*. Farnham.

Dench, E. (1995), *From Barbarians to New Men: Greek, Roman and modern perceptions of peoples of the Central Apennines*. Oxford.

Dench, E. (2013), 'Cicero and Roman identity', in C. Steel, ed., *The Cambridge Companion to Cicero*. Cambridge. 122–38.

Elmore, J. (1916), '*Municipia fundana*', *Transactions and Proceedings of the American Philological Association* 47: 35–42.

Fiori, R. (1998–9), '*Ius civile, ius gentium, ius honorarium*: il problema della 'recezione' dei *iudicia bonae fidei*', *Bullettino del Istituto di Diritto Romano* 51–2: 165–97.

Frier, B. W. (1985), *The Rise of the Roman Jurists: Studies in Cicero's* Pro Caecina. Princeton.

Galsterer, H. (1976), *Herrschaft und Verwaltung im republikanischen Italien: Die Beziehungen Roms zu den italischen Gemeinden vom Latinerfreuden 338 v. Chr. bis zum Bundesgenossenkrieg 91 v. Chr.* Munich.

Hardy, E. G. (1917), 'Cicero's argument in *Pro Balbo*, VIII.19–22', *Classical Review* 31: 132–4.

Harries, J. (2006), *Cicero and the Jurists: From citizens' law to the lawful state*. London.

Harries, J. (2013), 'The law in Cicero's writings', in C. Steel, ed., *The Cambridge Companion to Cicero*. Cambridge. 107–21.

Harris, W. V. (1972), 'Was Roman law imposed on the Italian allies?' *Historia* 21: 639–45.

Kendall, S. (2013), *The Struggle for Roman Citizenship: Romans, allies, and the wars of 91–77 BCE*. Piscataway, NJ.

Knapp, P. C. (1980), 'Festus 262L and *praefecturae* in Italy', *Athenaeum* 58: 14–38.

Lintott, A. W. (2008), *Cicero as Evidence: A historian's companion*. Oxford.

Mouritsen, H. (1998), *Italian Unification: A study in ancient and modern historiography*. London.

Nagle, D. B. (1973), 'An allied view of the Social War', *American Journal of Ancient History* 77: 367–78.

Roselaar, S. T. (2010), *Public Land in the Roman Republic: A social and economic history of* ager publicus *in Italy, 396–89* BC. Oxford.

Roselaar, S. T. (2013a), 'The concept of *commercium* in the Roman Republic', *Phoenix* 66: 381–413.

Roselaar, S. T. (2013b), 'The concept of *conubium* in the Roman Republic', in P. J. du Plessis, ed., *New Frontiers: Law and society in the Roman world.* Edinburgh. 102–22.

Roselaar, S. T. (forthcoming), *Italy's Economic Revolution: Economic relations and the integration of Roman Italy.*

Salmon, E. T. (1967), *Samnium and the Samnites.* Cambridge.

Sherwin-White, A. N. (1973³), *The Roman Citizenship.* Oxford.

Sotty, R. (1977), *Ricerche sur les* utiles actiones: *La notion d'action utile en droit romain classique.* Grenoble.

Subacus, M. (2015), Duae patriae: *Cicero and political cosmopolitanism in Rome.* New York University PhD thesis.

Watson, A. (1961), *Contract of Mandate in Roman Law.* Oxford.

Chapter 10

Jurors, Jurists and Advocates: Law in the Rhetorica ad Herennium *and* De Inventione

Jennifer Hilder

1. INTRODUCTION

For Jill Harries, the anonymous *Rhetorica ad Herennium* and Cicero's early *De Inventione*, written in the 80s BC, read 'at times like textbooks on law rather than rhetoric'.[1] This is surely a reflection of the great emphasis both works place on the Judicial type of oratory, to which the *Rhetorica ad Herennium* devotes two books. Law and the legal context are manifest in the examples used in these two handbooks written in the 80s BC, giving an insight into the practice as well as the theory of legal oratory in this period.

In fact, the two handbooks are a rich source of information for several aspects of trials – from the jurists who advise on civil law cases to the advocates who speak at trials and the jurors who judge them. In this chapter I will explore these three groups of people involved in trials (who may not, in reality, be separate individuals) to build a picture of the legal system in Cicero's youth.

The *Rhetorica ad Herennium* and Cicero's *De Inventione* are often studied together, to the detriment of one or other of the texts. As will become apparent, the two texts are significantly different, although this is often not explicitly recognised. There is little to gain, therefore, from trying to reason away their disagreements. Instead, these points of difference make the picture of the Roman Republic richer, emphasising the choices that were available to the people involved in the legal world and giving a glimpse of the variety that is frequently lacking in the surviving sources.

Despite their differences, the texts are still worth studying together for two reasons: their date and their common source. Both texts were almost certainly written in the 80s BC before Cicero began his legal career and before his earliest surviving speech, *Pro Quinctio* (81 BC). The commonly agreed dating of the *Rhetorica ad Herennium* falls between 86 and 82 BC.[2] The termi-

---

[1] Harries 2006: 93.

[2] See Caplan 1954 for a brief but valuable introduction to the issues surrounding the text, including its authorship and dating. Other major commentaries are Calboli 1969; Achard 1989.

nus post quem refers to the death of Marius in 86 BC,[3] the latest datable event mentioned in the text, and the fact that there is no mention of Sulla's dictatorship is used as evidence for it being written before 82 BC. Although the *terminus ante quem* is less certain, and some scholars have argued for a much later date,[4] the concentration of examples relating to the late 90s and early 80s strongly suggests that the work was written around this time.

The *De Inventione* is also undated but scholars have placed the work in the middle of the 80s BC.[5] The work was once thought to have been written prior to the Social War, but Cicero's very young age at this time makes it unlikely. His own reference to the work as being written when he was *puer et adulescentulus* is probably intended to mislead.[6] Instead, the work fits into the later period of Cicero's rhetorical and legal education in Rome under figures such as Q. Mucius Scaevola the Pontifex and Apollonius Molon of Rhodes.[7] Its unfinished state, treating only the first of five duties of an orator (*inventio*), may well reflect his growing interest in philosophy or the beginning of his legal career.[8] Hence the strong likelihood that the two rhetorical handbooks were written around the same time and reflect a similar historical and legal context; although it cannot be determined which one came first.

The common source of the two works is another important issue in understanding the relationship between the *Rhetorica ad Herennium* and the *De Inventione*. The identical wording of the texts in some places must mean that they both used the same written source in Latin.[9] It is not known who or what this common source might be, but it is clear that either one or both authors deviate from it as there are significant structural differences that underlie the superficial similarities.[10]

The deeper structural divergences are particularly important when considering the legal aspects of the texts as the two authors choose to instruct their readers quite differently on the use of legal evidence. For example, the anonymous Auctor of the *Rhetorica ad Herennium* restricts his methods of argumentation, the Issues or *constitutiones*, to three: *coniecturalis, legitima,*

---

[3] *Rhet. Her.* 4.54.68.

[4] See Douglas 1960, who suggests that the date could be as late as the 50s BC. Henderson 1951: 73 fn.18 takes 75 BC as the *terminus ante quem*, the date that a C. Herennius was killed in Spain in Sertorius' army.

[5] See Achard 1994: 6–10.

[6] Cic. *De or.* 1.2.5.

[7] Cic. *Brut.* 304–16. On Cicero's education see Corbeill 2002, 2007.

[8] Negri 2007: 190–1.

[9] See Herbolzheimer 1926 for a detailed comparison of such similarities, for example the identical definition of *inventio* at Cic. *Inv. rhet.*1.7.9 and *Rhet. Her.* 1.2.3. A common Latin source is supported by Marx 1894: 111–33; Herbolzheimer 1926; Adamietz 1960; Achard 1989: 48; Achard 1994: 20.

[10] Calboli 1972 argues for a strong connection between the *Rhet. Her.* and the work of M. Antonius (cos. 99); see Cic. *De or.* 1.21.94, 1.47.206, 1.48.208. Others have suggested that there were many such rhetorical works being produced at this time; see Calboli 1969: 19–23.

iuridicialis.[11] Two of these are specifically about the law: in a *iuridicialis constitutio* the Auctor explains how to employ the different sources of law, and how to beg forgiveness despite breaking the law.[12] By contrast, in using a *legitima constitutio* the advocate aims to resolve difficulties with the laws themselves, such as whether to follow the letter or the spirit of the law.[13]

In the *De Inventione* on the other hand, there are four *constitutiones* (*coniecturalis, definitiva, generalis, translativa*)[14] and a separate section about written documents,[15] which is parallel to the *legitima constitutio* of the *Rhetorica ad Herennium*. Cicero chooses to keep the section about legal difficulties isolated from the main method of argumentation.[16] One effect of this is that Cicero is able to focus more clearly and expansively on these legal aspects of a rhetorical argument. In general, the text of the *De Inventione* is much longer than the equivalent books of the *Rhetorica ad Herennium* and Cicero's tendency to add further details is particularly evident in these legal sections.

These specific discussions of law and legal culture take place in the context of the wider discussion of forensic oratory that predominates in the *Rhetorica ad Herennium* and the *De Inventione*. Both texts devote the majority of the first two books to the Judicial style of speech and give only short explanations of *inventio* for Epideictic and Deliberative speech, which are less commonly used in court.[17] Despite this focus on forensic oratory, neither text makes an explicit distinction between civil or criminal trials, either in terms of the rhetorical techniques required or the legal processes involved. In this chapter I will also treat both civil and criminal trials, although their discussion will largely fall into separate sections.

The two texts can by no means provide a complete picture of the Roman legal system in the early first century BC. Indeed, it would be surprising if this were the case, given that they are both principally guidebooks on rhetorical theory. But by carefully analysing the evidence they do contain, it is possible to think further about the people involved in the legal cases: jurists, advocates and jurors. In the first section I will examine the influence that Cicero

---

[11] *Rhet. Her.* 1.11.18–5.25.

[12] Idem: 2.13.19–7.26.

[13] Idem: 2.9.13–2.18.

[14] Cic. *Inv. rhet.* 1.8.10.

[15] This section begins at idem: 2.40.116. Cicero explains it (2.39.115): 'But I have said quite enough about the *constitutiones*, now it seems I must speak about the *controversiae* that relate to written documents' (*Ac de constitutionibus quidem satis dictum est: nunc de iis controversiis, quae in scripto versantur, dicendum videtur*).

[16] Without going into too much detail about the history of rhetorical theory here, Cicero's system follows the division of the mid-second century rhetorician Hermagoras, while the Auctor says he is using the three *constitutiones* of his own teacher, *noster doctor* (*Rhet. Her.* 1.11.18). For the theory of *constitutiones* see Heath 1994.

[17] The Auctor explains this by saying that the Judicial is the most difficult of the three types of speech (2.1.1). For Epideictic and Deliberative: *Rhet. Her.* 3.2.2–8.15; Cic. *Inv. rhet.* 2.52.157–9.178.

attributes to the jurists (while the Auctor does not mention them explicitly) and the way that this is reflected in the legal cases around inheritance that recur in both texts. I will then turn to the role of the advocates in each of the texts, and particularly the challenge that the ill-defined law about *maiestas* presented to contemporary figures. Finally, I will look at the way in which the jurors or *iudices* are addressed in examples from both texts, and what this reveals about expectations of their legal knowledge and what they would respond to.

2. JURISTS

Jurists were legal experts who advised primarily in the field of civil law in Rome.[18] The juristic tradition can be traced back into the third century but Cicero saw a high point in the mid-second century with Sext. Aelius, M'. Manilius and P. Mucius Scaevola.[19] The next generation included Q. Mucius Scaevola the Augur and Q. Mucius Scaevola the Pontifex, who were the leading figures immediately prior to and at the time that the *Rhetorica ad Herennium* and the *De Inventione* were being written. Until Q. Mucius Scaevola the Pontifex and his influential work *De Iure Civili*, the juristic profession had been closely tied to the *pontifices* and pontifical law. His work, which was also probably written in the 80s BC, is said to have helped to create a separate role for the jurists beyond the religious sphere.[20] Their role was typically described by Cicero as *respondere, agere, cavere*,[21] but it is the first of these – the giving of *responsa* – for which they are perhaps best known. It is these *responsa* that comprise much of the later collected writings on law, such as Justinian's Digest.

Jurists appear twice in Cicero's *De Inventione* and both references attest to the importance and involvement of the jurists in the field of *ius civile*, civil law. The examples that Cicero uses alongside these references can help to further understand where and how jurists participate in the wider legal system. Although jurists are not mentioned by the Auctor in the *Rhetorica ad Herennium*, a number of similar examples imply that jurists must also figure in his conception of the Roman courts, as I will discuss below. Elsewhere, although I will not discuss this in detail here, the Auctor's assumptions about his audience's legal knowledge imply that they would either have received a

---

[18] See Frier 1985 and Harries 2006 for the two major discussions of the jurists; see also Watson 1974: 101–10. For an overview of Cicero's attitude to jurists in his writings, see Harries 2013: 107–12. For Cicero and the law generally, see Harries 2004; Gildenhard 2011: 168–95.

[19] Cic. *De or.* 1.48.212.

[20] Harries 2006: 13–14, 19.

[21] Cic. *De or.* 1.48.212. For the different roles of jurists, see Frier 1985: esp. 139–96; Harries 2006: esp. 27–50. Bauman's discussion of Q. Mucius Scaevola the Pontifex is a good case study of the range of roles such a figure could play: 1983: 340–424. On where and how jurists were consulted, see Tuori 2010. Cicero refers to different juristic specialisms at *Balb.* 45.

level of legal education from jurists or that jurists were widely available for consultation on legal matters.[22]

The references that Cicero makes to jurists in the *De Inventione* (*iure consulti, iuris consulti*) occur when he is discussing the *negotialis* (Legal) subdivision of the *constitutio generalis* (Qualitative issue).[23] As opposed to the *constitutio coniecturalis*, where the dispute is about what actually happened, in this Issue the advocates debate what kind of thing happened (*qualis res*) and whether it qualifies as being against the law.[24] As recommended in the *negotialis* subdivision, one way of doing this is to look at the law itself, or perhaps more specifically, what the law is according to the custom of the community (*civilis mos*) and equity (*aequitas*).[25] As Cicero says explicitly, the type of law that is under consideration in this Issue is the *ius civile*.[26]

When introducing the *negotialis* subdivision in Book 1, Cicero states that the people who have command over the way in which *mos* and *aequitas* are interpreted are the jurists themselves (*cui diligentiae praeesse . . . iure consulti*).[27] As mentioned, the remit of the jurists is clearly specified as being *ius civile* and they are given the full responsibility for this, at least in Rome (*apud nos*). The task that Cicero is assigning to the jurists here, essentially that of deciding *quid iuris*, is no small one. Although the Auctor does not mention the jurists in the parallel section of the *Rhetorica ad Herennium*, he does give this Issue equal significance, saying that it should be used to argue 'whether a thing was done legally' (*iurene sit factum*).[28] When each text goes into further detail about this Issue in its second book, the list of the six parts of *ius* that follows demonstrates the incredible scope of topics that the jurists assisted with. The references to laws from the Twelve Tables in this section also provide a further connection to the jurists; I discuss these further below.

Cicero's second reference to the jurists comes at the end of his extended discussion of the same *negotialis* subdivision in his second book.[29] Here he says that it is a commonplace in arguing this kind of case to speak either for or against the authority of a jurist (*ab auctoritate iuris consultorum et contra auctoritatem*).[30] This is particularly interesting, because Cicero precedes this by saying that it is impossible to suggest any other definite topics or commonplaces (*certi . . . loci*) for this issue. The frequent presence of the

---

[22] For example, the Auctor's discussion of *translatio* at *Rhet. Her.* 1.10.18.

[23] This is part of the *absoluta* subdivision within the *iuridicialis constitutio* in the *Rhetorica ad Herennium*: 1.14.24, 2.13.19–20.

[24] Cic. *Inv. rhet.* 1.8.10.

[25] Idem: 1.11.14.

[26] Idem:. 2.22.68. For the Roman distinction between *ius civile* and *ius publicum*, see for example Harries 2006: 59–66. Cic. *Top.* 28.

[27] Cic. *Inv. rhet.* 1.11.14.

[28] *Rhet. Her.* 2.13.19.

[29] Cic. *Inv. rhet.* 2.21.61–22.68.

[30] Idem: 2.22.68.

jurists is one of the only things his reader can be sure of. Cicero's reluctance or inability to propose any specific commonplaces also gives the impression that this is somehow a different kind of case. It prompts Cicero to remind his reader to look out for other *loci communes* arising from the case itself (*ipsa res . . . ostendat*); it was necessary for the advocate to respond directly to a particular argument being made on the basis of the jurist's advice, and the way for them to do this could not be predicted in general terms. The advocates' interaction with the jurists when attending such a case is implicit.[31]

With this in mind, it is useful to examine the example that Cicero has chosen to explain the *negotialis* issue as a whole:[32]

> Quidam pupillum heredem fecit; pupillus autem ante mortuus est, quam in suam tutelam venit. De hereditate ea quae pupillo venit, inter eos qui patris pupilli heredes secundi sunt et inter agnatos pupilli controversia est.

> A certain man made a ward his heir; however the ward died before he came of age. A dispute arose about the inheritance the ward came into between those who were the reversionary heirs of the ward's father and the agnates of the ward.

The example goes on to discuss the arguments on either side, which are based on whether or not the father's will was also the ward's will as long as he was a minor.[33] The need for jurists in a case such as this is clear: as the writers of wills (as expressed by *cavere*), jurists would be well placed to advise on such topics and their *auctoritas* would be valuable.

Significantly, this example is very similar to an example of 'letter versus spirit' that Cicero gives in his later discussion of written documents, which describes the case known to modern scholars as the *causa Curiana*.[34] This was another case involving inheritance and a dispute between the reversionary heirs and the agnates that took place in 92 BC, just a few years before the two rhetorical handbooks were written:[35]

> Paterfamilias cum liberorum haberet nihil, uxorem autem haberet, in testamento ita scripsit: si mihi filius genitur unus pluresve, is mihi heres esto. Deinde quae assolent. Postea: si filius ante moritur, quam in tutelam suam venerit, tum mihi, dicet, heres esto. Filius natus non est. Ambigunt adgnati cum eo, qui est heres, si filius ante, quam in tutelam veniat, mortuus sit.

---

[31] Harries discusses the overlap and tension between advocates and jurists: 2006: 92–100, 114.

[32] Cic. *Inv. rhet.* 2.21.62.

[33] This may or may not have originated in a real case; it is quite usual for Cicero to anonymise the examples he uses in the *De Inventione*, see Harries 2006:107.

[34] Cic. *Inv. rhet.* 2.42.122. Other references to the case appear in Cic. *De or.* 1.39.180, 1.57.242–5, 2.6.24, 2.32.140–1, 2.54.220–3; *Brut.* 39.144–6, 52.194–53.199; *Top.* 10.44; *Caecin.* 18.52–3, 67–70; Quint. *Inst.* 7.6.9–10. See Vaughn 1985 for a comprehensive overview and further references.

[35] Cic. *Inv. rhet.* 2.42.122.

A head of a household, when he had no children, but he had a wife, wrote this in his will: if I have one or more sons, let him be my heir. Then the usual phrases. Afterwards: if the son dies before he comes of age, then let so-and-so be my heir. A son was not born. The next of kin disputed with the man who was heir if the son died before he came of age.

The structural resemblance between this and the previous example already suggests that there must have been a similar need for jurists in the case, but in fact the advocates involved make this even clearer. Cicero describes the two men, L. Licinius Crassus and Q. Mucius Scaevola the Pontifex, as the most learned in law of the eloquent men and the most eloquent of the men learned in law respectively.[36] Crassus spoke in favour of Manius Curius, the reversionary heir, by arguing for the spirit of the law and Scaevola was the advocate for the next of kin, Coponius, arguing that the letter of the law should be prioritised.[37] Although Crassus' argument was more persuasive for the jury on this occasion, Scaevola's contribution to the case confirms the active role that jurists could play in legal trials.

Cicero's personal connection to the two advocates, who were both his mentor at one time, may explain why he chooses to use this example of the *causa Curiana* as well as the previous inheritance case despite their similarity. But his use of this example may also reflect a broader tendency of both rhetorical handbooks to repeatedly use cases of inheritance.

One instance of this occurs in the lists of the six parts of *ius* that both authors give to illustrate the *negotialis/absoluta* Issues discussed above. In fact, Cicero and the Auctor use the same two examples of problematic inheritance cases, which may mean that the examples come from the common source that the texts share. The first example demonstrates a case of ambiguity, when the will specifies that the heir should give his mother certain silver vessels 'as they wish' (*quae volet*), but doesn't say who is to do the choosing.[38] The dispute arises between a son and a mother, each claiming the right to choose. The wording of the example in each of the two texts is very similar.

The second example is an example of reasoning by analogy.[39] The authors list a series of relevant laws (*leges*) before describing an actual situation in further detail. In this case, a condemned man made a will and the question is whether the will is valid or not. The three laws that are cited by both

---

[36] Cic. *Brut.* 39.145. Although Cicero separates the two men here into different specialisms, it should be remembered that they were colleagues in magistracies for most of their careers, and indeed had been consuls together only a few years previously in 95 BC. On Scaevola's career, see for example Balsdon 1937; Bauman 1983; Kallet-Marx 1989, 1990.

[37] Cic. *Brut.* 193–9; see Vaughn 1985. As Vaughn argues, Scaevola followed the theoretical advice of the *Rhetorica ad Herennium* in structuring his argument: 1985: 215.

[38] *Rhet. Her.* 1.12.20; Cic. *Inv. rhet.* 2.40.116.

[39] Cic. *Inv. rhet.* 2.50.149, cf. 2.41.120; *Rhet. Her.* 1.13.23.

authors can be securely attributed to the fifth book of the Twelve Tables.[40]
The Auctor gives the name of the individual involved, Malleolus, and both
authors explain that he had been convicted of murdering his mother, made
a will, and was thrown in a sack to be drowned in the river. Livy's *epitoma-
tor* confirms that this was a real case from 101 BC.[41] As mentioned above,
the reference to the Twelve Tables connects this discussion to the jurists,
including Scaevola, whose work *De Iure Civili* was a somewhat traditional
commentary on the ancient statutes.[42] Cicero's decision not to include the
name of Malleolus, just as he did not refer to any names in the *causa Curiana*,
may show the additional influence of the juristic hypothetical case on his
writing.[43]

Why are these examples significant? The prevalence of such examples,
many of which I have not discussed here for reasons of space,[44] must be
a reflection of the frequency of such cases in the Roman civil law courts.
Their use in the rhetorical handbooks also suggests that they place particular
demands on the advocates taking part. From the context of the first unknown
inheritance case that I discussed within Cicero's work and its subject matter,
it is clear that the *responsa* of jurists were involved. In the case of the *causa
Curiana*, this involvement deepened to include the jurist Scaevola directly
as an advocate. In the examples of the silver vessels and Malleolus' will,
the advice of jurists must also have played an important role in shaping the
arguments of the advocates on either side. For this reason, these and the
many other examples of inheritance in the two rhetorical handbooks serve
as evidence for the supporting role played by jurists in many Roman trials.

The references that Cicero makes to the jurists acknowledge their prominent and essential role in the field of civil law from an advocate's point of
view. It is no coincidence that Cicero uses the example of inheritance to
illustrate the domain over which they have such mastery: the frequent inter-
vention of the jurists' expert advice about these cases must be assumed. The
recurrence of these examples touching on inheritance in both texts may in
fact reflect a discussion sparked by the *causa Curiana* about its significance.
Yet it may also simply be a sign of how frequently this issue arose in the

---

[40] Twelve Tables 5.7a ('Si furiosus est, agnatum gentiliumque in eo pecuniaque eius potestas esto'); Twelve Tables 5.3 ('Paterfamilias uti super familia pecuniaque sui legassit, ita ius esto'); Twelve Tables 5.4–5 ('Si paterfamilias intestato moritur, familia pecuniaque eius agnatum gentiliumque esto'). The Auctor also gives one further law, which cannot be securely attributed to the Twelve Tables but may derive from there.

[41] Livy *Per.* 68.

[42] Harries 2006: 43: the commentary may have been 'both traditionalist and revolutionary'. See Watson's reconstruction: 1974: 143–4.

[43] For Scaevola and the hypothetical case, see Frier 1985: 166–9; Harries 2006: 105–8.

[44] Examples that mention inheritance but I do not discuss here are: *Rhet. Her.* 2.13.19, 2.21.33, 3.20.33, 4.23.33, 4.29.40, 4.38.50, 4.40.52, 4.53.67; Cic. *Inv. rhet.* 1.45.84, 1.48.89, 2.21.62, 2.40.118.

Roman courts. In either case, the position of the jurists at this time seems to be assured.

3. ADVOCATES

Unsurprisingly, advocates are not as hard to locate in the two rhetorical handbooks as the jurists in the previous section; the orator of the *Rhetorica ad Herennium* and the *De Inventione* are both implicitly situated in the law courts for much of the time. They are also shown using the law explicitly in several locations. The anonymous Auctor of the *Rhetorica ad Herennium* comes back to the case of *maiestas* three times in the work, a reflection of the difficulties arising from new legislation. Yet the Auctor shows how a case involving *maiestas* can be argued from both sides, presenting an opportunity for the advocate to reframe the law.

The role of advocates in a Roman court is best introduced by the *Rhetorica ad Herennium* itself. In the fourth book of the *Rhetorica ad Herennium*, the Auctor gives an example addressed to the judge L. Cassius Longinus Ravilla, known for his strictness and severity:[45]

> Accusatoris officium est inferre crimina; defensoris diluere et propulsare; testis dicere quae sciat aut audierit; quaesitoris est unum quemque horum in officio suo continere. Quare, L. Cassi, si testem praeterquam quod sciat aut audierit argumentari et coniectura prosequi patieris, ius accusatoris cum iure testimonii commiscebis, testis inprobi cupiditatem confirmabis, reo duplicem defensionem parabis.

> It is the duty of the prosecutor to bring the charges; of the defence counsel to explain and oppose them; of the witness to say what they know or what they have heard; of the court official to keep each one of these to their duty. Therefore, Lucius Cassius, if you allow the witness to describe more than what they know or have heard using arguments and conjectures, then you will confuse the right to prosecute with the right to give evidence, you will encourage the ambition of a dishonest witness, and you will prepare a double defence for the defendant.

This is an example of *distributio*, assigning roles to people or things. The Auctor praises this rhetorical technique and the reference to Cassius Longinus gives it grounding in a recognisable (and datable) Roman context. It clearly describes the ideal role of the two advocates, the role of the court official (*quaesitor*), and the witnesses. The prosecutor (*accusator*) brings the charges, makes arguments and attacks the opposition with conjectures, while the defence (*defensor*) explains and rebuts them.

---

[45] *Rhet. Her.* 4.37.47. See Cic. *Rosc. Am.* 84–5; *Brut.* 97; Asc. *Mil.* 34C for Longinus' reputation. It may be Crassus speaking here or another defendant at the trials for corruption of the Vestal Virgins in 114/3.

This example is intended to make the process sound simple, but the reality is more complicated. As seen in the section above, an advocate in a civil trial would have to take into account the arguments of the jurists, as well as the disposition of the judge. In a criminal trial too, as I discuss in the next section, the advocate would have to assess his audience of *iudices* to pitch his argument in the most persuasive terms.[46]

But while these factors were obviously important, an additional consideration for advocates recurs throughout the texts, and that is the laws themselves.[47] The *Rhetorica ad Herennium* and the *De Inventione* both point to a very contemporary issue with one particular, new law: the *lex Appuleia de maiestate*. In full, this law about *maiestas* (sometimes translated as 'treason' or *lèse majesté*) was intended to protect against *maiestas populi Romani minuta*, 'damage to the dignity of the Roman people'.[48] The law was passed by L. Appuleius Saturninus, the tribune of 103/100.[49]

The issue of *maiestas* recurs throughout the two handbooks in much the same way that inheritance does, both as the central focus of examples and also incidentally as the background to examples. The main figure linked with *maiestas* in the *Rhetorica ad Herennium* is Q. Servilius Caepio; his alleged offence in obstructing Saturninus' attempt to pass a grain law is described early in Book 1.[50] The Auctor's decision to use this particular occurrence of (potential) *maiestas* is significant because the offence involved Saturninus, who had passed the law *de maiestate*. By using this incident to illustrate *maiestas* the Auctor draws a direct line for future advocates between Saturninus' legislation and the actions of Caepio, an exemplary justification for Saturninus' *maiestas* law.

The key information for the reader comes afterwards: the Auctor explains that this example illustrates *definitio* because 'the term itself is defined when it is examined what "damaging *maiestas*" is'.[51] This highlights the scope that the advocate had to determine exactly what *maiestas* was in terms that were favourable to their client's situation. *Maiestas* was a subjective term and Saturninus' law clearly allowed for some manipulation.[52] As this suggests,

---

[46] See also Alexander for the differences between the role of a prosecutor and defence counsel: 2002: 1–54, esp. 8–15. See for example the specific advice given to the prosecutor or defence counsel for a *narratio* in *Rhet. Her.* (2.2.3) or the *loci communes* for the *coniecturalis constitutio* in *Inv. Rhet.* (2.16.51). Also found in Quint. *Inst.* 5.13.2–3; Cic. *Rosc. Am.* 56–7.

[47] See Burnand's comments on Cic. *Clu.* 146–7, 155: 2000: 116–21.

[48] Fantham 2004: 34. See Bauman 1970 for a full overview of the history and significance of the charge.

[49] Cic. *De or.* 2.25.107, 49.201.

[50] *Rhet. Her.* 1.12.21. Saturninus is mentioned twice more in the *Rhetorica ad Herennium*: 4.22.31, 4.54.67.

[51] 1.12.21: 'vocabulum enim definitur ipsum cum quaeritur quid sit minuere maiestatem.'

[52] Fantham 2004: 122 (see also 123–30). Seager 2001 uses D. 48.4.7.3, 48.4.4 pr. to argue that some specific examples of improper conduct may have been included in the law, although *seditio* would not have been. Harries discusses the acknowledged limitations of written law

the advocate's own interpretation of 'damaging *maiestas*' could prove crucial in winning or losing the case.

In Book 2, the Auctor illustrates for the reader the way in which an advocate could construct his interpretation or definition when faced with this type of cause. He gives two examples that define *maiestas* in different ways, using the same phrase of *amplitudo civitatis* but reappropriating the meaning to suit opposing perspectives.[53] In this way, the Auctor illustrates for the future advocate how to speak on either side of such a case. The two examples represent fragments of the prosecution and defence in Caepio's trial, with the defence example given in the first person.[54]

In the first definition, the prosecutor argues that *maiestas* is diminished when the things that make up the *civitatis amplitudo*, 'greatness of the state', are taken away. According to him, these are *suffragia, magistratus*: the right to vote and the magistracies. These two things are political and they relate to the people's involvement in the state and their protection by it. In the contrasting definition, the defence claims to have guarded the treasury and opposed the desires of evil people in order to prevent the state's decline.[55] Here the focus is on the economic stability and moral rectitude of the state. These definitions provide the crux of either argument, containing themes that could be expanded persuasively throughout the remainder of the speech to convince the audience that this interpretation was the most important one. The Auctor makes it clear that each phrase can be construed in various ways and hence demonstrates the options available for an advocate defending or prosecuting in a *maiestas* trial.

The similarity of the approach in *De Inventione* suggests that was a widely recognised approach, at least in the *quaestio de maiestate*. In Cicero's text *maiestas* is used to illustrate the technique of *definitio* once again, although the example that Cicero chooses is one from much earlier in Republican history – the case of C. Flaminius being removed from the *rostrum* by his father when he was tribune of the plebs in 232 BC.[56]

---

more generally: 2004: 156–7. Sulla's *lex Cornelia de maiestate* did not succeed in clarifying the law satisfactorily, according to Cicero: *Part or.* 105; cf. Lintott 1968: 118.

[53] 2.12.17: 'Maiestatem is minuit, qui ea tollit, ex quibus rebus civitatis amplitudo constat. Quae sunt ea, Q. Caepio? Suffragia, magistratus. Nempe igitur tu et populum suffragio et magistratum consilio privasti, cum pontes disturbasti.'

[54] Caepio's defence advocate was L. Licinius Crassus and the prosecutor was T. Betutius Barrus. It is not known whether Caepio did speak in his own defence either at his trial or on another public occasion, or whether the example represents an imagined speech act. See Cic. *Brut.* 169; Alexander 1990: fn.88.

[55] 2.12.17: 'Maiestatem is minuit, qui amplitudinem civitatis detrimento <adficit. Ego non adfeci, sed prohibui detrimento:> aerarium enim conservavi, libidini malorum restiti, maiestatem omnem interire non passus sum.' The bracketed section is omitted by some manuscripts, but has been included by editors from Marx onwards. The sense of the fragment in contrast with the former is nevertheless clear for the purposes of this discussion.

[56] Cic. *Inv. rhet.* 2.27.52.

The term *amplitudo* appears again in Cicero's opposing definitions for *maiestas*, but the emphasis has shifted towards the significance of the term *potestas* instead.[57] This suggests that Saturninus' *maiestas* law had left yet another avenue of debate open to be taken advantage of by advocates. Despite the different focus, Cicero's two opposing definitions follow quite similar themes to those found in the *Rhetorica ad Herennium*. One foregrounds the *potestas* of the people and the elected magistrates, while the other gives priority to the unlawful *potestas* of those who have not been elected, perhaps equivalent to the *libido malorum* in the *Rhetorica ad Herennium*.

The concern with defining and using *maiestas* continues in several other examples from both texts that refer to the offence directly or indirectly.[58] For example, the Auctor and Cicero mention the defeat of L. Popilius by the Gauls in 107 and say explicitly that he was brought to trial for *maiestas*.[59] Cicero uses the Popilius example while discussing the Qualitative (*generalis*) issue, but he acknowledges that the action could also be prosecuted using one of two Conjectural (*coniecturalis*) arguments. This recognition, that there were several possible methods of argument for the same *maiestas* case, is a particularly interesting aspect of Cicero's presentation. In a very pragmatic way, it is a further confirmation that the topic of *maiestas* was not straightforward but presented advocates with a choice.

The same debate about the right approach for advocates is also explored in Cicero's much later work, *De Oratore*. Although written around 55 BC, the text is set in 91 BC and includes several key figures from *maiestas* trials in the 90s,[60] including Crassus who spoke on behalf of Caepio, as mentioned above. Cicero also gives voice to the characters of M. Antonius and Ser. Sulpicius Rufus who were defence counsel and prosecutor respectively for a parallel *maiestas* case involving C. Norbanus.[61]

In this latter case, Cicero has Antonius explain that the whole case (*tota illa causa*) rested on the way that he and Sulpicius interpreted *maiestas* in the *lex Appuleia*.[62] Although Antonius claims that neither of the advocates gave a strict definition of *maiestas*, which would be vulnerable to attack, he does later give the same sort of description that is found in the *Rhetorica ad Herennium* and the *De Inventione*.[63]

---

[57] Idem: 2.27.53, 2.28.55.
[58] The Auctor gives another definition of *maiestas* in Book 4 (4.26.35; alongside *iniuria, fortitudo* and *diligentia*) where he discusses *definitio* as a rhetorical technique. The Auctor's example of the style at the beginning of Book 4 (4.9.13) is also thought to represent part of L. Varius' speech in favour of his own *lex Varia de maiestate* during the Social War; see Caplan 1954: *ad loc*. See Gruen 1965; Seager 1967 for the *lex Varia*.
[59] *Rhet. Her.* 1.15.25, 4.24.34; Cic. *Inv. rhet.* 2.24.72.
[60] For the importance of trials in the 90s, see Gruen 1966, 1968.
[61] Cic. *De or.* 2.25.107–9, 47.197–50.202. Cf. Badian 1957, 1983.
[62] Cic. *De or.* 2.25.107. See Fantham 2004: 122.
[63] Cic. *De or.* 2.39.164.

Si maiestas est amplitudo ac dignitas civitatis, is eam minuit, qui exercitum hosti-
bus populi Romani tradidit, non qui eum, qui id fecisset, populi Romani potestati
tradidit.

If *maiestas* is the greatness and the dignity of the state, then it is lessened by the
man who hands over the army of the Roman people to the enemy and not by the
man who brings the one that did it to the authority of the Roman people.

Antonius here sets up the contrast between the severity of what Caepio did
and what Norbanus did. To do this, he again uses the key words *amplitudo*
. . . *civitatis* and *potestas*, which were found in Cicero and the Auctor's definitions.[64] These seem to be the key terms that an advocate would have to
think about and prepare his response to. The slight differences within each
text show how each pair of advocates could redefine the terms for their own
individual cases.

An advocate in the early first century BC would face many challenges, but
the focus on *maiestas* that I have discussed in this section shows one particular aspect of an advocate's role that both Cicero and the Auctor found
important. The ability of the prosecutor to bring the charges and the defence
counsel to rebut them were both significantly impaired by the ambiguity
of the definition of *maiestas*, which could leave even the most convincing
arguments vulnerable. However, both authors take the opportunity to
quote both sides of the argument and thereby give their readers the skills
necessary to take advantage of such a scenario. For a would-be advocate, this
could be a chance to practise arguing on both sides of a case. For historians,
this evidence shows how advocates in the Roman Republic were able to re-
appropriate language like *amplitudo* and adapt definitions in order to succeed
in court.

4. JURORS

On the receiving end of these definitions were the jurors, *iudices*. In a civil
trial there would typically be a single judge (*unus iudex*) who was appointed
by the urban praetor.[65] The *causa Curiana* was a slightly different type of
civil case that was heard by a group of *iudices* called the *Centumviri*.[66] In a
criminal trial, the board of *iudices* was drawn from a list that would be set
annually by the praetor.[67] The individuals involved in either type of case

---

[64] See Hellegouarc'h 1963: 314–20 for the political significance of *maiestas* and its connection
with the term *amplitudo*.

[65] Kelly 1976: 112–33.

[66] Cic. *Brut.* 144. For more on legal procedure see Lintott 2004; Metzger 2010.

[67] As stipulated in the *lex repetundarum*, 123/2 BC: Crawford 1996: fn.1 ll.15–26. See also Frier
1985: 199–201 for the normal process of selecting *iudices* and the different procedure for
selecting *recuperatores*; Harries 2006: 15. See Cicero's discussion in *Planc.* 62.

were likely to have a similar background, in that they were all members of the Roman elite, highly educated and relatively wealthy. However there was an ongoing debate about whether equestrians or senators (or both) should staff the criminal courts, the *quaestiones*.[68] The situation went back and forth in the thirty years between Gaius Gracchus' controversial legislation and the writing of the two handbooks, but in 87 the *lex Plautia* was passed, resulting in mixed juries.[69]

Jurors, the *iudices*, are mentioned in sixteen examples from the *Rhetorica ad Herennium* and seven examples from the *De Inventione*.[70] The *iudices* are addressed in the form of an apostrophe, usually towards the beginning of an example. If these examples do come from real speeches, then the plural form of *iudex* means that it is likely these jurors are addressed as part of a *quaestio* in criminal law.[71] This is important because it provides a context in which the role of the *iudices* can be assessed. I will study the way they are addressed and the assumptions made about what is persuasive in that context. However, as I will show in this section, there are important differences in the realism and approach of the examples chosen by the Auctor and Cicero that employ this rhetorical device.

Neither author intends these disparate examples to be representative of the *iudices*; each of them is used to illustrate different techniques at different points of the text. In the *Rhetorica ad Herennium* all but one of the examples comes from the final book, where the Auctor gives positive recommendations about style. The single negative example in the *Rhetorica ad Herennium* is matched by two consecutive examples in the *De Inventione* that illustrate the faulty techniques of a *commune* or *vulgare* argument. But despite the rather accidental nature of these two groups, there are common themes running through the examples that reference the *iudices* in each work.

In the *Rhetorica ad Herennium*, the examples addressing the *iudices* tend to use *pathos* rather than legal argument (*logos*), arousing fear in the audience through a variety of techniques.[72] By contrast, Cicero in *De Inventione* uses examples from non-Roman contexts, which mostly refer explicitly to the use of the law. Cicero also devotes a long passage to the applicability and utility of laws to the *iudices* themselves.[73]

A typical example in the *Rhetorica ad Herennium* addressing the *iudices* will

---

[68] For a brief treatment of the various changes, see Suárez Piñeiro 2000. See also Weinrib 1970; Griffin 1973.

[69] Asc. *Corn.* 79C. Suárez Piñeiro 2000: 264–5.

[70] *Rhet. Her.* 2.21.34, 4.8.12, 4.9.13, 4.21.29, 4.24.33, 4.31.42, 4.35.47, 4.36.48, 4.37.49, 4.38.50, 4.39.51 (x3), 4.40.53–41.53, 4.49.63, 4.50.63–51.64; Cic. *Inv. rhet.* 1.33.56, 1.39.68, 1.39.70, 1.48.90 (x2), 1.52.100, 2.43.104.

[71] The term does not appear in Cic. *Quinct.*, Q *Rosc.*, *Tull.*, *Caecin.*

[72] See Wisse 1989: 77–104 for *ethos* and *pathos* in the rhetorical handbooks.

[73] Cic. *Inv. rhet.* 2.45.131–2.

attempt to persuade the jurors by emphasising and exaggerating the negative consequences that would result from making the wrong decision:[74]

> Quodsi istum, iudices, vestris sententiis liberaveritis, statim, sicut e cavea leo emissus aut aliqua taeterrima belua soluta ex catenis, volitabit et vagabitur in foro ... Quare, iudices, eicite eum de civitate, liberate omnes formidine; vobis denique ipsis consulite.

> But if, men of the jury, you set that man free with your verdicts he will swoop and skulk around the forum at once like a lion let out of its cage or another terrible wild beast released from its chains ... Therefore, men of the jury, throw him out of the city, free everyone from fear, and finally, consider yourselves.

This example illustrates Vivid Description (*descriptio*) and, indeed, seems to do so very successfully. The advocate addresses the *iudices* directly to reinforce and awaken them to the connection between their votes and the potential threat of the defendant. He describes at length the terrible actions that the free man could undertake, and then encourages them to make their judgement on the basis of this knowledge for the sake of the state, all the citizens and themselves. Two other examples for Vivid Description also address the *iudices* and use a similar combination of threats and encouragement to attempt to persuade them,[75] while the Auctor's examples of the Grand and Middle styles of speech also take place in this context.[76]

The personal threat that is hinted at the very end of the example is also taken up elsewhere. An example of *licentia*, Frankness of Speech, berates the *iudices* for failing to pass judgement on the defendant in the first hearing of the trial.[77] The speaker says that the *iudices* have themselves suffered 'very great misfortunes, both private and public' (*maximae publicae et privatae calamitationes*) and that many more (*maiores*) threaten them. The misfortunes are not specified, and the speaker may have left the details purposefully vague for greater effect. Yet even if this is another exaggeration, it gives the responsibility implied in the above example a sense of reality, and shows how the job of a *iudex* could be an unpleasant and burdensome one.

It is not certain whether some, all or none of these examples originate in a real Roman *quaestio*. At the beginning of this fourth book, the Auctor makes a strong case for writing his own examples throughout the work, but this does not seem to always be the case.[78] Commentators on the *ad Herennium* have previously identified influences on some of these examples addressed to

---

[74] *Rhet. Her.* 4.39.51.

[75] Also at *Rhet. Her.* 4.39.51.

[76] Idem: 4.8.11–9.13.

[77] Idem: 4.36.48.

[78] This has been discussed by many scholars, see Marx 1894: 114–18; Caplan 1954: 31–2; Barwick 1961: 300–14; Calboli 1969: 42–6; Ungern-Sternberg 1973: 149–52; Adamik 1998: 271.

iudices such as Demosthenes, Plautus and possibly also Varius, who passed the *lex Varia* during the Social War.[79] It seems unlikely that the Auctor would have wholly invented a lengthy 438-word character description of a poor man said to have been involved in an elaborate pretence.[80] There are other details too that locate these examples within a Roman context, such as mentions of the senate and the equestrian order, as well as references to the Roman people and the forum.[81] Wherever these examples come from, then, they have at least been adapted to fit the context of a Roman *quaestio*. In order to be appropriate and useful teaching tools, they must be intended to resemble the kinds of speech that might be found there. Hence they are useful evidence of the kinds of addresses to the *iudices* that the Auctor considers successful in the legal context of a *quaestio*.

Reading the *Rhetorica ad Herennium*, then, gives an impression of a *quaestio* environment that functions primarily through the use of emotional appeals and is staffed by a board of *iudices* who respond best to this approach. To some extent, this presentation of the *quaestio* system makes sense in the Roman context as it is understood by modern scholarship. *Iudices* are not chosen for their legal knowledge or expertise, although as members of the elite (either equestrians or senators) they would have had some legal education. In the *quaestiones*, too, the jurists did not play a major role in advising or supporting legal interpretation. Hence emotional appeals and general themes may have been more understandable to this audience.[82]

And yet, the *iudices* addressed in Cicero's examples in the *De Inventione* are quite different. One explanation for this might be that it is much less clear that the *iudices* Cicero refers to are meant to resemble *iudices* from a Roman *quaestio*, unlike those in the *Rhetorica ad Herennium*. The three most substantial passages come from Book 1 and describe an argument with five, four or three parts. While many of the points are of a general nature and discuss the *res publica* in a familiar way, the specifics relate to Thebes and the general Epaminondas.[83] Cicero also glosses one of the examples, ending with 'For what more do you want, *iudices*, when this and this [*hoc et hoc*] have been made clear to you?'[84] Cicero supplies only the information that is relevant to the example itself, which illustrates a method of summing up in the conclusion. Although understandable, this is a contrast to the Auctor's tendency to make his examples sound as authentic as possible.

Nevertheless, as in the *Rhetorica ad Herennium*, it ought to be true that

---

[79] See Caplan 1954: *ad loc.* 4.9.13 (Varius), 4.22.33 (Demosthenes), 4.50.63–51.64 (Plautus).

[80] *Rhet. Her.* 4.50.63–51.64.

[81] See e.g. 4.9.13 for *populi Romani*, 4.35.47 for *senatus* and *locus equester*, 4.39.51 for *in foro*.

[82] As discussed by Harries 2004: 149. See also Riggsby 1997, 2004 for the relevance of non-legal arguments.

[83] Cic. *Inv. rhet.* 1.33.56, 1.38.68, 1.39.70.

[84] Idem: 1.52.100.

Cicero's examples are intended to serve as models for the reader, and the arguments contained within them are relevant for persuading Roman *iudices* too. Indeed, as proof of this, Cicero makes much the same arguments in Book 2 in his authorial voice.

The discussion relates to the argument between the letter and the spirit of the law. Two of the three Theban examples argue in favour of the letter of the law, that is, that the way that the law is written should be interpreted literally. The examples explicitly refer to the legal knowledge of the *iudices* and the relevance of the laws to the *iudices* personally. In the first example the speaker says:

> Quod ergo ascribi ad legem nefas est, id sequi, quasi ascriptum sit, rectum vobis videatur? Novi vestram intellegentiam; non potest ita videri, iudices.[85]

> Therefore, would it seem right to you that something was done as if it had been added to law, which it is illegal to add to the law? I know your intelligence; it cannot seem right to you, *iudices*.

The *intellegentia* of the *iudices* surrounding the laws is also relied upon in the third example. The speaker argues that the *iudices* must obey the laws, but in order to do so they must follow what has been written there. If they themselves are reliant on and bound by the written word of the law, then it is obvious that the defendant ought to be too.

Cicero picks up on this idea when he returns to explain the arguments based on letter and spirit in Book 2 (rather than how to piece together an argument, which is the focus of the examples above).[86] Among other arguments that can be made in favour of the letter of the law, including the reading out of *exceptiones* from other laws to prove that they can be written in if necessary, Cicero comes back to the *iudices*' own reliance on the law. The *iudices* need laws to base their judgements on, and to justify their actions to others afterwards. The *iudices* are bound by many annoying details of the law (*obstricti in tantis molestiis*) and, therefore, why should others not be too?

The idea that the *iudices* should consider the law is made explicit in these sections of the *De Inventione*. Cicero's use of this topic to illustrate how arguments can be formed and adapted suggests that this was a clear-cut argument in itself, a relatively straightforward proposition that could be made (or had been made) in different ways. When Cicero goes into greater detail in Book 2, he provides an argument that counters the points above by also appealing to the experience of the *iudices*: the writer of the law knew the kind of men who would be judging the case, not stupid or foreign ones, and not simple legal clerks, but interpreters: *interpretes*.[87]

---

[85]   Idem: 1.33.56.
[86]   Idem: 1.45.131–2.
[87]   Idem: 2.57.139.

Cicero's glossed example, mentioned above, also places the *iudices* in the position of interpreting and understanding the law. In this case, the speaker asks the *iudices* 'What if the laws could speak? Would they not ask you these things?'[88] The *iudices* must listen to the laws, which the speaker connects directly to their argument and the outcome of the case as a whole.

In Cicero's examples involving the *iudices*, they are presented as a group of people with real legal responsibility and an ability to interpret the laws in complex and meaningful ways. This is in contrast to the way that the *iudices* appear in the *Rhetorica ad Herennium*, where they are not connected to the law by any of the speakers chosen by the Auctor.

There is one example from the *De Inventione* that more closely resembles the examples from the *Rhetorica ad Herennium*.[89] This example illustrates *deprecatio*, a plea for mercy, and addresses the *iudices* with persuasive language that is founded on their own character, the character of the accused and their emotional response. The speaker says that it would be worthy of their clemency and the defendant's virtue for them to forgive him this one error. This discussion of the defendant in the third person by an advocate suggests that this speech comes from a Roman context rather than a Greek one, where the defendant would speak for themselves. It is possible that this is a real Roman example, which might suggest that there were genuinely different expectations of legal knowledge when speaking to a Greek and a Roman audience.

There is not enough evidence here to conclude definitively what is representative of the interaction between Roman advocates and *iudices* in the *quaestiones*, or of the legal knowledge of the *iudices* more generally. But in the context of the two rhetorical handbooks it is notable that the dominant approach to the *iudices* in the two works is very different, with the *Rhetorica ad Herennium* demonstrating the rhetorical success of emotional appeals and the *De Inventione* showing repeatedly that the law ought to be the deciding factor. Two models of speaking to the *iudices* are set up, which represent two of the different options for the advocates of the 80s BC.

5. CONCLUSION

This last section highlights an important question: to what extent can the guidelines provided by a rhetorical handbook be taken as historical evidence? Although there cannot be a definitive answer, both texts were intended to be relevant and useful to readers at the time hence their evidence ought to be taken seriously. Yet this argument applies more convincingly perhaps to the Auctor, who was experienced enough in Herennius' eyes to be an authority *de ratione dicendi*, than to Cicero, who was still a young man without any personal experience of being an advocate. This may be reflected in the more

---

[88] Idem: 1.52.100.
[89] Idem: 2.34.104.

theoretical and idealised approach to rhetoric that is apparent throughout the *De Inventione*. On the other hand, Cicero's years of education and training with highly experienced statesmen, as well as his demonstrable ability to discuss legal issues at length in the *De Inventione*, mean that the in-depth legal arguments presented in his Theban example should not be dismissed as irrelevant to the Roman context.

Instead, by examining the *Rhetorica ad Herennium* and *De Inventione* I hope to have shown that both works are rich sources of evidence for this period and can significantly add to our understanding of the legal context. By looking at these works it is possible to better appreciate the post-Social War legal system, the context of Cicero's legal education, and the potential for the influence of jurists such as Scaevola to be widely felt. These two rhetorical handbooks show that the law courts in the early first century BC were complex and challenging places, but the Auctor and Cicero saw the need to present solutions and offer guidance in order to train the next generation of advocates. In spite of the disturbance of the Social War and the following years – or perhaps because of it – the Roman law courts continued to function and these texts are important evidence of the people and processes involved.

BIBLIOGRAPHY

Achard, G. (1989), *Rhétorique à Herennius*. Paris.

Achard, G. (1994), *Ciceron: De L'Invention*. Paris.

Adamik, T. (1998), 'Basic problems of the *Ad Herennium*: author, date, its relation to the *De Inventione*', *Acta Antiqua Academiae Scientiarum Hungaricae* 38: 267–85.

Adamietz, J. (1960), *Ciceros de inventione und die Rhetorik ad Herennium*. Dissertation. Marburg.

Alexander, M. C. (1990), *Trials in the Late Roman Republic: 149 BC to 50 BC*. Toronto.

Alexander, M. C. (2002), *The Case for the Prosecution in the Ciceronian Era*. Ann Arbor.

Badian, E. (1957), 'Caepio and Norbanus: notes on the decade 100–90 BC', *Historia* 6: 318–46.

Badian, E. (1983), 'The Silence of Norbanus', *American Journal of Philology* 104: 156–71.

Balsdon, J. P. V. D. (1937), 'Q. Mucius Scaevola the Pontifex and *Ornatio Provinciae*', *Classical Review* 51: 8–10.

Barwick, K. (1961), 'Die Vorrede zum zweiten Buch der rhetorischen Jugendschrift Ciceros und zum vierten Buch des *Auctor ad Herennium*', *Philologus* 105: 307–14.

Bauman, R. A. (1970), *The* Crimen Maiestatis *in the Roman Republic and Augustan Principate*. Dissertation. Johannesburg.

Bauman, R. A. (1983), *Lawyers in Roman Republican Politics*. Munich.

Burnand, C. J. (2000), *Roman Representations of the Orator during the Last Century of the Republic*. Dissertation. Oxford.

Calboli, G. (1969), *Rhetorica ad C. Herennium*. Bologna.

Calboli, G. (1972), 'L'oratore M. Antonio e la *Rhetorica ad Herennium*', *Giornale italiano di filologia* 24: 120–77.

Caplan, H. (1954), *[Cicero]: Rhetorica ad Herennium*. Cambridge, MA.

Corbeill, A. (2002), 'Rhetorical education in Cicero's youth', in J. May, ed., *Brill's Companion to Cicero: Oratory and rhetoric*. Leiden. 23–48.

Corbeill, A. (2007), 'Rhetorical education and social reproduction in the republic and early empire', in W. Dominik and J. Hall, eds, *A Companion to Roman Rhetoric*. Oxford. 69–82.

Crawford, M. H., ed. (1996), *Roman Statutes*, volume 1. London.

Douglas, A. E. (1960), '*Clausulae* in the *Rhetorica ad Herennium* as evidence of its date', *Classical Quarterly* 10: 65–78.

Fantham, E. (2004), *The Roman World of Cicero's De Oratore*. Oxford.

Frier, B. W. (1985), *The Rise of the Roman Jurists: Studies in Cicero's Pro Caecina*. Princeton.

Gildenhard, I. (2011), *Creative Eloquence: The construction of reality in Cicero's speeches*. Oxford.

Griffin, M. (1973), 'The "*leges iudiciariae*" of the pre-Sullan era', *Classical Quarterly* 23: 108–26.

Gruen, E. (1965), 'The *Lex Varia*', *Journal of Roman Studies* 55: 59–73.

Gruen, E. (1966), 'The Quaestorship of Norbanus', *Classical Philology* 61: 105–7.

Gruen, E. S. (1968), *Roman Politics and the Criminal Courts, 149–78 BC*. Cambridge, MA.

Harries, J. (2004), 'Cicero and the law', in J. Powell and J. Paterson, eds, *Cicero the Advocate*. Oxford. 147–63.

Harries, J. (2006), *Cicero and the Jurists: From citizens' law to the lawful state*. London.

Harries, J. (2013), 'The law in Cicero's writings', in C. Steel, ed., *The Cambridge Companion to Cicero*. Cambridge. 107–21.

Heath, M. (1994), 'The substructure of *stasis*-theory from Hermagoras to Hermogenes', *Classical Quarterly* 44: 114–29.

Hellegouarc'h, J. (1963), *Le vocabulaire latin des relations et des partis politiques sous la République*. Paris.

Henderson, M. I. (1951), 'The process "*De Repetundis*"', *Journal of Roman Studies* 41: 71–88.

Herbolzheimer, G. (1926), 'Ciceros *Rhetorici Libri* und die Lehrschrift des *Auctor ad Herennium*', *Philologus* 81: 391–426.

Kallet-Marx, R. (1989), 'Asconius 14–15 Clark and the date of Q. Mucius Scaevola's command in Asia', *Classical Philology* 84: 305–12.

Kallet-Marx, R. (1990), 'The trial of P. Rutilius Rufus', *Phoenix* 44: 122–39.

Kelly, J. M. (1976), *Studies in the Civil Judicature of the Roman Republic*. Oxford.

Lintott, A. (1968), *Violence in Republican Rome*. Oxford.

Lintott, A. (2004), 'Legal procedure in Cicero's time', in J. Powell and J. Paterson, eds, *Cicero the Advocate*. Oxford. 61–78.

Marx, F. (1894), *Incerti Auctoris de Ratione Dicendi ad C. Herennium Libri IV*. Leipzig.

Metzger, E. (2010), 'Civil procedure in classical Rome: having an audience with the magistrate', in F. de Angelis, ed., *Spaces of Justice in the Roman World*. Leiden. 27–41.

Negri, M. (2007), 'Il 'giovane' Cicerone, la *lex Cornelia de sicariis et veneficiis* e la datazione del *De inventione*', *Athenaeum* 95: 183–201.

Riggsby, A. (1997), 'Did the Romans believe in their verdicts?', *Rhetorica* 15: 235–51.

Riggsby, A. (2004), 'The rhetoric of character in the Roman courts', in J. Powell and J. Paterson, eds, *Cicero the Advocate*. Oxford. 165–85.

Seager, R. (1967), '*Lex Varia de Maiestate*', *Historia* 16: 37–43.

Seager, R. (2001), '*Maiestas* in the late Republic: Some observations', in J. W. Cairns and O. F. Robinson, eds, *Critical Studies in Ancient Law, Comparative Law and Legal History*. Oxford. 143–53.

Suárez Piñiero, A. M. (2000), 'Las "*leges iudiciariae*" ante la crisis de la República Romana (133–44 AC[BC])', *Latomus* 59: 253–75.

Tuori, K. (2010), 'A place for jurists in the spaces of justice?', in F. de Angelis, ed., *Spaces of Justice in the Roman World*. Leiden. 43–65.

Ungern-Sternberg, J. von (1973), 'Die popularen Beispiele in der Schrift des *Auctor ad Herennium*', *Chiron* 3: 143–62.

Vaughn, J. W. (1985), 'Law and rhetoric in the *Causa Curiana*', *Classical Antiquity* 4: 208–22.

Watson, A. (1974), *Law Making in the Later Roman Republic*. Oxford.

Weinrib, E. J. (1970), 'The judiciary law of M. Livius Drusus (tr. pl. 91 B.C)', *Historia* 19: 414–43.

Wisse, J. (1989), Ethos and Pathos from Aristotle to Cicero. Amsterdam.

Chapter 11

Multiple Charges, Unitary Punishment and Rhetorical Strategy in the Quaestiones of the Late Roman Republic

Michael C. Alexander

1. INTRODUCTION

This chapter addresses an apparent contradiction in Roman criminal trials between multiple charges and unitary punishment. If the punishment for a defendant who was found guilty was the same whether he was found guilty of one charge or many charges, why were multiple charges common?

I will first attempt to establish that the *causa coniuncta*, the case involving several charges, was, in fact, common. In order to support this point, I will argue against the belief that many of what I consider to be actual charges were merely character defamation of the defendant, although character defamation of the defendant was typically employed by prosecutors to make a conviction more likely. I will try to make my case not only on the evidence of Cicero's forensic orations, but on the advice provided to orators in the extensive rhetorical literature of the late Republic and early Empire. This rhetorical literature helps us see Cicero as a typical orator, albeit the leading orator of Rome for much of his life, rather than as an anomalous 'star player' in the Roman courts.

I hope to show in this chapter that it can be more fruitful to view rhetoric as a means employed by ancient orators, such as Cicero, to implement a strategy that they developed to meet the specific legal environment of a trial, rather than as a way merely to obfuscate the legal issues that the trial needed to address. Rhetoric, I will argue, should not be viewed as an unfortunate but necessary way to confuse the jurors, but rather primarily as a highly developed tool that enabled orators to present the facts and the law to the jurors in a comprehensible and persuasive manner.

Legal history involves an inherent tension between formalism and legal realism. My approach pushes the needle somewhat towards the former and away from the latter, while, I hope, avoiding the pitfalls of an extreme formalist approach.

2. MULTIPLE CHARGES

Prosecutors typically cast many aspersions against the defendant in Roman criminal trials, which we usually know about because the *patronus*, speaking for the defendant, attempts to refute these aspersions. (The main exception where we know about the prosecution directly from the prosecutor's words is, of course, all the charges that Cicero made when he prosecuted Verres in 70 BC, which are contained in the orations that he delivered at that trial and from those of the Second *Actio* that he published, although he never actually delivered these speeches in court.) Quintilian describes the difference between a simple case (*causa simplex*) and a complex case (*causa coniuncta*):

> Ceterum causa omnis, in qua pars altera agentis est, altera recusantis, aut unius rei controversia constat aut plurium: haec simplex dicitur, illa coniuncta. Una controversia est per se furti, per se adulterii. Plures aut eiusdem generis, ut in pecuniis repetundis, aut diversi, ut si quis sacrilegii et homicidii simul accusetur. Quod nunc in publicis iudiciis non accidit, quoniam praetor certa lege sortitur, principum autem et senatus cognitionibus frequens est et populi fuit.

> Every Cause, in which one side is the plaintiff's and the other the defendant's, is based either on a Controversy involving a single matter or on one involving several. The first type is called 'simple', the second 'compound'. A theft taken by itself or an adultery taken by itself form a single Controversy. Where there are several charges, these may be of the same kind (for example, in extortion cases) or of different kinds (for example, if a man is accused at the same time of sacrilege and homicide). This does not now happen in the public courts, because the praetor allots cases according to the relevant law, but it often happens in hearings before emperors or the senate, as it did once in trials by the people.[1]

Quintilian makes here a distinction between cases where there is only one question at issue and those where several questions are at issue, and then divides the latter between those in which the issues are all the same (that is, all the same kind of charge, for example, all extortion charges), and those in which different kinds of questions are involved. The final sentence quoted above refers to this second kind of complex case, which is likely to occur, in Quintilian's time, before imperial and senatorial courts, and in Republican times in trials before the People (*iudicia populi*). In a later passage,[2] Quintilian gives the example of a *causa coniuncta* in which there are charges that the defendant arranged for someone to be killed, for another person to be wounded, and for someone else to be killed, and an example of the several kinds of issues may be raised, if, for example, the defendant disputes one

---

[1] Quint. *Inst.* 3.10.1, translation Russell 2001.
[2] Quint. *Inst.* 7.1.9.

fact, justifies another, and argues that a third is not the business of the court. An example of a *causa coniuncta* from imperial times is the trial of Apuleius before the Roman proconsul in Sabrata in the province of Africa, on three charges of magic, towards the end of AD 158 or the beginning of the following year;[3] since the only non-Ciceronian forensic speech (Apuleius' self-defence) comes from this trial, it provides important confirmation that multiple charges were not a peculiarity of trials of the Ciceronian era, but a normal feature of Roman judicial practice.[4]

I am admittedly a 'maximalist' in terms of classifying aspersions against the defendant as actual charges rather than as character defamation, as can be seen in an appendix to my book that attempts to reconstruct the case for the prosecution on the basis of eleven speeches of Cicero for the defence. Here is the number of charges I detected in the ten criminal cases in which the following were defendants:[5]

Fonteius: 5
Flaccus: 10
Scaurus: 2
Murena: 3
Plancius: 3
Roscius of Ameria: 1
Cluentius: 4
P. Cornelius Sulla: 8
Sestius: 2
Caelius: 7

There are forty-two charges in ten trials, thus, on average, slightly more than four per trial.

This is the maximum number of charges, since I marked some of them with a question mark, and I have not included Rabirius Postumus, since he did not face an actual criminal charge, but rather had been called into court as the recipient of extorted funds.[6] Thus, for example, Cluentius was charged not only with 'judicial murder', the matter to which Cicero devotes most of his speech, but also to three acts of poisoning.[7] In his defence of P. Cornelius Sulla, although most of the case involves the Catilinarian Conspiracy of 63, Hortensius, Cicero's co-counsel, also answers charges related to the so-called 'First Catilinarian Conspiracy' of 66.[8]

---

[3] Hunink 1997: vol. 1, 12.
[4] See Pellecchi 2012: 261 and 273 fn.61.
[5] Alexander 2002, Appendix One ('List of *Crimina*'): 251–3.
[6] Cic. *Rab. Post.* 8.
[7] Cic. *Clu.* 164–91.
[8] Gell. *NA* 1.5.2–3.

The conceptual basis for this maximalist approach was provided by an article of mine that starts with the Roman concept of double jeopardy, as we see it in the epigraphically preserved extortion law of the Gracchan era, and concludes that the law envisaged the prosecutor being authorised to bring up all offences against that statute committed by the defendant up to the time of the trial. This article then contemplates the possibility that this was a general principle of the Roman statutes that established standing criminal courts in the late Republic.[9] Admittedly, such a principle rests on a very narrow evidentiary foundation, but it is consistent with what we see as Ciceronian practice.[10]

Corroboration for the proposition that multiple charges in criminal trials were a product of the specific legal environment of Roman criminal law is provided by a contrast with private law cases, which, though not as numerous as criminal cases within the Ciceronian *corpus* of forensic speeches, nevertheless are numerous enough (four in number) to provide a test of the proposition. These are the cases in which Cicero delivered these speeches: the *Pro Quinctio* (81 BC), the *Pro Tullio* (71 BC), *Pro Roscio Comoedo* (late 70s or early 60s), and in the *Pro Caecina* (early 60s), In these four cases, the issue or issues that the court was going to decide had been established by the formulary procedure or by some subsidiary procedures before speeches were delivered, and Cicero, as *patronus*, sticks fairly closely to speaking on behalf of his client in relation to those specific issues.

A minimalist approach with regard to the number of formal charges, on the other hand, can be based on two approaches. The first is that the actual charges mattered little because cases were actually decided primarily on political grounds:

> Conviction or acquittal was more often an index of political power than a testimony to the effectiveness of legal argument.[11]

> Legal sophistries abounded on both sides; the slippery character of *maiestas* encouraged them. But it would be a mistake to dwell on legal arguments. Politics was the central issue in this case . . .[12]

> The technical charge against C. Antonius, it seems, was *res repetundae*, in connection with alleged misbehaviour in Macedon. But the technical charge was a minor

---

[9] Alexander 1982. I doubt that my thesis has found general acceptance, although Riggsby 1999: 54 and Riggsby 2004: 172–3 express approval.

[10] In fact, the actual charges made by the prosecution in extortion trials were probably normally limited to one province, because of the practical fact that the prosecutor had time to conduct an *inquisitio* (Asc. *Scaur.* 19C; Ps. Ascon. 205 Stangl) in only one province. Thus, in the *interrogatio legibus*, Cicero made the statement against Verres, 'Aio te Siculos spoliasse' (Ps. Ascon. 207 Stangl). Santalucia 2007: 4996.

[11] Gruen 1968: 6.

[12] Trial of Cornelius for *maiestas* in 65: Gruen 1974: 264–5.

issue. The prosecutors, as in all Republican trials, had a free hand to raise any matter that might bring discredit upon the defendant.[13]

These quotations recall an era of English language scholarship on the history of the Roman Republic, starting in the 1950s and going into the 1980s, in which there was great interest in Roman criminal trials as indices of political coalitions and feuds, but almost no interest in Roman criminal law itself.[14]

This inclination to minimise the legal element in Roman trials may originate, in the case of scholars living in Common Law jurisdictions such as England and the United States, in the perception that the respects in which Roman trials differed from trials in the Anglo-Saxon world must have rendered them political rather than legal events. In the nineteenth century Heitland described some of these differences in order to describe 'the spirit of Roman trials': the use of non-professional pleaders, *praevaricatio* (collusion between the prosecutor and the accused), the importance of the personal influence of individual pleaders, emotional appeals to the jurors, including defendants dressed in rags, the bribery of jurors, and, perhaps most importantly from the viewpoint of someone with Common Law expectations about the training and function of the presiding magistrate,[15]

> 4. There was no professionally trained judge to sift the evidence in a summing-up. The praetors were changed from year to year, and merely acted as chairmen of the Courts. With such presidents, no wonder that irrelevant considerations often were the most powerful in determining a verdict.

While it is true that a Roman praetor exerted much less control over the actual trial than an English or American judge, in terms of ruling on what kinds of evidence could be introduced, and what questions could be asked of witnesses, one should not ignore the active role that a praetor or *quaesitor* played in the legal preliminaries leading up to the actual trial, as Santalucia has elucidated in a series of articles.[16] Moreover, the dominance of rhetoric at the high level of Roman education that most presiding magistrates and *patroni* in Roman Republican trials would have received, and the important role that legal issues and argumentation played in that education, mitigated the amateur standing of these participants.

The other way to minimise the formal charges that formed the basis of a criminal trial is to emphasise the rhetorical tricks used by the speakers. Zetzel, in a review of Craig's book on the use of dilemma, expresses this point of view very openly:

[13] Trial of Antonius in 59: idem: 288.
[14] On the prosopographical approach to Roman criminal trials, see Alexander 2007: 103.
[15] Heitland 1878: 116–17. Appendix A.
[16] Santalucia 1997, 1998, 2007, 2009.

truth itself, the guilt or innocence of Cicero's client, was rarely very important
... The blatant fraud of most dilemma-arguments establishes a collusive bond
between advocate and jury: a recognition on both sides of the fraud, and a simultaneous recognition that it is both entertaining and unimportant.[17]

In other words, Zetzel claims that Cicero as the advocate for the defendant
was not really addressing the charges, and the jurors did not expect him to
do so, and therefore the trial was a form of entertainment – though, I would
add, presumably not entertaining for the defendant, whose whole mode
of life was at risk, even if his life itself was not. For those scholars whose
primary skill is the exegesis of speeches, it is natural to focus on the speech,
rather than the occasion that gave rise to it.

I find Zetzel's critique of Craig misleading for two reasons. First, when it
assumes that the fraud created by Cicero's use of dilemma was evident to the
jurors, it fails to take sufficient account of the difference between hearing a
live oration as a juror, and reading a written text of an oration as a scholar,
and in fact rereading it many times, as Craig must have done. As Powell and
Paterson write, 'it would be an acute juror indeed who could see the logical
flaws in Cicero's arguments on a first hearing'.[18] And as May points out,
digressions that seem unnecessary in a written document may have served
to reinforce points that make the speech easier to follow as a listener rather
than a reader.[19]

Second, Zetzel's criticism confuses two different things: (1) a trial, and (2)
one oration delivered within a trial. The oration is just part of the trial; there
were, in fact, at least two orations, for the prosecution and for the defence,
and often many orations, important legal preliminaries that led up to the
receptio nominis by the presiding magistrate before the actual criminal trial
took place, the testimony of witnesses and the interrogation of witnesses,
and some kind of debate between the speakers on the two sides. A Roman
trial provided many ways for factual information to be presented before the
jurors to use in deciding their verdict. The importance of witnesses is emphasised by Powell, and in particular he argues that the rules of Roman procedure, in putting the testimony after the speeches, restricted what the *patronus*
could say about what witnesses were going to say, and therefore make the
whole trial appear to be less focused on matters of fact than it actually was.[20]

Zetzel's depiction of a Roman criminal trial as 'a collusive bond between
advocate and jury: a recognition on both sides of the fraud, and a simultaneous recognition that it is both entertaining and unimportant' (quoted
above) in my view underestimates the seriousness of a criminal trial. In

[17] Zetzel 1994.
[18] Powell and Paterson 2004: 44.
[19] May 2002: 54.
[20] Powell 2010: 27.

fact, Quintilian[21] says that the defence *patronus* can claim, as an argument for acquittal, that the prosecutor has, as a last resort, introduced false slurs against the defendant so as to predispose the jurors to convict him.

> hanc fiduciam fuisse accusatoribus falsa obiciendi, quod laesum et vulneratum reum speraverint hac invidia opprimi posse.

> the prosecutors felt confident in making false allegations because they hoped that a damaged and wounded defendant could be crushed by the odium thus aroused.[22]

The legal reality of the specific charge or charges accepted by the court as the basis of the prosecution, both as a limitation on the scope of the charges that could provide the basis of the prosecution, and as a requirement that the prosecutor substantiate that charge or charges, is illustrated by an example of a *constitutio translativa* ('procedural issue') provided by Cicero in his rhetorical treatise the *De Inventione*.[23] Earlier in the *De Inventione*[24] Cicero defined a *constitutio translativa* in the following manner:

> At cum causa ex eo pendet, quia non aut is agere videtur quem oportet, aut non cum eo quicum oportet, aut non apud quos, quo tempore, qua lege, quo crimine, qua poena oportet, translativa dicitur constitutio, quia actio translationis et commutationis indigere videtur.

> But when the case depends on the fact that it is brought by the wrong person, and that it is brought against the wrong person, or in the wrong court, at the wrong time, under the wrong statute, with the wrong charge, or with the wrong penalty, it is called a procedural issue, because the suit seems to need a different venue or procedural modification.

This specific example falls in the category of *quo crimine*. In a trial in which the defendant was accused of poisoning (*venefici*), the *nominis delatio* made a specific charge of parricide (*parricidi*). This specific kind of charge carried two legal consequences: the case was heard out of order (*extra ordinem*) and the penalty for the defendant, if found guilty, would be more severe (drowning in a sack, without the possibility of voluntary exile) than in an ordinary poisoning case.[25] However, in the actual trial, while the prosecutor was able to prove through testimony and argumentation other poisoning charges, he only barely mentioned the parricide charge. Therefore, in this case the defence should argue vociferously that since a guilty verdict will result in a specific penalty, and since the basis for this specific penalty

---

[21] *Inst.* 7.2.30.
[22] Adapted from Russell 2001.
[23] At 2.58; on *translatio*; see also *Auct. ad. Her.* 1.22.
[24] At 1.10.
[25] Cic. *Rosc. Am.* 30, 71; *Inv. rhet.* 2.149; Modestinus in D. 48.9.9 pr.

has not been established, the defendant should be acquitted.[26] While Cicero does not say, and therefore we cannot assume, that this defence was successful, his account suggests that it had a chance of success, and (we may conclude) that the court had registered a specific charge or charges that needed to be proven. Nevertheless, it is interesting that Cicero recommends that the defence counsel should, in addition to pursuing this legal line of defence, also attempt to refute the other charges of poisoning;[27] this recommendation suggests that it can be unwise to rely too much on a legal technicality.[28]

3. *PROBABILE EX VITA ANTE ACTA*

It may be objected that we know from rhetorical manuals, as well as from Cicero's forensic orations, that the character of the defendant played a large role in a trial, and that the prosecutor levelled many allegations against the defendant that are not formal charges, but rather personal slurs meant to arouse the jurors' emotions against the defendant and thus make a conviction more likely, even those these slurs did not relate directly to the charges. However, an analysis of the advice offered in the rhetorical literature suggests that a more nuanced understanding of the strategies of the opposing advocates is needed. This understanding bears out the truth of what Powell and Paterson suggest about the role that character played in Roman courts:[29]

> It is evident from Cicero that a defence counsel had to be ready to fend off personal abuse of the defendant, as well as substantive allegations; and it can be difficult for a modern reader to take seriously Cicero's own protestations of the unimpeachable character of some of his clients. It is easy to get the impression that, in Roman courts, issues of general character were more important than the actual charges. Perhaps, however, the phenomena are better accounted for by supposing that the Roman courts were indeed interested in guilt and innocence, but that they regarded questions of general character as supremely relevant to deciding such issues.

In an era in which scientific forensic evidence (fingerprints, DNA, blood types, electronic digital records, and so on) was not available, it was natural that the character of the defendant, along with eyewitness testimony, assumed great probative importance. Nevertheless, rather than simply throwing mud against defendants in the hope that something would stick, the prosecutors used (or at least were advised to use) the *probabile ex vita ante acta* in a highly disciplined way to corroborate, in the best possible way given the facts available to each prosecutor, the charges brought by them, and the

---

[26] See Santalucia 1997: 416, and Giuffrè 2009: 259–63.

[27] Cic. *Inv. rhet.* 2.59.

[28] See Alexander 2000.

[29] Powell and Paterson 2004: 36.

patroni similarly used the defendant's prior life to undermine those charges according to the same logic.

A belief in the fixity of an individual's character, at least in adulthood, was strong in ancient thinking. How strong it was may be debated, and in any era people may be able to entertain simultaneous contrary ideas in their belief system, but fixed character was certainly one belief in the jurors' minds, and both prosecutor and defence speaker needed to take it into account.[30] Directly relevant to the theme of multiple charges is Riggsby's observation, 'A belief that character predicts action tends to increase the burden of proof for the prosecution, who must prove multiple crimes, not one',[31] since it did not appear plausible that someone would commit just one crime and no more. (Quintilian does offer a way for a prosecutor to attack a defendant whose past life furnishes no obvious corroboration that the defendant was likely to commit the crime with which he is now being charged [below, 198], but clearly this was a tactic of last resort.) The strength of argument from character is revealed in an account given in the second century AD by a young Aulus Gellius about his first experience of serving as an *iudex* in a case of private law.[32] A plaintiff of good character was suing a defendant with a bad reputation for repayment of a loan. The defence maintained vociferously that the parties' past lives and characters should play no role in a private lawsuit such as this: 'rem enim de petenda pecunia apud iudicem privatum agi, non apud censores de moribus' ('this was a case conducted before a private judge about money, not before the censors about character').[33] Because the plaintiff lacked adequate support in documents or witnesses, Gellius received advice from friends that the case should be dismissed. He writes that he was reluctant to do so, and, torn between finding for the plaintiff against the defendant because of their characters, and finding for the defendant because of a lack of evidence, in the end he prevaricated by ruling *non liquet*.[34] Although this case could be viewed in legal terms as simply revolving around the credibility of the two parties, it is clear that the layman Gellius found it very hard to rule in favour of a man whom he regarded as wicked, and against a man whom he regarded as virtuous, and perhaps we can extrapolate that many jurors, who were of course also laymen, would have been similarly swayed by their perception of the parties' probity.

The rhetorical writers advise the speaker to use the most relevant and

---

[30] Riggsby 2004: 165–6 summarises recent discussion. Berry 1996: 275 argues that the idea of fixed character is used by orators to suit their own purposes, and that their expression of it may not convey their sincere belief. As Riggsby 2004: 167 points out, however, while forensic orations do not necessarily provide reliable evidence for Cicero's beliefs about character, they do provide better evidence about the beliefs held by his audience, the jurors.

[31] Idem: 169.

[32] Gell. NA 14.2.

[33] Idem. 14.2.8.

[34] Idem. 14.2.25. On this episode, see Holford-Strevens 2003: 295–7.

convincing argument that the defendant's character and past deeds make available:

> et in eo debebit esse occupatus ut ad eam causam peccati quam paulo ante exposu-
> erit vita hominis possit adcommodari, hoc modo: si dicet pecuniae causa fecisse,
> ostendat eum semper avarum fuisse, si honoris, ambitiosum; ita poterit animi
> vitium cum causa peccati conglutinare.

> and it will devolve upon him (the prosecutor) to make every effort to relate the
> defendant's manner of life to the motive which he has just exposed. For example,
> if the prosecutor contends that the motive for the crime was money, let him show
> that the defendant has always been covetous; if the motive was public honour,
> ambitious; he will thus be able to link the flaw in the defendant's character with
> the motive for the crime.[35]

The author of this early-first-century BC treatise advises prosecutors to find the kind of character flaws in the defendant that would plausibly have induced him to commit the crime or crimes with which he has been charged.

In Cicero's early treatise on rhetoric, he gives similar advice, but with one better option, if it is available to the prosecutor, and a less desirable, but still usable option, if it is not:

> Quare vitam eius, quem arguit, ex ante factis accusator inprobare debebit et
> ostendere, si quo in pari ante peccato convictus sit: si id non potuerit, si quam
> in similem ante suspicionem venerit, ac maxime, si fieri poterit, simili quo in
> genere eiusdemmodi causa aliqua commotum peccasse aut in aeque magna re aut
> in maiore aut in minore, ut si qui, quem pecunia dicat inductum fecisse, possit
> demonstrare aliqua in re eius aliquod factum avarum.

> Therefore the prosecutor ought to discredit the life of the accused on the basis of
> his past acts, and to point out if he has previously been convicted of any similar
> crime. If this is impossible, he should prove the defendant has been under sus-
> picion of a crime of the same kind before, and particularly, if possible, that in
> similar circumstances he committed an offence because under the influence of
> some motive of the same kind, either in a matter of equal, or greater or less impor-
> tance; an example would be a case in which a prosecutor could prove that the man
> who he alleges acted from desire for money, has acted avariciously on some other
> occasion.[36]

The first choice of the prosecutor is to show that the defendant has already been convicted of a similar crime. Failing that, he should show that the defendant has been suspected of a crime of the same kind, and specifically, if possible, has acted on a motive such as would also lead him to commit the crime with which he has been charged in this trial. Thus, in an extortion trial

---

[35] *Rhet. Her.* 2.5. Translation Caplan 1954.
[36] Cic. *Inv. rhet.* 2.32. Adapted from translation by H. M. Hubbell (1949).

it would be relevant to show that the defendant had previously committed theft or embezzlement or some other crime in which the motive is greed. Cicero does not recommend that the prosecutor list other offences of the same kind as the one or ones with which the defendant has been charged in this trial, but which are not formal charges in this trial, because, I would argue in keeping with my understanding of the scope of a criminal trial, that line of argument would raise the issue as to why the prosecutor did not present those offences as formal charges.

Cicero goes on to advise that if it is not possible to find faults of a similar kind, to make use of any faults of a different nature. Further down the chain of desirability, from the point of view of the prosecutor, is that if the defendant has a clean reputation, then the crimes with which he has been charged demonstrate that he must have been concealing his true nature, and as a last resort, the prosecutor should resort to the argument that the defendant's unblemished reputation only shows that there has to be a first time for everything.[37]

This order of desirable arguments from the defendant's past life is reversed for the defence speaker, who if possible will show that the defendant's blameless life renders the current charges implausible. If the defendant has a bad reputation, the *patronus* will argue, if possible, that while his client has displayed faults, they are not faults that would logically lead to the commission of the crime with which he has been charged, and as a last resort, *negare oportebit de vita eius et de moribus quaeri, sed de eo crimine quo de arguatur; quare, ante factis omissis, illud quod instet id agi oportere* ('he will have to say that the investigation is not about his life and character, but about that charge with which he is accused; therefore, his past deeds should be set aside, and only the case at hand should be pursued').[38]

Quintilian offers similar advice. Like Cicero, he focuses on faults revealed in the defendant's past life that are consistent with the charges levelled at the defendant:

> Accusatoris autem est efficere, ut, si quid obiecerit, non solum turpe sit, sed etiam crimini, de quo iudicium est, quam maxime conveniat. Nam si reum caedis inpudicum vel adulterum vocet, laedat quidem infamia, minus tamen hoc ad fidem valeat quam si audacem, petulantem, crudelem, temerarium ostenderit.

> It is the accuser's business to ensure that any attacks on character he makes are not only shaming but, so far as possible, appropriate to the charge which is before the court. If he calls a man accused of murder a debauchee or an adulterer, the discredit would indeed be damaging, but it would not do as much for the accuser's credibility as if he showed him to be bold, insolent, cruel, and reckless.[39]

---

[37] Cic. *Inv. rhet.* 2.33–4.
[38] Idem. 2.35–7
[39] Quint. *Inst.* 7.2.28, translation Russell 2001.

Quintilian goes on to point out that the defence must deny these character allegations, or show that they are not relevant to the issue at hand. In fact, some allegations, although shameful, may make the charges less plausible. Quintilian gives the example of someone charged with theft who has been described as extravagant; the contempt for money implied by extravagance is not consistent with the desire for money implied by theft. As a last resort, the defence should argue that the character aspersions are irrelevant to the business of the court, which is to investigate the actual charges.[40] On the other hand, if the defendant has led a blameless life, the *patronus* will use that fact in support of his client, while it will be the prosecutor who will argue that the charge or charges are the only business of the court. Clearly, in making this argument the prosecutor is making the best of what is for him a bad situation. Quintilian advises that if the prosecutor cannot attack the defendant's character with aspersions that are significant and true, he would be better off not to attack the defendant's past life at all, because false allegations will lessen the credibility of everything that he says, but he should convey the impression that he has chosen not to attack the defendant's character rather than that he was unable to do so.[41]

For example, in the trial of Caelius, charged under the *lex Plautia de vi*, the defendant was charged with (by my reckoning) seven offences against that statute: assault on a senator[42] sexually molesting women,[43] causing disturbances at Naples,[44] attacking an Alexandrian delegation at Puteoli,[45] something to do with goods of Pallas,[46] borrowing money from Clodia to bribe slaves to commit the murder of Dio,[47] and finally bribing the slaves of Clodia to murder their mistress.[48] The prosecution endeavoured to corroborate these seven charges with eight *maledicta*: the low status of Caelius' father,[49] Caelius' lack of respect for his father,[50] Caelius' low repute among his own townsmen, the *Interamnates Praetuttiani*,[51] Caelius' support for Catiline in the 60s,[52] Caelius' violation of campaign laws,[53] serious personal debts,[54] disloyalty: first supporting a candidate and then prosecuting

---

[40] Quint. *Inst.* 7.2.29–30.
[41] Idem. 7.2.33–4. See Riggsby 2004: 175.
[42] Cic. *Cael.* 19.
[43] Idem. 20.
[44] Idem: 23.
[45] Idem: 23.
[46] Idem. 23.
[47] Idem: 23–5, 51–5.
[48] Idem: 56–7. See Alexander 2002: 236–8; Dyck 2013: 2–4.
[49] Cic. *Cael.* 3.
[50] Idem: 3.
[51] Idem: 5.
[52] Idem: 10–5.
[53] Idem: 16.
[54] Idem: 17.

him[55] and finally, and most notoriously, *impudicitia*.[56] These personal failings render more plausible the specific charges, because someone who is of low status, who fails to respect his father, whom his neighbours dislike, who supports the (in Cicero's eyes) archetypal man of violence and sedition, who will do anything to get elected to office, whose debts render him desperate, who stabs his friends in the back, and who flouts sexual strictures, is the sort of person who is likely to commit the violent and desperate offences with which Caelius has been charged.

In the case of Roscius of Ameria, the defendant is not charged with any other murder than the murder of his father. In the apparent absence of misdeeds in the defendant's past, either criminal in nature or merely opprobrious, the prosecution tries to make the charge plausible by portraying him as an antisocial rube.[57] One might expect that Cicero, as the speaker for the defence, would simply point out to the court the failure of the prosecutor to provide examples of specific acts committed in the past by the defendant. Instead, 'C[icero] does not so much contradict as reinterpret the prosecution's picture. He puts a positive face on Roscius' rustic life, emphasising his skill at and devotion to agriculture (§49); the failure to appear in society is the inevitable concomitant (§52)'.[58]

Giuffrè and Santalucia, in two short articles, have debated with each other whether in the standing criminal courts a sharp line was drawn between the *crimen proprium quaestionis* and the *vita anteacta*, with Santalucia taking the more restrictive viewpoint.[59] This debate revolves around the proper interpretation of one passage in Quintilian.[60] As Santalucia points out, the contrast is here not between all imperial trials and all Republican trials, because trials in the standing criminal courts were also held *certa lege*;[61] Quintilian sees a similarity between senatorial and imperial trials, on the one hand, and trials before the Roman people (*iudicia populi*), on the other. Therefore, I would reject the view of Giuffrè that various considerations were taken into consideration even if there was no connection *stricto iure* between the principal crime and the other facts that were charged.[62] Conceptually, there was a difference between the two, although individual jurors might put more or less weight on that distinction.

---

[55] Idem: 1, 16, 26, 56, 76, and 78.
[56] Idem: 25, 44. See Alexander 2002: 230–3; Dyck 2013: 7–8.
[57] Cic. *Rosc. Am.* 74.
[58] Dyck 2010: 5.
[59] Giuffrè 1998, Santalucia 1998.
[60] Quint. *Inst.* 3.10.1, quoted above, 188.
[61] Santalucia 1998: 463.
[62] Giuffrè 1998: 99.

4. UNITARY PUNISHMENT

Having established that multiple charges were normal in the criminal courts of Cicero's time, I turn now to what might seem to be a characteristic contrary to multiple charges: unitary punishment. By 'unitary punishment' I mean that in the standing criminal courts of this period, a single punishment was usually the only one available when the defendant was found guilty, rather than, as in modern times, a sliding scale, such as a range of fines or a range of years of incarceration. As Kunkel explains,[63]

> Als erstes gilt es zu erkennen, welches der Gegenstand des römischen Strafverfahrens in dieser Periode gewesen ist: In dieser Hinsicht ist festzustellen, daß das Verfahren allein der Feststellung diente, ob der Beschuldigte die ihm zur Last gelegte Tat begangen hatte oder nicht. Dementsprechend lautete das vom Magistrat verkündete Urteil nicht, wie heute bei uns: der Angeklagte wird wegen Mordes zur Todesstrafe (oder zu lebenslänglichen Zuchthaus) verurteilt, sonder ganz schlicht: er hat es getan (*fecisse videtur*), oder er hat es nicht getan.

> First it is worthwhile recognising what the object of the Roman criminal trial of this period was: in this respect, it is to determine that the trial served only for the determination whether the accused had committed the act that was ascribed to him as a charge or not. Accordingly, the verdict pronounced by the magistrate was not, as it is with us, the defendant is sentenced for murder to capital punishment (or to a lifelong penitentiary sentence), but quite simply: he did it (*fecisse videtur*) or he did not do it.

As Kunkel says, unitary punishment is related to a unitary form of a guilty verdict: *fecisse videtur*. If the defendant seems to have committed the offence – not necessarily every offence with which he had been charged, but possibly just one, he will suffer a fixed punishment.

In practice, in most of the standing criminal courts that punishment was a kind of exile from Rome. The convicted defendant was no longer part of the Roman citizen body. This was, however, not the only form of punishment. Each of the many *ambitus* laws stipulated some other punishment, which in each successive *ambitus* statute was more severe than in the previous one, but, as far as we know, each *ambitus* statute stipulated only one punishment for the convicted defendant. We have reason to believe that Sulla's law *de sicariis* contained a more severe punishment for parricide than for other forms of murder (above, 193).

The exceptions to the principle that criminal courts stipulated one fixed punishment are those courts (*repetundae* and *peculatus*, as far as we know) that created a two-stage procedure: first the trial, with a verdict, and second a *litis aestimatio* ('calculation of damages') that assessed appropriate

---

[63] Kunkel 1968: 116.

damages payable to the different victims. However, even in these courts the outcome of a guilty verdict became almost automatically bankruptcy and exile, though there might have been some variation in the consequences of a guilty verdict on the family members of the accused. Financial ruin and expulsion from the Roman citizen body became almost a certainty when the epigraphically preserved extortion law of the Gracchan period introduced double damages (for cases brought before 1 September of each year [line 6]), because, given the huge sums of money extorted, it was almost impossible that the defendant would be able to pay back twice that sum of money. A noteworthy exception – that is, an instance that was noted because it was so exceptional – was the case of C. Porcius Cato in 113 BC, who was charged and convicted with having extorted 4,000 HS, paid double that amount, and presumably walked away from court relatively unscathed, without having to go into exile.[64] All this is not to say that the *litis aestimatio* was meaningless, because that procedure determined how much compensation each victim would receive.

5. CONCLUSION

The juxtaposition of multiple charges and unitary punishment can best be explained as a logical strategy pursued by prosecutors to increase their chances of convicting the defendant. Given that only one charge had to be proven to achieve a conviction (*fecisse videtur*), it made sense to bring several charges to increase the odds of a conviction. As Quintilian writes, it was impossible to tell what points would be most persuasive to the jurors:

> Alius enim alio moveri solet: et qui factum putabit, iustum credere potest, qui tamquam iusto non movebitur, factum fortasse non credet. ut certa manus uno telo potest esse contenta, incerta plura spargenda sunt, ut sit et fortunae locus.

> People are moved by different arguments; a person who believes in the killing may think it was justly done, and a person who is not to be moved by the plea of justice may perhaps not believe in the killing. A sure hand may be content with one shot; an unsure one needs to spray them around, to give fortune a chance too.[65]

In general, the prosecutor increased his chances of obtaining a guilty verdict from the jury the more charges he brought, with the proviso that any charges that were clearly unsubstantiated or very flimsy would tend to discredit the solid charges that the prosecutor had to offer.

This solution to the coexistence of multiple charges and unitary punishment is based on the belief that orators used the guidelines of rhetoric to

---

[64] Cic. *Verr.* 2.3.184; Vell. Pat. 2.8.1. See Alexander 1990: 23, no. 45. 'Exile' is a mistake, and should be deleted.

[65] *Inst.* 4.5.14; translation Russell 2001.

fashion speeches that were most likely to achieve their aim – a conviction in the case of a prosecutor, and an acquittal in the case of a *patronus*. Rhetoric should not be viewed as at best a regrettable necessity that stood between the jury and the truth, and that stands as an obstacle between us and an accurate understanding of a legal case, but rather as part of a culture in which, to quote Crook, 'persuasion by means of the word (was) the most fully worked-out technology'.[66] While Cicero held first place among Roman orators after his successful prosecution of Verres in 70 BC, in his use of rhetorical guidelines to make a convincing legal case, his strategy and tactics must have been more typical than exceptional compared to the other orators of his day.

A remark made by Professor Fred Naiden (Department of History, University of North Carolina at Chapel Hill) helps put into focus the issue of squaring multiple charges with unitary punishment. He made the general observation that legal historians need to place their approach to legal history on a spectrum between the extremes of legal formalism and legal realism.[67] Legal formalism holds that the law functions apart from any normative or policy considerations as an autonomous, self-enclosed form of reasoning, like Euclidean geometry. Legal realism, on the contrary, holds that law is an instrument aimed at producing a desirable result, and that the outcome is the result not of logic but of experience. This chapter's approach has inclined more to formalism than legal realism, because it has attempted to explain the nature of the charges in terms of a legal norm – the availability to the prosecutor of all charges that were relevant to the statute under which the trial was being conducted, and could be made against the defendant. On the other hand, my approach avoids extreme formalism, and grants something to legal realism, in that it acknowledges that the verdict in a particular case was not totally determined by relevant legal norms and facts related to the case, but that the jurors had an opportunity and, indeed, an obligation to exercise their own independent judgement, and that, as a consequence, persuasion played a role in influencing their decision. Persuasion was exerted by advocates on each side of the case, and often, and perhaps usually in cases where both sides opted to go forward with a full trial, the outcome was in question until the jurors made up their own minds, and cast their votes.

Frier provides a very valuable insight that helps us adopt a somewhat formalist approach to understand the trials themselves, while still allowing for social and economic factors to influence the events that led up to the trial. He suggests that we should locate law either in the 'back region' or the 'front region' of people's interactions, using as his example the trial in which Caecina was involved. According to him, the law moved from the back region of the participants' minds to the front region, as social and economic factors that influenced whether or not they would turn to litigation yielded

---

[66] Crook 1995: 197.
[67] Naiden and Harris 2013.

to legal factors once litigation had actually begun. He argues that in the years before the trial, as the future parties sold or rented property, made dowries, and wrote wills, law was kept in the back region, and social and economic factors predominated in their thinking. After they began to quarrel over the will of Caecina's deceased wife, the law moved to the front region, and social and economic considerations receded.[68]

The contrast between 'back regions' and 'front regions' can be applied to criminal cases, as well as to civil cases like the trial in which Caecina was involved. Many non-legal factors influenced whether a prosecutor would attempt to bring charges against an individual: political animosity, desire for fame and glory, and just possibly burning moral indignation.[69] Once the case was admitted, however, the law became dominant, and the prosecutor marshalled all the evidence and his persuasive powers to persuade the jurors that the defendant had violated the statute in question on at least one count. If he was able to do that, the punishment for the convicted was, under most criminal statutes, fixed.

BIBLIOGRAPHY

Alexander, M. C. (1982), 'Repetition of prosecution, and the scope of prosecutions, in the standing criminal courts of the Late Republic', *Classical Antiquity* 1: 141–66.

Alexander, M. C. (1990), *Trials in the late Roman republic, 149 BC to 50 BC.* Toronto. [Phoenix Supplementary Volume 26.]

Alexander, M. C. (2000), 'The repudiated technicality in Roman forensic oratory', in M. Hoeflich, ed., Lex et romanitas: *Essays for Alan Watson.* [Studies in Comparative Legal History] Berkeley. 59–72.

Alexander, M. C. (2002), *The Case for the Prosecution in the Ciceronian Era.* Ann Arbor.

Alexander, M. C. (2007), 'Oratory, rhetoric, and politics in the republic', in W. Dominik and J. Hall, eds, *A Companion to Roman Rhetoric.* Malden. 98–108.

Berry, D. H. (1996), *Cicero pro P. Sulla Oratio. Edited with Introduction and Commentary.* Cambridge.

Craig, C. P. (1993), *Form as Argument in Cicero's Speeches: A study of dilemma* [American Classical Studies, 31] Atlanta.

Crook, J. A. (1995), *Legal Advocacy in the Roman World.* Ithaca, NY.

Dyck, A. R. (2010), *Cicero, Pro Sexto Roscio.* Cambridge Greek and Latin Classics. Cambridge.

Dyck, A. R. (2013), *Cicero, Pro Marco Caelio.* Cambridge Greek and Latin Classics. Cambridge.

Fantham, E. (2004), *The Roman World of Cicero's De Oratore.* Oxford.

Frier, B. W. (1985), *The Rise of the Roman Jurists: Studies in Cicero's Pro Caecina.* Princeton.

---

[68] Frier 1985: 29.
[69] On political advancement through forensic oratory, see Fantham 2004: 105.

Giuffrè, V. (1998), 'De "vita anteacta"'. *Labeo* 44: 98–101.

Giuffrè, V. (2009), 'Una singolare coerenza di Cicerone tra il *De inventione* la *Pro Cluentio oratio*', in B. Santalucia, ed., *La repressione criminale nella Roma repubblicana fra norma e persuasione*. Pavia. 251–64.

Gruen, E. S. (1968), *Roman Politics and the Criminal Courts, 149–78* BC. Cambridge, MA.

Gruen, E. S. (1974), *The Last Generation of the Roman Republic*. Berkeley.

Heitland, W. E., ed. (1878²), *M. T. Ciceronis oratio pro L. Murena*. Cambridge.

Holford-Strevens, L. (2003), *Aulus Gellius: An Antonine scholar and his achievement*. Oxford.

Hubbell, H. M. (1949), *Cicero's On Invention: The best kind of orator. Topics*. Edited and Translated. Loeb Classical Library 386. Cambridge, MA.

Hunink, V. (1997), *Apuleius of Madauros pro se de magia (Apologia)*, 2 volumes. Amsterdam.

Kunkel, W. (1968), 'Prinzipien des römischen Strafverfahrens', in J. A. Ankum, ed., *Symbolae iuridicae et historicae Martino David dedicatae*, I: *Ius Romanum*. Leiden. 111–33. = Kunkel (1974).

Kunkel, W. (1974), *Kleine Schriften zum römischen Strafverfahren und zur römischen Verfassungsgeschichte*. Weimar. 11–31.

May, J. M. (2002), 'Ciceronian oratory in context', in J. M. May, ed., *Brill's Companion to Cicero: Oratory and rhetoric*. Leiden. 49–70.

Naiden, F. and Harris, E. (2013), 'A new typology for sacred laws', Oral paper, delivered at the Association of Ancient Historians, Columbus, OH, 17 May.

Pellecchi, L. (2012), Innocentia eloquentia est: *Analisi giuridica dell'Apologia di Apuleio* [Biblioteca di Athenaeum 57] Como.

Powell, J. (2010), 'Court procedure and rhetorical strategy in Cicero', in D. H. Berry and A. Erskine, eds, *Form and Function in Roman Oratory*. Cambridge. 21–36.

Powell, J. and Paterson J. (2004), 'Introduction', in J. Powell and J. Paterson, eds, *Cicero the Advocate*. Oxford. 1–57.

Russell, D. A. (2001), *The Orator's Education: Quintilian*. Loeb Classical Library 125 and 126. Cambridge, MA.

Riggsby, A. M. (1999), *Crime and Community in Ciceronian Rome*. Austin.

Riggsby, A. M. (2004), 'The rhetoric of character in the Roman courts', in J. Powell and J. Paterson, eds, *Cicero the Advocate*. Oxford. 165–85.

Santalucia, B. (1997), 'Cicerone e la "nominis delatio"', *Labeo* 43: 404–17.

Santalucia, B. (1998), 'Ancora in tema di "nominis delatio"', *Labeo* 44: 462–6.

Santalucia, B. (2007), '*Nominis delatio e interrogatio legibus*: un'ipotesi', in C. Cascione and C. M. Doria, eds, Fides Humanitas Ius: *Studii in onore di Luigi Labruna*. Naples. VII, 4991–5005.

Santalucia, B. (2009), 'Le formalità introduttive del procsso per *quaestiones* tardorepubblicano', in B. Santalucia, ed., *La repressione criminale nella Roma repubblicana fra norma e persuasione*. Pavia. 93–114.

Zetzel, J. E. G. (1994), Review: Craig (1993). *Bryn Mawr Classical Review*, 94.01.05.

Chapter 12

Early-career Prosecutors: Forensic Activity and Senatorial Careers in the Late Republic

Catherine Steel

1. INTRODUCTION

The relationship between forensic and political activity in the Roman Republic is well known.[1] Much of what the *iudicia publica* dealt with were offences in public office: embezzlement, extortion, bribery and various kinds of misconduct by military commanders. The increasing prevalence of violence within domestic politics towards the end of the Republic further increased the overlap between politics and legal proceedings through the use of legislation *de vi*. Even if juries generally reached their decision on the basis of the evidence presented to them, rather than their pre-existing political dispositions, it is nonetheless the case that many of the trials heard by the *quaestiones* that dealt with the offences of *repetundae, ambitio* and *maiestas* involved defendants who were prominent in public life.[2] This aspect of Roman public life – the fact that prominent men were vulnerable to legal proceedings arising from their public activities, whose outcome, if a conviction, could have career-ending consequences – would not necessarily lead to forensic activity on the part of politicians, particularly since the Roman legal system allowed advocacy.[3] But in fact senators are found engaged in both prosecution and defence within the *iudicia publica*. This can be seen as an aspect of that distinctive lack of specialisation, or at least involvement in a range of activities, which is so characteristic a feature of the Republican elite.[4] In addition, prosecution in Rome depended on a private individual bringing a charge, rather than any action by the state: thus prosecution was, or was often perceived to be, motivated by personal animosity between politically active individuals, and undertaken by men who were

---

[1] Gruen 1968; Riggsby 1999.
[2] A similar proportional confidence cannot be expressed about the *quaestio de vi*, given the breadth of its scope, though political significant trials *de vi* are numerous. On the relationship between the offences tried in the *iudicia publica* and the interests of the *res publica*, Riggsby 1999.
[3] Crook 1995.
[4] Beard and Crawford 1985: 56–9.

themselves engaged in a political career.[5] Consequently, forensic ability is
generally regarded in modern research on the Roman Republic as a valuable skill for a politician to possess.[6]

The purpose of this chapter is to explore in more detail the ways in which
forensic activity played a part in the public careers of late Republican politicians through a close examination of cases where prosecution was undertaken by very young men. Roman writers on rhetoric from Cicero onwards
acknowledge the existence of a convention by which a young man prosecuted
a senior political figure with a view to becoming known favourably in the
community.[7] This convention is regularly acknowledged in modern treat-
ments of Republican oratory.[8] However, the narrow and precise constraints
within which this convention of early-career prosecution operated are often
ignored. Close analysis of the known cases demonstrates the criteria that
those who aspired to prosecute in this way needed to meet, and the characteristics their opponents had to possess. These parameters set this kind of
prosecution apart from other forms of prosecution, ensuring that it could
play a recognisable and constructive role in the creation of elite careers. In
addition, undertaking a prosecution at an early age did not necessarily mean
that the prosecutor subsequently became a specialist forensic orator, nor did
those members of the elite who specialised as forensic orators necessarily
begin their careers with a prosecution of this kind.

Early-career prosecution thus illuminates the role of forensic activity
in senatorial careers more generally, with particular relevance to how we
should understand that of Cicero. His is highly anomalous, despite his
attempts to present his trajectory as normative. Finally, this chapter also
illuminates the kinds of support from specialist advisors that members of
the senatorial elite – particularly those who were not experienced when they
prosecuted – could access.

The period studied is the century 149–49, that is from the establishment
of the first permanent *quaestio* at Rome to the outbreak of civil war between
Caesar and the *res publica*.[9] Within this period it is possible to identify more
than twenty trials, which form the basis of the following discussion.[10]

---

[5] Consequently, prosecution was itself a high-stakes activity: Cic. *Off*. On prosecution more
generally in the Republic, David 1992: 497–569; Crook 1995; Van der Blom forthcoming,
chapter 1.

[6] Fantham 1997; Van der Blom forthcoming.

[7] See below, section 2.

[8] So, for example, Fantham 1997: 120–21; Alexander 2002: 7.

[9] This is also the period covered by Alexander 1990, to whose data I acknowledge my debt.

[10] See Table 12.1

2. EARLY-CAREER PROSECUTION AS AN IDENTIFIABLE CONVENTION

In 119 L. Licinius Crassus prosecuted C. Papirius Carbo in one of the *iudicia publica*; Carbo was found guilty and subsequently committed suicide.[11] The case is unusually well attested and a recurrent interest in accounts of the trial is Crassus' age at the time of the prosecution. Cicero, who was certainly in a position to be accurate, given his personal connections to Crassus and his circle, gives his age as twenty-one.[12] The prosecution was the occasion of Crassus' first public speech; it also, almost certainly, marked his entry into public life more generally. Crassus, and his prosecution of Carbo, is regularly used as an example when Roman writers on oratory discuss the age of practitioners at the start of their careers. In addition to the discussion of the case in *De Oratore* and *Brutus*, Cicero puts Crassus at the head of his list when he discusses in *De Officiis* (2.49) the phenomenon of prosecution by *adulescentes*: his other examples are M. Antonius (cos. 99) and Sulpicius (tr. pl. 88).[13] Tacitus' list in *Dialogus* contains (in addition to Crassus, who is again mentioned first) Caesar, Calvus and Pollio.[14]

The significance of this case is not restricted simply to Crassus' age. It is an example of a phenomenon that could later be presented as a distinctive tactic: a prosecution undertaken by a young man in order to secure public recognition.[15] In *Pro Caelio*, one of the many difficulties that Cicero faces

---

[11] Cic. *Fam.* 9.21.3; *De or.* 1.121, 2.170, 3.74; *Brut.*159; *Off.* 2.47; Tac. *Dial.* 34.7; see further Gruen 1968: 107–9; Fantham 2004: 30–1.

[12] Tacitus has nineteen, probably an error.

[13] Interestingly, Antonius' prosecution of Carbo was *not* his first known public speech: that happened when he was prosecuted for sex with a Vestal in 113, a case to which Cicero does not refer. Moreover, he had already by then been elected quaestor. Fantham (2004: 29) suggests that he may have been active in civil cases. Cicero's attempt to make Antonius' career fit the more Crassan model is noteworthy, and may be related to the presentation of his own career: see below.

[14] Quint. (*Inst.* 12.6.1) gives Caesar, Calvus and Pollio as examples of men who undertook prosecutions well before they reached the age of eligibility to the quaestorship, but does not include Crassus, and concludes his list with Augustus; cf. *Inst.* 12.7.3–4 (prosecution of bad citizens).

[15] M. Fulvius Flaccus prosecuted Nasica Serapio in 132 (Alexander 18) for his part in Tiberius Gracchus' death, perhaps before he had been enrolled in the senate (consul in 125, his praetorship may be as late as 128, and if he did not hold the aedileship he may not have been enrolled by the censors of 130); but he was at least ten years older than Crassus. Numidicus' prosecution of Messalla (Alexander 1990, no. 29) cannot be dated with any precision; if it is as early as 119, as Alexander suggests, then it offers a parallel to Crassus that may even be prior to his prosecution of Carbo (Numidicus was consul in 109, and therefore at least a decade older than Crassus; but would not have been a senator in 119). But Gellius, our only source for this trial, does not comment on the prosecutor's youth, and Numidicus does not feature as an example of a youthful prosecutor in the lists that Tacitus and Apuleius provide, which perhaps point to a later date. Examples can be found pre-149 of young men initiating

in defending his protégé Caelius is the latter's active and provocative judicial career, including the successful prosecution of Gaius Antonius in 59 with which Caelius began his forensic activity. In justifying Caelius' action, Cicero invokes what he claims was precedent for this behaviour if undertaken to secure a good reputation with the Roman people:

> He wished, following the established practice and the example of those young men who later emerged in the community as outstanding men and distinguished citizens to let his diligence become known to the Roman people through some noteworthy prosecution.[16]

Two centuries later, when Apuleius wanted to construct a list of justifiable prosecutions by young men, to contrast with the behaviour of his own prosecutor Aemilianus, he invoked a very similar pattern of behaviour, using cases that can be found in Cicero's works:

> He does not prosecute me for the sake of glory, as Marcus Antonius did Gnaeus Carbo, Gaius Mucius Aulus Albucius, Publius Sulpicius Gnaeus Norbanus, Gaius Furius Marcus Aquillius and Gaius Curio Quintus Metellus. These learned young men underwent this, for the sake of praise, as the first task of forensic activity, so that they might be known to their fellow citizens through some striking trial.[17]

Apuleius' treatment poses its own problems.[18] It is, however, a clear demonstration of the persistence of a particular model of understanding forensic activity in the Roman Republic, where prosecution was a justifiable activity for young men as a means to becoming known by the Roman people.[19]

---

judicial proceedings, though direct comparison is difficult with the circumstances under which trials took place prior to the establishment of *quaestiones*. Livy's description of Ser. Galba's attempt to disrupt Paullus' triumph in 167 as 'si in L.Paulo accusando tirocinium ponere et documentum eloquentiae dare voluit' (45.37.3, 'if he wished by prosecuting Lucius Paullus to lay aside his apprenticeship and give evidence of his eloquence'), a description he includes in a speech he ascribes to M. Servilius, may well reflect later understandings of forensic careers; Galba himself acted during the passage of the law authorising Paullus' triumph, speaking in response to an invitation from the tribune of the *plebs* Sempronius Gracchus.

16 Cic. *Cael.* 73, 'voluit vetere instituto et eorum adulescentium exemplo qui post in civitate summi viri et clarissimi cives exstiterunt industriam suam a populo Romano ex aliqua illustri accusatione cognosci.'

17 Apul. *Apol.* 66, 'neque autem gloriae causa me accusat, ut M. Antonius Cn. Carbonem, C. Mucius A. Albucium, P. Sulpicius Cn. Norbanum, C. Furius M. Aquilium, C. Curio Q. Metellum. quippe homines eruditissimi iuvenes laudis gratia primum hoc rudimentum forensis operae subibant, ut aliquo insigni iudicio civibus suis noscerentur.'

18 On Apuleius' Ciceronian sources, and his errors, Hammerstaedt et al. 2002: 269. One peculiarity is the way that Apuleius avoids cases that seem elsewhere to compose a standard list, and relies instead on more obscure names and cases.

19 Compare Tac. *Dial.* 34.7: Tacitus similarly looks back to Republican oratory as a model of good practice but his focus is on the nature of training that young orators received and, as a result, their capacity to engage in prosecution at very young ages; he does not share Apuleius'

Table 12.1 lists cases that may fall under this heading. The criteria for inclusion are that (1) the case is the first in which the prosecutor is known to have spoken at a *iudicia publica*; (2) the prosecutor was not, or probably not, a senator at the time of the trial because he was too young to have stood for a qualifying magistracy; and (3) the prosecutor went on to enter the senate.[20] I give the prosecutor, the defendant, date, whether the prosecutor had consular ancestry, whether he is known to have continued as a forensic speaker after this prosecution, and, for convenience, the reference number in Alexander's *Trials*. There is a degree of imprecision about some of these examples: the dating of the trial is often not secure; consequently it is not always possible to define beyond doubt the relationship between the act of prosecuting and the prosecutor's career. In addition, we seldom know whether men reached the offices they are attested to have held *suo anno*, and as a result when they might have held earlier magistracies, which can be hypothesised even if not attested. Finally, our knowledge of specific forensic cases is evidently very patchy, insofar as a number of the men under consideration are discussed in Cicero's *Brutus* in terms that suggest that they were forensically active, yet cases in which they were involved other than a career-starting prosecution cannot be identified. Absence of specific evidence about subsequent forensic careers needs to be interpreted with some care. These caveats in place, the cases identified are ones where the probable age and stage of the prosecutor are compatible with the prosecution being his first major public act, where no earlier occasion on which he spoke in public is known, and where a public career is known to have followed this initial prosecution.[21] It does

---

observation that prosecution can be a route to *gloria* and public recognition. Another point of contrast is that those whom Tacitus identifies, Crassus, Caesar, Asinius and Calvus, all continued their forensic careers after these débuts and were known as orators.

[20] P. Valerius Triarius is included although his subsequent career is not attested, as he is spoken of in *Pro Scauro* as though he intended to pursue a political career.

[21] This second caveat is worth making insofar as it is usually impossible to say anything about the relationship between career development and a particular prosecution if the prosecutor did not hold public office. The wider implication that underlies the distinction, however – namely, that there was such a thing as a prosecutor within the Roman forensic system who regularly brought charges, itself deserves scrutiny. The problem is well illustrated by the case of Cicero's cousin Gratidius and his prosecution of Fimbria (Alexander 1990, no. 61) in perhaps 106. Gratidius' death in 102 ruled out a senatorial career, but this case may represent ambition for public life, particularly as he was a protégé of M. Antonius. M. Antonius himself is not included as a possibility, despite his identification by Cicero in *De Officiis* as an example, since his prosecution of Carbo was apparently preceded by a trial at which he defended himself, on a charge of sexual relations with a Vestal: see above, fn.13. I do however include Sulpicius, despite the fact that he had spoken in a civil case before he prosecuted Norbanus (Cic. *De or.* 2.88), since civil cases were less high profile than those in the *iudicia publica*. The prosecution of Eburnus (Alexander 62) is not included, because of uncertainty over the identification of the prosecutor and, if he was Pompeius Strabo, the relative dating of this trial and Strabo's quaestorship. The trial of P. Sulla in 62 (Alexander 201) is not included, despite the involvement of L. Manlius Torquatus, because of the likelihood that

not however include cases where the prosecutor was holding the tribunate of the plebs at the time of the trial or those where a man was prosecuted *de repetundis* by his quaestor,[22] even though such prosecutors may well, prior to Sulla's constitutional changes, not yet have been members of the senate, since the holding of either office indicates that a public career had begun.[23]

Prosecution was an activity that might be undertaken at a very early stage of a career, in contrast to most other forms of public activity, particularly those that involved public speech. Roman public life was hierarchical: what an individual could do was heavily constrained by what he had already done and what he had been authorised to do by the Roman people and by those to whom they delegated their authority. In particular, citizens had no right to address their peers at an assembly: they required an invitation from the magistrate who had summoned the meeting.[24] Within this context, the forensic sphere offered unusual flexibility. A prosecutor had to convince the praetor to permit him to bring the charge; in some cases he had also to demonstrate at a *divinatio* that he was more competent to prosecute than another.[25] But that was the only barrier that a prosecutor had to clear: he did not need to hold or have held any office, and there were no formal qualifications that those speaking in the courts needed to possess. Even fewer constraints surrounded defence oratory: someone facing charges could, as far as we know, ask whomever he or she wished to speak on their behalf. But in selecting an advocate, we must assume, defendants looked for competence, ideally demonstrated by prior performance, particularly in cases where the defendant was a prominent public figure and the charge one that related to his conduct in public life. So forensic prosecution provided a way to speak to an audience of Roman citizens about weighty topics of wide public concern and interest earlier in a man's career than any other form of public speaking. Its

---

the lead prosecutor was his father. Cotta's prosecution of Carbo (Alexander 244) is omitted because nothing is known of the prosecutor's subsequent career, though senatorial ambition can be expected from the son of a consul (identification with the senatorial governor of Sardinia in 49 [Caes. *BCiv.* 1.30.2] is tempting but chronologically difficult given that Cotta embarked on his prosecution on the day he took up the *toga virilis* and that this is probably to be dated to 60 or 59.) In other respects this prosecution fits some of the patterns identified in this chapter well, in terms of the youth of the prosecutor, his senatorial connectedness and the motive of familial revenge.

22　Cf. Cic. *Div. Caec.* 63.

23　The *lex Atinia* did not, it seems, circumvent the actual procedure of senatorial *lectio*.

24　A magistrate who could summon a *contio* could ask anyone he chose to address the people: but it is not clear what benefit the holder of *contio* might gain from an inexperienced and unknown speaker, particularly given what is known of the volatility of contional audiences. Interestingly, both Lucius Crassus and Hortensius are known to have addressed *contiones* very early in their careers – but in both cases after their initial prosecution. On procedure in the *contio*, Pina Polo 1996; Hiebel 2009.

25　Of the cases considered in this chapter, Caesar Strabo's prosecution of Albucius involved a *divinatio* (Cic. *Div. Caec.* 63).

attractiveness to those looking to pursue a public career, and particularly to those who did not wish to invest heavily in military activity, is not surprising. Of all the forms of public speaking at Rome, it was the one over which the potential speaker had the greatest control: he did not need to be invited to speak or elected to a particular office. If he could identify a target and convince the praetor that a case existed, he could autonomously create an opportunity to speak in a system that otherwise tightly controlled access to a public audience.

Nonetheless, the act of bringing a prosecution was not without its risks. Because the act of bringing a prosecution was that of an individual, not the community, it was easily interpreted as the act of an *inimicus* and one that would almost inevitably sour subsequent relationships between prosecutor and defendant. Even if the prosecution was successful, and the defendant convicted, his family might undertake a revenge prosecution at a later date; if the defendant was acquitted, his hostility could affect his former prosecutor's subsequent career and success. Although the development of a convention around a career-starting prosecution may have provided some justification for the activity, care was needed, as is evident from Cicero's attempts to explain away Caelius' behaviour. There were also practical issues. Although there were no requirements of a prosecutor in terms of his formal qualifications, to bring a prosecution successfully to court required technical knowledge and understanding of forensic procedure. These skills and knowledge were acquired through the *tirocinium fori*, a process of shadowing and practice, which introduced young men to the legal system. As a result, prosecution was in practice an option available only to those who had access to a network containing more experienced individuals.

3. EARLY-CAREER PROSECUTIONS: A CHRONOLOGICAL SURVEY

Analysis of the prosecutions that fall into this category of early-career prosecution, as defined above, reveals recurrent features as well as a range of differences between the men involved and the circumstances of the trials.[26] The nature of the evidence for most of these trials makes systematic comparison across each example impossible. However, a more impressionistic survey does reveal some suggestive variation around the circumstances behind decisions to prosecute and the relationship between initial forensic activity and subsequent career, as well as similarities in the profiles of the objects of prosecution.

In the case of Crassus' prosecution of Carbo, assessment is potentially clouded by the way in which the trial became exemplary of a career-initiating

---

[26] For the careers of these men, see Sumner 1973; David 1992: 721–902.

prosecution and the fundamental role that Crassus played in Cicero's repeated attempts to create a history of Roman oratory. Nonetheless, Crassus' youth at the time of prosecution is a fixed point, as is the prominence of the man he prosecuted: Carbo had been consul the previous year. The trial seems to been related to the continuing reverberations from the recent death of Gaius Gracchus, insofar as Crassus' speech referred to the fact that Carbo had defended Opimius the previous year despite what were thought to be Gracchan sympathies earlier in his career.[27]

It is however not entirely clear how far Crassus used the speech to articulate a political stance of his own, though it seems likely that his performance in this case, which ended in Carbo's conviction, paved the way for his participation as *tresvir* in the foundation of a colony in Gaul, at Narbo, the following year, despite his age.[28] Crassus also had close links to powerful men; his consular father Mucianus had died a decade earlier but he was connected to the Mucii Scaevolae through both his father's biological family and his wife Mucia.

In the same year, 119, T. Albucius prosecuted Scaevola, Crassus' father-in-law, on *repetundae* charges arising from his proconsulship in Asia Minor; Scaevola, who spoke for himself, was acquitted. Albucius' inclusion in this category is questionable to the extent that he may possibly have held the quaestorship by this point; he was praetor in the first half of the 100s. Unlike Crassus, he was a new man; according to Lucilius, Scaevola claimed Albucius was motivated by hostility towards Scaevola, who had publicly mocked Albucius' philhellenic tendencies when the two met in Athens.[29] Lucilius seems to have dedicated an entire book of *Satires* to the case, which suggests it attracted considerable attention; though it is difficult to determine from the surviving fragments and testimony what line Lucilius took in his treatment. Scaevola was acquitted, and Albucius is not known to have been forensically active after this case. Finally he himself was the victim of a successful *repetundae* prosecution after his praetorship, and went into exile at Athens; the case is discussed in more detail below, as it appears to have marked his prosecutor Strabo's forensic début.

The next example chronologically in the table is Gaius Claudius Pulcher's prosecution of a Calpurnius Piso on *repetundae* charges, though the reconstruction of the case is rather less secure than the two considered so far. It depends on the combination of two pieces of information. The first is evidence from *De Oratore* of a trial or trials of a Piso, defended by Scaurus and by Crassus.[30] The second is an anecdote from Valerius Maximus about

---

[27] Cic. *De or.* 2.170. The quotation also suggests that Crassus disseminated a written version of his speech.

[28] Fantham 2004: 31–2.

[29] Lucil. 2.87–93; Gruen 1992: 289–91.

[30] Cic. *De or.* 2.265 (Scaurus as advocate; a hint that the charge was *repetundae*, as one witness

a trial in which the prosecutor, L. Claudius Pulcher, lost an almost certain conviction of a Lucius Piso because the defendant's emotional appeal was powerfully supplemented by a shower of rain.[31] The *praenomen* 'Lucius' raises suspicions as it was not generally used by the patrician Claudii, and if this case in Valerius Maximus is to be connected with the one discussed in *De Oratore* the consul of 92 is the best fit for the prosecutor. But the reconstruction cannot bear very much weight, though it does seem to be an example of the Claudii Pulchri as prosecutors, a trend that is continued in subsequent generations.

Caesar Strabo's prosecution of Albucius, on *repetundae* charges arising from his governorship of Sardinia following his praetorship, is unambiguously attested, including as one of Apuleius' examples, and can be dated to the second half of the 100s.[32] According to Cicero in *De Officiis*, Strabo took care to present it as a defence of the Sardinians; some care is needed in interpreting this passage, as Strabo acts as parallel to Cicero's own prosecution of Verres. But it seems unlikely that Cicero could have radically recast Strabo's tactics, even if he had chosen where to place the emphasis, particularly if a written text was still in existence. Strabo was aedile only in 90, so this prosecution probably dates from his early twenties; he was also exceptionally well connected in political terms. This case is also the only one discussed in this chapter where a *divinatio* is known: Strabo won the right to prosecute ahead of Albucius' quaestor Pompeius Strabo (cos. 89). Unfortunately, the account of how Caesar Strabo managed this derives entirely from Cicero's account in his *Divinatio in Caecilium*, and his attempts there to find parallels for his prosecution of Verres (ahead of Verres' quaestor Caecilius); Caesar Strabo's arguments may have involved more than a eulogy of the bond between quaestor and pro-magistrate and the fact that the Sardinians had asked him to act, though if so they are not recoverable.[33]

The prosecution that the Luculli launched against a Servilius can be datable only broadly: it followed their father's prosecution, and conviction, on *repetundae* charges by the same Servilius after the elder Lucullus' promagistracy in Sicily, which followed his praetorship in 104. It appears to have been the prosecutors' first public act, and they may have been not yet twenty at the time; but the open motive of revenge sets this trial apart from

---

was a *Gallus*); 2.285 (Crassus as advocate). We cannot, however, be completely sure that these two anecdotes refer to the same trial.

[31] Val. Max. 8.1.absol.6.

[32] Cic. *Div. Caec.* 63 links Albucius and Caesar Strabo; Strabo's prosecution is also mentioned at *Off.* 2.50 and Suet. *Iul.* 55 (the latter passage suggesting also that a written version of the prosecution speech was disseminated); the fact of Albucius' conviction at Cic. *Scaur.* 40 and *Pis.* 92. On the trial, Gruen 1964.

[33] See also Thompson 1969, who argues that Pompeius Strabo was attempting a collusive prosecution.

the others considered hitherto.[34] The Luculli may have acquired public recognition through their actions, but this was recognition ultimately derived from their defence of their father's interests (unsuccessfully, as Servilius was acquitted) rather than from an entirely new affair. Neither brother is known to have spoken in the courts again; Cicero does describe L. Lucullus as spending his youth *in forensi opera*,[35] but as the point of that passage is to bring out how surprising his later military competence was the impression of a great deal of activity may be misleading.

C. Scribonius Curio's prosecution of Metellus Nepos is one of Apuleius' examples, but precise dating is elusive; Asconius[36] implies that the trial took place after Nepos' consulship in 98, which would put Curio in his mid-twenties. Nothing is known about the charge or the outcome, though Curio did go on to a successful if at times idiosyncratic career as a forensic orator, as well as reaching the consulship in 76.[37] The inclusion of Fufius' prosecution of Aquillius as an example of an early-career prosecution is not very secure: it is not identified as his first forensic speech.[38] However, Cicero cites the prosecution in *De Officiis* (2.50) as an example in a context that implies that Fufius was not a habitual prosecutor, and perhaps even that he initiated his career by so doing. Fufius was a new man, as far as can be ascertained, and sufficiently active as an orator to have a distinctive style, criticised by Crassus in *De Oratore* (3.50), and one who spoke in deliberative as well as forensic contexts.[39] Sulpicius too built an oratorical career before his early death after his prosecution of Norbanus *de maiestate*, the case that forms the centrepiece of Cicero's *De Oratore*;[40] he is regularly spoken of by Cicero and those who follow his rhetorical history as one of the two pre-eminent younger orators of the period immediately prior to the Social War, the other being Cotta.[41] There is however no specific forensic case in which Sulpicius is known to have participated after his unsuccessful prosecution of Norbanus (which was not his first forensic case: he was involved in what Antonius in *De Oratore*[42] describes as a *causa parvula* a year before the Norbanus case, possibly a civil

---

[34] Cic. *Acad.* 2.1 describes L. Lucullus as *admodum adulescens* at the time of the prosecution; he was probably about fifteen at the time of his father's conviction, assuming his quaestorship in the early 80s was not significantly delayed. Revenge: Cic. *Off.* 2.50; Plut. *Luc.* 1; Quint. *Inst.* 12.7.3–4. On revenge and the courts, Flaig 2003: 145–7.

[35] Cic. *Acad.* 2.1.

[36] At 63 C.

[37] On Curio as an orator, Rosillo Lopez 2013: 294–6.

[38] It gave Antonius the opportunity to deliver one of his most notorious defences, involving the ripping off of Aquillius' tunic to reveal his scars: Cic. *Verr.* 2.5.3; *De or.* 2.194–9; Hall 2014: 19–21.

[39] Cic. *De or.* 2.91, where *furit in re publica* implies deliberative oratory, perhaps in the context of a tribunate.

[40] At 2.197–204.

[41] On Sulpicius, see Powell 1990.

[42] At 2.88.

law case). Hortensius' forensic début can be dated firmly to 95, with his age as nineteen, on the basis of the discussion of his career in *De Oratore* and *Brutus*.[43] More detail of his first case is however hard to secure.[44] What is evident however is that it was one with significant broader political implications that led to Hortensius addressing the senate in the same year, where 'he defended the cause of Africa'.[45] This opportunity for a nineteen-year-old to speak in the senate is remarkable and difficult to parallel. The final possible example of an early-career prosecution datable prior to the Social War is Marcius Censorinus' attempt to prosecute Sulla after his proconsulship in Cilicia on what seem to have been *repetundae* charges.[46] However, the case was dropped before it came to trial.[47]

There is a hiatus in prosecutions by young men from the outbreak of the Social War until the re-establishment of the courts during Sulla's dictatorship: the intense judicial activity that was sparked by the *lex Varia* in 90 did not, as far as we know, provide opportunities for début activity. Sulla's transformation in the *respublica* affected, if it did not fundamentally alter, the framework for this kind of prosecution. In the early 70s particularly, the prosecution of high-profile public figures inevitably involved engagement with recent history. It is possible, too, that the heightened competition that followed from the rise in the number of junior magistracies relative to senior ones increased the pressure on political aspirants to find ways to become known to the voting public. In 79 the Metelli brothers Celer and Nepos (the future consuls of 60 and 57 respectively) brought a prosecution of Aemilius Lepidus for *repetundae* following his proconsulship in Sicily; the prosecution was dropped, apparently because the praetor refused to bring the case to trial. Lepidus was about to secure the consulship for 78, apparently against Sulla's wishes, and seek to unravel some aspects of his political reforms; how far his political programme was an element in the Metelli's decision to prosecute is unclear. More can be said about the following two prosecutions, of the homonymous Cn. Cornelii Dolabellae. Aemilius Scaurus, Sulla's stepson, successfully prosecuted the praetor of 81; the following year, Julius Caesar (having narrowly escaped death during the proscriptions) unsuccessfully prosecuted the consul of 81. That we have here a contrast between a piece of self-regulation by the ruling elite and an attack on it seems

---

[43] Especially *De or.* 3.228–9 and *Brut.* 228–30. The calculation that the latter passage does of the period of time (from this forensic début down to his death) as one in which Hortensius was a *patronus* confirms that 95 involved a forensic case, even though it is only described here as in *foro*.

[44] The object of Hortensius' prosecution is not identifiable, nor the outcome of the trial.

[45] Cic. *De or.* 3.229, 'in senatu causam defendit Africae[.]'

[46] Plut. *Sull.* 5.

[47] Censorinus' qualities as an orator are noted by Cicero in *Brut.* 237, where he is also described as 'iners et inimicus fori' ('lazy, and an enemy of the forum'); no occasion when he actually spoke in public is attested.

a convincing interpretation.[48] Scaurus and Caesar are both known to have continued their forensic careers.

The trial of Terentius Varro in 74 for extortion in Asia is perhaps best known for the blatant bribery of the jury that took place during it. The prosecutor was App. Claudius Pulcher, then in his mid-twenties; he was faced with Hortensius as Varro's advocate, and Varro was acquitted. The next possible case is nine years later, when his younger brother Publius Clodius prosecuted Catilina, also on *repetundae* charges. Cicero's allegation that Clodius prosecuted Catilina in order to ensure his acquittal is difficult to disentangle from the later hostility between the two men. Clodius was perhaps twenty-seven at the time; he had already spent some years with Lucullus' army in the east and been involved in the mutiny of Lucullus' troops, though how far that episode coloured his reputation once back in Rome is far from clear, particularly as the emphasis on his role as instigator of the mutiny depends heavily on the way that his subsequent political career developed.[49]

Caelius Rufus' prosecution of Antonius in 59 has already been mentioned; his is the name most closely linked as prosecutor to this trial, though he was in fact part of a team; the other two prosecutors cannot be securely identified, though neither appears to have been experienced.[50] How far the jurors shared the hostility to Antonius, which led sympathisers with Catilina to rejoice in his conviction is unclear, but his reputation more generally (including expulsion from the senate in 70) may have made him vulnerable. Cicero felt obliged to defend him because of their shared tenure of the consulship.[51] Also in 59 D. Laelius prosecuted Valerius Flaccus, again as part of a team.[52] The most visible of the other prosecutors was C. Appuleius Decianus, a Roman *eques* resident in Asia. It could be argued that this case involved an inexperienced but ambitious speaker, Laelius, joining forces with a collaborator, Decianus, who supplied a detailed understanding of the case and whose own motives were not related to political life in Rome but to the maintenance of his interests outside Italy.[53] But Laelius had been in Asia himself, as a legate of Pompeius, and could therefore present the prosecution as one in which he had some personal stake. Furthermore, Cicero records in his defence of Flaccus complaints by Laelius that Decianus had been suborned by Flaccus.[54] It seems unlikely that Laelius would have made so damaging an admission in his speech itself, and it is clearly in Cicero's interests to suggest a divided prosecution; but the fact that Cicero makes

---

[48] Gruen 1966.
[49] On Clodius' early career, Tatum 1999: 44–55.
[50] See Alexander 1990: 119–20.
[51] Crawford 1984: 124–31
[52] Alexander 2002: 79–81.
[53] On Decianus, Steel 2001: 58–66.
[54] Cic. *Flac.* 81.

this point at least suggests that the prosecution team looked heterogenous and could be presented as motivated by different factors. It was not successful, and Laelius himself is not known to have been involved in forensic cases subsequently. Licinius Calvus' prosecutions of Vatinius were canonical texts for subsequent generations, pre-eminent among an extensive *corpus* of written works by one who was regularly identified, with Caelius, as the greatest orator of the generation after Cicero.[55] There appear to have been at least three speeches against Vatinius, and the chronology of Calvus' attacks on Vatinius is difficult to establish securely.[56] However, Tacitus *Dialogus* 34 implies that an attack on Vatinius marked Calvus' forensic début.[57] That is probably to be dated to 58, since Calvus' involvement in other forensic cases is attested for the year 56, and he was constantly active in the courts throughout the 50s until his death. Sempronius Atratinus' prosecution of Caelius *de vi* in 56 had the justification of revenge, as Caelius was prosecuting his natural father Calpurnius Bestia; this was also an occasion where there was a large prosecution team, though Atratinus was the *nominis delator*. No further forensic activity by Atratinus is known, though he survived the Civil War and held a suffect consulship in the 30s. Asinius Pollio's first prosecution or prosecutions, of Gaius Cato in 54, are mentioned in Tacitus *Dialogus* 34; Pollio may have been prosecuting alongside Calvus, though the precise circumstances are difficult to unravel.[58] Pollio went on to an oratorical career of considerable distinction, though only after the Civil War; the prosecution or prosecutions of Cato are his only known forensic activity prior to 49.

Valerius Triarius, the prosecutor of Scaurus in 54 on *repetundae* charges following the latter's proconsulship in Sardinia, is described by Asconius (at 18 C) as *adulescente parato ad dicendum et notae industriae*; Douglas suggests that the praenomen Publius, given to him by Asconius, may be an error for Gaius and the prosecutor of Scaurus identical to the C. Valerius Triarius whom Cicero praises in *Brutus* but whose forensic activity cannot otherwise be identified.[59] Triarius had a connection with Sardinia: his father had been governor there in the 70s BC. Thanks to the survival of large fragments from Cicero's speech defending Scaurus, and Asconius' commentary on it, it is possible to say more about the backing that Triarius might have drawn on. There was a team of prosecutors, though its other members were not politically active; Appius Claudius Pulcher, one of the consuls of the year,

---

[55] Tac. *Dial*. 21.1–2 identifies twenty-one *libri* by Calvus.

[56] Gruen 1967; Sumner 1973: 149.

[57] Gruen 1967: 217–18 is sceptical, though, on the grounds only that information in the *scholia Bobiensia* (the only source for Calvus' involvement in the trial of Vatinius in 58, in other respects well-attested) is often unreliable. But it seems unlikely that Tacitus would, in a passage about the youth of prosecutors in the Republic, chosen a case that was not Calvus' first.

[58] Sen. *Controv*. 7.4.7.

[59] Douglas 1966:194; Alexander 2002: 99 fn.3.

supported the prosecutors; and Asconius notes that Scaurus was initially apprehensive that the close friendship of Triarius and his mother Flaminia with M. Cato's half-sister Servilia might affect Cato's impartiality as presiding praetor. It was a case where we know a young prosecutor drew on support and advice from more senior and experienced men.

The inclusion of Pompeius Rufus' prosecution of Messalla Rufus in 54 is questionable, because of the age of the prosecutor: he was born no later than the early months of 87 and so well into his thirties; his quaestorship is not attested but could well be prior to this prosecution.[60] The Claudii Pulchri's prosecution of Milo for the murder of their uncle Clodius was driven immediately by the external necessity of the death of a relative, though that motive was compatible with the reputational and career development aspects of these prosecutions. In addition, the Pulchri must have seemed to the rest of Clodius' family capable of carrying out the task.

The final case of a youthful prosecutor attested before the outbreak of the Civil War is P. Cornelius Dolabella, who prosecuted App. Claudius twice after his return from Cilicia early in 50: first for *maiestas* and then, when that was unsuccessful, for bribery, probably in relation to Appius' campaign for the censorship. This too was unsuccessful. At the second trial one of Appius' advocates was Hortensius, in what turned out to be his final case. This was Dolabella's first (and only) attested forensic activity as a speaker, but he had already faced two prosecutions himself, on capital charges, and had Cicero as his advocate.[61] This was not, then, Dolabella's first appearance on the public scene, and it is possible that he had already been elected quaestor. Dolabella's actions were a considerable embarrassment to Cicero, whose daughter had just married him, and Cicero had been trying very hard to maintain good relations with Appius. In an attempt to distance himself, he describes Dolabella's action, in a letter to Appius, as *permirum* (rather strange), and comments that Dolabella lacks *ornamenta* and *praesidia*, marks of distinction and resources, in comparison to Appius. Elsewhere, however, Dolabella's motivation becomes clearer: Caelius notes that the *invidia* against Appius is less than he expected.[62] This suggests that Dolabella had opportunistically identifed a target, action against whom he hoped would be popular.[63]

On the basis of these cases, we can amplify the pattern that Cicero and subsequent writers describe by identifying further features, which many or

---

[60] The *terminus ante quem* for his birth is his father's death during violent disturbances in Rome during 88.

[61] Cic. *Fam.* 3.10.5.

[62] Idem: 8.6.1

[63] Idem: 3.10.5 implies that there was no pre-existing ill-feeling between the two men, as he describes the prosecution as one through which Dolabella will assume a state of enmity with Appius.

all of them share. Perhaps the most obvious is the social position of these early-career prosecutors. Of the twenty-five prosecutors in the twenty-two cases I have identified, seventeen were the descendants of consuls; two more were the sons of praetors. Ten were patricians.[64] Thus in most cases youthful prosecutors possessed considerable social and political capital in terms of their ancestry. If we consider the small number of prosecutions undertaken by men who did not have consular or immediately praetorian ancestry, we can see that in most cases there were some other relationships that could approximate. Sulpicius was a protégé of Antonius, a consular and leading orator (even if the prosecution in question involved his facing Antonius as the defence advocate). Laelius' father had served with Pompeius as a legate during the campaign against Sertorius and died there; and the family connection with Pompeius continued. Caelius had the support and friendship of Cicero, if not specifically for the prosecution of Antonius; and Pollio may have been working with Calvus who, although very junior in career terms, had already made a considerable impact as a forensic speaker. Caelius and Pollio were also making their débuts in the 50s, by which point the role of forensic oratory in political life had shifted somewhat. Not only had the volume of activity seemingly increased following Sulla's reforms to the law courts; Hortensius and above all Cicero had established forensic activity as the basis for a highly successful public career in a way that is difficult to parallel in the period before Sulla. Caelius and Pollio were both very talented speakers; given that forensic brilliance was now demonstrably a credible route to political eminence their willingness to take on the risks of an early-career prosecution despite the lack of robust family connections makes sense.[65] It may also be relevant that neither Antonius nor Gaius Cato commanded wide support among the elite.[66] The exceptions to this pattern are Albucius and Fufius, where we can only hypothesise strong motives for prosecution and engagement by both men with the forensic sphere. An early-career prosecution was in most cases only undertaken by men who had the support of experienced political actors, whether that was family support or not.

In most cases the man prosecuted was senior, a former praetor or former consul: this confirms that the search for reputation was a major factor in motivating such prosecutions. Obscure defendants and trivial crimes would not have the same effect. More speculatively, there is some indication that even when undertaken by a young man as his début, a prosecution needed to

---

[64] Cicero's remarks about Dolabella are a useful check on assuming that patrician status automatically conferred significant advantage; however, in that case he is comparing two patricians.

[65] Sulpicius is an important precursor in this respect.

[66] Antonius' shortcomings are discussed above; for Gaius Cato's career and alliances, see Gruen 1967.

be justified by appeal to the motives that Cicero claims justified prosecution more generally: either the interests of the *res publica*, or revenge, or the obligations of patronage. The Luculli, Cotta and the Claudii Pulchri were acting on behalf of a close relative; Caesar Strabo and Triarius, prosecutors in *repetundae* cases dealing with Sardinia, could both point to connections with the island. Too little is known about the tactics and backgrounds of most of these prosecutions to make a confident assertion, but it seems that prosecutors in these cases needed to justify their actions in the same way as any other prosecutor, even if the audience understood that there were distinct motives of personal ambition involved as well.

Early-career prosecutions were almost always undertaken by young men who belonged to the elite or who had already secured significant support and backing from an eminent individual. The eminence of their targets supports the ambition inherent in the activity: it was a designedly high-profile act, to draw the attention of the citizen body to a young man of energy and talent and prepare voters to accept him in subsequent years as an appropriate recipient of their support for public office. However, this route to notoriety did not, at least prior to the fifties BC, open the door to talented outsiders, but rather offered the elite another forum for internal competition that did not seriously undermine their overall dominance of the system. Indeed, the senatorial class was probably an important element within the audience who evaluated these initial performances. Whilst the acquisition of elected office required candidates to develop a public profile among the Roman citizen body as a whole, other opportunities could follow from impressing members of the senate, the body to which this group of young prosecutors, we can assume, aspired to join as soon as possible. Forensic activity was also a method by which young men could demonstrate how promising they were as potential members of the governing elite.

4. EARLY-CAREER PROSECUTION AND FORENSIC CAREERS

Despite these recurrent features there is one respect in which these cases are not uniform. Some of these prosecutors continued to be active in the courts; others did not. Prosecution was not the inevitable precursor to a forensic career.

If we look in more detail at the prosecutors, it is evident that many, though by no means all, of the most distinguished orators of the late Republic began their careers with a prosecution. In addition to Crassus' exemplary prosecution, such a list would include Caesar Strabo, Sulpicius, Hortensius, Julius Caesar, Clodius, Calvus and Pollio. On the other hand, it does not include Aemilius Scaurus (cos. 115), M. Antonius, Gaius Cotta, Q. Calidius, M. Crassus, M. Marcellus or Cicero himself. A forensic career could be built without this initial step; but for the young man whose training indicated that he possessed the necessary talent it does seem to have been an attractive route. However, it was also a route followed by men who did not continue to be forensically active: of our twenty-five orators, thirteen are not known to have spoken in the courts subsequently, whether in prosecution or defence. It seems likely, as noted above, that this proportion is inflated by under-reporting of cases; for example, both Furius and Sulpicius are spoken of in *De Oratore* as though they were active in the courts, though in fact no other forensic case in which either was involved is securely known. The violence of the period plays a part, too: Censorinus was killed during the civil war of 84–82 and the orators who made their débuts in the late 50s had little time to take their careers forward before the hiatus in legal activity of the Civil War, during which Dolabella and Triarius died. Nonetheless, there are still examples of men whose public careers are known to have continued with great success, yet who apparently did not exercise their forensic skills after this first foray: L. Licinius Lucullus, his brother M. Lucullus Varro, Metellus Nepos, Metellus Celer and Appius Claudius, all of whom reached the consulship.[67] There are at least two possible lines of interpretation of this phenomenon. One is that a single prosecution was enough: it announced the young man's identity and commitment to public service, whether successful or not, and once completed he could turn his attention to the other tasks that should occupy the aspirant politician. There was no need for him to continue with the time-consuming business of defending men in court in order to demonstrate his skill or cement his reputation. Another possibility is that actual experience of the courts revealed aptitude and ability in ways that training had not done; that is, those who did not continue with foren-sic activity made that decision at least in part because they found the work uncongenial or realised that they were not effective. This latter observation is much more speculative: there is no direct evidence for it (though Cicero's emphasis on the sheer hard work involved in successful forensic pleading may suggest that he thought his contemporaries underestimated what was involved), but we may note that Censorinus abandoned his prosecution of Sulla and the Metelli theirs of Lepidus, examples where a decision by a young man or men to prosecute was not even carried through to the trial itself.

The practical inexperience of these prosecutors combined with the signifi-cance of the cases they undertook should also prompt us to reflect further on the ways in which they prepared for their first cases. As discussed above, these young men were in general well connected to the political elite. Their education hitherto involved not only theoretical training in rhetoric but also exposure to what happened in the Forum in the company of senior and

---

[67] At *Brut.* 247, describing the Metelli, most manuscripts read *non nihil in causis versati*, but L's reading of *nihil* is attractive. It may imply more than this initial prosecution of Servilius. Nonetheless, there is nothing to suggest that they were significant figures on the forensic scene.

experienced participants, whose oratorical performances they could witness – as any citizen could – but in addition discuss and study from the inside.[68] They could also participate in the meetings in private space, which preceded and underpinned forensic proceedings.[69] Their introduction to public life took place within an intimate network that involved competition – elite young Romans were surely alert from a very young age to their contemporaries, who would be their electoral rivals in the future – but also collaboration, as established men sought to ensure the success of their protégés, whether they were sons, nephews or other connections. In this context, it strains credulity that early-career prosecutors were acting on their own in any substantial sense. Rather, we should assume that the decisions to undertake a prosecution and the choice of target were reached through debate and discussion, and that the legal tactics to be adopted were also the object of collective consideration. The support available may even have involved some degree of speech writing. Speechwriters are attested in the late Republic; whilst the available evidence clusters around the trials that took place under the *lex Varia* and funeral speeches, it is at least possible that the help that inexperienced prosecutors received extended in some cases as far as detailed drafting.

Different orators will have used these kinds of support in different ways. Nor did every début prosecution necessarily have the unanimous support of all the speaker's circle. Cicero makes it clear that he did not approve of Caelius' prosecution of Antonius in 59, and he was clearly appalled by Dolabella's move against Appius Claudius in 50.[70] The key point to emerge is that early-career prosecutions were not a phenomenon confined to the oratorically and forensically brilliant. The support networks existed to enable the less talented still to make a credible appearance in the role of prosecutor. Forensic procedure, and the conventions of elite society, combined to create a space in Rome, which could be put to a variety of different uses. Early-career prosecution was a tactic that could enable the young and brilliant to make their mark on public life at an advantageously early stage. But it was also a means by which the elite could police itself whilst using the licence extended to young men as prosecutors to prevent the escalation of internal conflicts. And in many cases it will have served both ends. But it did not involve a commitment, or even an expectation, that the prosecutor himself would remain forensically active.

Consideration of this aspect of Republican forensic practice also throws important light on Cicero's early career. It becomes strikingly obvious that

---

[68] On rhetorical education in the Republic, see Bonner 1977; Bloomer 2015.

[69] The *locus classicus* for this aspect of elite training in the Republic is the opening of Cicero's *De Amicitia* 1–3, which describes young men, including Cicero and Atticus, attending consultations held by Mucius Scaevola the Augur.

[70] Cic. *Cael.* 74; *Fam.* 3.10.5.

Cicero's prosecution of Verres becomes even more distinctive, and in need of explanation, when viewed alongside these examples. Verres himself was a target who shared many characteristics with those prosecuted in the cases considered so far. He had held the praetorship and was planning his consular campaign. The charges against him were *repetundae* in the province, which he had governed after his praetorship. And his behaviour in Sicily had already faced unfavourable scrutiny in the senate, a fact that might reassure a prosecutor about the support he could expect and the grounds on which he could justify the prosecution. But Cicero could not claim the protection of early-career prosecution. He himself was a member of the senate, an aedile-elect, and a man with a decade's worth of forensic practice and experience. The contrasts between his position and those of the other prosecutors discussed in this chapter support the view that his prosecution of Verres was not only unusual but also risky, and thus perhaps, in a career whose early stages are in general marked by caution and restraint, an indication that Cicero's forensic career was not proceeding as smoothly as his later presentations of it would suggest.[71]

Early-career prosecution existed as a distinct tactic within the forensic sphere, though with defined conditions. The prosecutor needed to have the support and advice of established figures. The less integrated he was with the elite through birth, the more likely it is that he possessed considerable oratorical talent, and that this talent was a key motivator in choosing this route towards a political career. The target was a senior figure, someone who had been elected to an *imperium*-holding office, and the charge was one of concern to the *res publica* such as *repetundae* or *maiestas*. And the existence of the convention of prosecution by the very young helped the prosecutor in such cases evade the social disapprobation that generally attended the act of prosecuting, though did not entirely dispel it. However, there is no clear link between undertaking a prosecution of this kind and subsequent forensic distinction: it was neither a necessary nor a sufficient condition. And since it was not an essential part of forensic career development, each case should be analysed as the result of a significant choice on the part both of the prosecutor and his circle. Finally, these prosecutions imply the existence of technically skilled support networks available to these young men as they planned their prosecutions. In this case, as in others, the Republican elite supported its 'myth of universal aristocratic competence' through effective teams as much as through native ability and individual training.[72]

---

[71] Steel 2013.
[72] Rosenstein 1990: 172.

Table 12.1 A list of early-career prosecutions

Prosecutor	Defendant	Date	Consular ancestry?	Subsequent forensic career	No. in Alexander
L. Licinius Crassus (cos. 95)	C. Papirius Carbo (cos. 120)	119	Yes	Yes	30
T. Albucius (pr. c. 105)	Q. Mucius Scaevola (cos. 117)	119	No	No	32
C. Claudius Pulcher (cos. 92)	Calpurnius Piso	?second half of the 110s	Yes	No	48
C. Caesar Strabo	T. Albucius	c.103	Yes	Yes	67
Luculli (coss 74, 73)	Servilius	?90s	Yes	No	71
C. Scribonius Curio (cos. 76)	Q. Caecilius Metellus Nepos (cos. 98)	?soon after 98	No (praetorian)	Yes	82
L. Fufius (tr. pl. 91 or 90)	M.' Aquillius	first half of the 90s	No	?Yes	84
P. Sulpicius (tr. pl. 88)	C. Norbanus (cos. 83)	96–91	?No	?Yes	86
Q. Hortensius (cos. 69)	?Q. Marcius Philippus (cos. 91)	95	Yes	Yes	90
C. Marcius Censorinus (leg. 82)	L. Cornelius Sulla (cos. 88)	second half of the 90s	Yes	No	92
Metelli Celer and Nepos (coss 60, 57)	L. Aemilius Lepidus (cos. 78)	79	Yes	No	131
M. Aemilius Scaurus (pr. 56)	Cn. Cornelius Dolabella (pr. 81)	78	Yes	Yes	135
C. Iulius Caesar (cos. 59)	Cn. Cornelius Dolabella (cos. 81)	77	Yes	Yes	140
App. Claudius Pulcher (cos. 54)	Terentius Varro	74	Yes	No	158
P. Clodius Pulcher (aed. 56)	L. Sergius Catilina (pr. 68)	65	Yes	Yes	212

M. Caelius Rufus (pr. 48)	C. Antonius (cos. 63)	Yes	No	59	241
D. Laelius (tr. pl. 54)	L. Valerius Flaccus (pr. 63)	No	No	59	247
C. Licinius Calvus	P. Vatinius (cos. 47)	Yes	Yes	58	255; cf. 274, 292
L. Sempronius Atratinus (cos. suf. 34)	M. Caelius Rufus	274	No	56	
C. Asinius Pollio	C. Porcius Cato (tr. pl. 56)	Yes	No	54	283, 286
P. Valerius Triarius	M. Aemilius Scaurus (pr. 56)	No	No (praetorian)	54	295
M. Valerius Messalla Rufus (cos. 53)	Q. Pompeius Rufus (tr. pl. 52)	No	Yes	54	299
Claudii Pulchri (cos. 38 and cousin)	T. Annius Milo	No	Yes	52	309
P. Cornelius Dolabella (cos. suf. 44)	App. Claudius Pulcher (cos. 54)	No	Yes	50	344, 345

For the purposes of this table, pr. refers to Praetor and leg. to Legate. All other abbreviations are noted in the List of Abbreviations at the front of the volume.

BIBLIOGRAPHY

Alexander, M. (1990), *Trials in the Late Roman Republic 149 to 50* BC. Toronto.

Alexander, M. (2002), *The Case for the Prosecution in the Ciceronian Era*. Ann Arbor.

Beard, M. and Crawford, M. (1985), *Rome in the Late Republic: Problems and interpretations*. London.

Bloomer, W. M., ed. (2015), *A Companion to Roman Education*. Hoboken.

Bonner, S. (1977), *Education in Ancient Rome: From the elder Cato to the younger Pliny*. London.

Crawford, J. (1984), *Cicero: The lost and unpublished orations*. Göttingen.

Crook, J. (1995), *Legal Advocacy in the Roman World*. London.

David, J.-P. (1992), *Le Patronat Judiciare au dernier siècle de la Republique romaine*. Rome.

Douglas, A. E. (1966), *M. Tulli Ciceronis Brutus*. Oxford.

Fantham, E. (1997), 'The contexts and occasions of Roman public rhetoric', in W. Dominik, ed., *Roman Eloquence: Rhetoric in society and literature*. London. 111–28.

Fantham, E. (2004), *The Roman World of Cicero's* De Oratore. Oxford.

Flaig, E. (2003), *Ritualisierte Politik: Zeichen, Gesten und Herrschaft im Alten Rom*. Göttingen.

Gruen, E. S. (1964), 'Politics and the courts in 104 BC', *Transactions of the American Philological Association* 95: 99–110.

Gruen, E. S. (1966), 'The Dolabellae and Sulla', *American Journal of Philology* 97: 385–99.

Gruen, E. S. (1967), 'Cicero and Licinius Calvus', *Harvard Studies in Classical Philology* 71: 215–33.

Gruen, E. S. (1968), *Roman Politics and the Criminal Courts 149–78* BC. Cambridge.

Gruen, E. S. (1992), *Culture and National Identity in Republican Rome*. Cornell.

Hall, J. (2014), *Cicero's use of Judicial Theatre*. Ann Arbor.

Hammerstaedt, J., Habermehl, P., Lamberti, F., Ritter, A. and Schenk, P. (2002), *Apuleius: De Magia*. Darmstadt.

Hiebel, D. (2009), *Rôles institutionnel et politique de la* contio *sous la République romaine: 287–49 av. J.-C.* Paris.

Pina Polo, F. (1996), Contra arma uerbis: *der Redner vor dem Volk in der späten römischen Republik*. Stuttgart.

Powell, J. (1990). 'The tribune Sulpicius', *Historia* 39: 446–60.

Riggsby, A. (1999), *Crime and Community in Republican Rome*. Austin.

Rosenstein, N. (1990), Imperatores victi: *Military defeat and aristocratic competition in the middle and late Republic*. Berkeley.

Rosillo Lopez, C. (2013), 'The common (*mediocris*) orator of the late republic: the *Scribonii Curiones*', in C. Steel and H. van der Blom, eds, *Community and Communication: Oratory and politics in republican Rome*. Oxford. 287–98.

Steel, C. (2001), *Cicero, Rhetoric, and Empire*. Oxford.

Steel, C. (2013), 'Cicero's autobiography: narratives of success in the pre-consular orations', *Cahiers du centre Gustave-Glotz* 23: 251–66.

Sumner, G. (1973), *The Orators in Cicero's* Brutus: *Prosopography and chronology.* Toronto.

Tatum, W. J. (1999), *The Patrician Tribune: Publius Clodius Pulcher.* Chapel Hill.

Thompson, L. A. (1969), 'Pompeius Strabo and the trial of Albucius', *Latomus* 28: 1036–9.

Van der Blom, H. (forthcoming), *Oratory and Political Career in the Late Roman Republic.* Cambridge.

Postscript

Paul J. du Plessis

The authors included in this volume were asked to revisit the traditional narratives of Roman law during the late Republic with a view to establishing whether and to what extent a greater focus on Cicero and his works would affect these. They were instructed not to treat Cicero as 'an outsider', but as part of a broader 'legal culture' of the late Republic, while at the same time remaining aware of the biases inherent in his œuvre.

The first section of this book focused on various interrelated narratives regarding the state of Roman law during the late Republic. Thomas shows the extent to which much of the modern narrative regarding the rise of the Roman jurists and the Roman legal profession remains subtly, yet profoundly affected by notions of specialisation and intellectual isolation created at the turn of the nineteenth century in German legal scholarship. This, in turn, affects modern understanding of the significance of Republican Roman law for the emergence of classical Roman law. By counterbalancing this narrative with the evidence provided by Cicero (while at the same time making allowances for the biases present in his works), it allows the modern reader to obtain a broader, more inclusive picture and, in turn, to reflect more closely on the importance of issues such as rhetoric and of philosophy for the development of Roman law during the late Republic. This latter point finds a natural *locus* in the chapter of Tellegen-Couperus and Tellegen who, using an aspect of the law of succession as their example, proceed to question the commonly held belief that Stoicism was the driving force behind much of Republican Roman law. In fact, as they show, the jurists drew on a variety of philosophical influences, often also from the New Academy, when debating matters of law. This chapter, in turn, allows the modern reader to draw greater inferences regarding the impact of philosophy upon Republican Roman law, especially in light of the claims often made regarding the philosophical inclinations of some of the great Republican jurists. This insight percolates into the final chapter in this section in which Forschner grapples with the knotty issue of Cicero's 'theory of law'. Using a variety of sources, Forschner concludes that Cicero did in fact arrive at a 'general theory of law' in the latter part of his life. This theory was not based on a juxtaposition between human and divine law, as is often assumed, but was rather a holistic theory about law in general based on human nature. In sum, these three contributions show that Cicero, despite his self-representation, remains indispensable to any reconstruction of the law and the legal culture of the period.

The legal profession is the focus of the second part of this volume. Benferhat cautions that Cicero's utterances about the jurists of his time need to be viewed in the larger context of his political ambitions. While he admired the jurists, he was also critical of them. For Cicero, juristic expertise was not enough. In order to make an impact on the Republic and to secure its survival, more was needed. Never a shrinking violet, Cicero believed that only a blend of skilful eloquence and juristic knowledge, visible in himself, could effect real and meaningful change. Issues of perspective dominate the remainder of this section. Lehne-Gstreinthaler demonstrates that Cicero's presentation of the jurists was undoubtedly coloured by his social position as a *novus homo* wishing to be accepted in Rome's upper classes. In reality the legal profession was much more diverse and open-ended. This contribution does much to argue against a narrow conception of the jurist prevalent in nineteenth-century scholarship. It also demonstrates how much work still needs to be done on the Roman legal profession in all its forms. The final two chapters in this section focus on Cicero's subsequent legacy. Wibier, tracing Cicero's reception by the jurists of the early Empire, demonstrates that the Roman jurists at times treated Cicero as one of their own and used his works to answer substantive points of law. This raises interesting questions about the persistent view in modern literature about Cicero as 'an outsider'. Harries takes a long perspective and investigates the idea of the loss of constituent power of the citizenry towards the end of the Republic and the role of the intellectual in facilitating such change from collective government to autocracy. This insightful contribution does much to uncover Cicero's views of the role of the people in the preservation of the Roman Republic. In sum, Cicero was a many-sided figure who played an important part, not only in the development of law, but also in the transformation of the Roman state (even if not consciously). As these chapters collectively show, the 'legal culture' of the late Republic by no means operated in isolation from politics. Furthermore, despite the biases visible in Cicero's work, he remains an indispensable source for uncovering the legal culture of the late Republic.

The final section of this volume deals with the legal environment in which Cicero operated. Roselaar shows the close relationship between the expansion of the Roman state and the availability of Roman law in the late Republic. This is a point that bears reinforcing. The legal environment of the late Republic was a pluralist one where differing peoples of differing legal statuses were obliged to engage (not without legal prejudice) using the legal framework created piecemeal by the Roman authorities. In such a situation, where different laws applied to different peoples and the principle of personality of law reigned supreme, we see glimpses of what is to come in the Roman Empire thereafter. This theme is taken up further by Hilder. She convincingly shows that those studying Roman law of this period need to take more account of manuals of rhetoric in order to form an appreciation of context. Rhetorical manuals can indeed provide us with much information of law and legal practice. The final two chapters in this section paint a broader picture of this environment. Alexander, making various important points about the relationship between formalism and realism when investigating the law, examines the practice of bringing multiple charges in criminal trials and the relationship between said charges and the unitary punishment that resulted from a conviction. In doing so, he engages with the important debate about the significance of the rhetoric of character in the Roman courtroom in the late Republic and its impact on proof of guilt. Steel, carries this theme further through her investigation of the peculiar practice of young men prosecuting more established public figures as a test of 'fitness for office'. This important contribution underscores the centrality of social networks in upper class Roman society of the late Republic as well as the very public nature of reputation and standing in this period.

So what does this all amount to? In their pithy introduction to the late Republic, Beard and Crawford observed that: 'Cicero would not have approved of this [their] book'.[1] I am not sure Cicero would have approved of this one either. But, at the very least, it is an attempt to start a conversation about Cicero, not as 'an outsider', but as a valuable source for uncovering the legal culture of the late Republic. And once this has been done, it becomes possible to ask further questions about the state and the shape of the law and legal institutions during this period. As Lawrence Rosen famously put it: 'To understand how a culture is put together and operates, therefore, one cannot fail to consider law, one cannot fail to see it as part of culture'.[2] Given the importance of late Republican Roman law for the classical period, we owe it to ourselves as scholars of Roman law to revisit this period with much greater care. A systematic study of Roman legal culture of the late Republic remains to be written. This is the first attempt to start the conversation.

---

[1] Beard, M. and Crawford, M. (1999)[2]. *Rome and the Late Republic: Problems and interpretations.* London. Introduction.

[2] Rosen, L. (2006). *Law As Culture: An invitation.* Princeton. At 5.

Index

Note: n indicates footnote, t indicates table; the standard abbreviations have been employed for Roman personal names